Walt Whitman's Selected Journalism

The Iowa Whitman Series

Ed Folsom, series editor

Walt Whitman's Selected Journalism

EDITED BY DOUGLAS A. NOVERR
AND JASON STACY

University of Iowa Press, Iowa City

University of Iowa Press, Iowa City 52242

www.uiowapress.org
Printed in the United States of America
Design by Ashley Muehlbauer

The University of Iowa Press is a member of Green Press Initiative and is committed to preserving natural resources.

Printed on acid-free paper
ISSN: 1556–5610

Library of Congress Cataloging-in-Publication Data
Whitman, Walt, 1819–1892.
[Works. Selections. 2014]
Walt Whitman's selected journalism / Walt Whitman; edited by Douglas A. Noverr and Jason Stacy.
pages cm. — (The Iowa Whitman series)
Includes bibliographical references and index.
ISBN 978-1-60938-315-2 (pbk), ISBN 978-1-60938-316-9 (ebk)
1. Whitman, Walt, 1819–1892—Political and social views. 2. Journalism—United States. 3. United States—Civilization—19th century. I. Noverr, Douglas A., editor. II. Stacy, Jason, 1970– editor. III. Title.
PS3203.N68 2014
818'.308—dc23 2014034886

Contents

Acknowledgments

We are grateful to many institutions for their support and resources. The Brooklyn Public Library graciously provided scans of three years' worth of the *Brooklyn Daily Times*. We are also thankful for the Brooklyn Public Library's online *Brooklyn Daily Eagle*, which continues to be a rich and useful resource for Whitman scholars. Thanks, also, to the Walt Whitman Archive (whitmanarchive.org) for the scans of full issues of the *New York Aurora*, which, until only a few years ago, were difficult to access. We would also like to thank Pennsylvania State University Press for allowing us to transcribe hard-to-find articles from Joseph Jay Rubin's *The Historic Whitman*, and Peter Lang Publishers for the use of *The Complete Journalism* for transcriptions we could not access in the original.

We also appreciate the support of our institutions, Michigan State University and Southern Illinois University Edwardsville, for giving us the time and resources to complete this project, and to the University of Iowa Press for making a beautiful book.

Thanks, especially, to Ed Folsom, series editor, for his close readings of the manuscript and his insightful suggestions.

Finally, Jason Stacy sends his thanks to friends, family, and far-flung correspondents. Without the love and support of Michelle, Abigail, and Margaret this book would not have been possible. Douglas Noverr acknowledges with deep appreciation the daily support and encouragement of his wife, Betty, as well as recalls fondly the team of Herbert Bergman and Edward Recchia, with whom he worked on *The Journalism, Volume I: 1834–1846* and *The Journalism, Volume II: 1846–1848*.

Introduction

Walt Whitman's Journalism Career in New York and Brooklyn

DOUGLAS A. NOVERR AND JASON STACY

When Walt Whitman published the first edition of *Leaves of Grass* in 1855, he had been a journalist for fifteen years. Even upon assuming his first major position as editor of the *New York Aurora* in 1842, he had already founded and edited one small newspaper, the *Long Islander*; worked as a printer's devil and apprentice and then typesetter for two other Long Island papers and the *New World* in New York City; and contributed short pieces, articles, and fiction to sixteen different newspapers and literary magazines during a remarkably productive period in 1840–1841. Even at nineteen years old, Walt Whitman was already a prolific writer on a range of topics in a wide variety of styles.

But Whitman's journalism was often surprisingly conventional. In the "Sun-Down Papers," for example, Whitman aligned himself with a contemporary form of Christianity that cultivated a reader's moral sensibilities, going so far in No. 4 of the series to criticize strongly the use of tobacco, tea, and coffee for the "evil" they worked on the mind, body, and nervous system. He concluded that his outlook was not narrowly puritanical, but rather one grounded in reason:

> In conclusion, I would remark, that I am not one of those who would deny people any sensual delights, because I think it is a sin to be happy, and to take pleasure in the good things of this life. On the contrary, I am disposed to allow every rational gratification, both to the palate, and the other senses. I consider that we were placed here for two beneficent purposes; to fulfill our duty, and to enjoy the almost innumerable comforts and delights he has provided for us. (Whitman, *The Journalism, Vol. I*, 20)

In "Sun-Down Papers" No. 8 (the longest of the series) Whitman described a dream that transported his speaker into a land where "the temple of Truth" stood and where "inquirers" examined the temple through various shapes and types of optical glasses in an attempt to discern Truth. Rather than look through a man-made device, the speaker, like the Bard of *Leaves of Grass*, asked the reader to filter the cosmos through herself or himself:

> "Behold!" thus it spoke, "and learn wisdom from the spectacles which have this day unfolded to thine eyes. Thou hast gazed upon the altar of Nature; but hast seen how impossible it is to penetrate the knowledge which is stored within it. Let pride therefore depart from thy soul, and let a sense of the littleness of all earthly acquirements bow down thy head in awe before the mighty Creator of a million worlds. Thou hast seen, that whatever of the great light of truth it has been deemed expedient to show to mortals—can be most truly and usefully contemplated by the plain eye of simplicity, unaccompanied by the clogs and notions which dim the gaze of most men—and hast with wonder seen how all will still continue to view the noblest object of desire through the distorted medium of their own prejudices and bigotry." (Whitman, *The Journalism, Vol. I*, 26–27)

This remarkable article, appearing in the *Long Island Democrat* on October 20, 1840, positions Whitman in the Protestant Christian tradition of the seeking believer who accepts duty and enjoyment of life's pleasures as concurrent while also situating himself, in his critique of prejudice and bigotry, in the tradition of the freethinking ecumenicalism of Thomas Paine. One could practice restraint and avoid excesses, yet savor and enjoy the delightful experiences of the senses. One could assume humility and a sense of one's "littleness" and thus through "the plain eye of simplicity" see "whatever of the great light of truth it has been deemed expedient to show to mortals." Denominationalism and sectarianism in their extremes resulted from men viewing "the noblest object of desire ['the temple of Truth'] through the distorted medium of their own prejudices and bigotry." By the time he was twenty-one, Whitman was already inviting his readers to see with "the plain eye of simplicity," unhindered by presuppositions or the presumed advantages of doctrinal systems (Stacy, *Walt Whitman's Multitudes*, 27–33).

When Whitman became the "leading editor" of the *New York Aurora* on March 28, 1842, the paper had been in full production for only about four months. Its first lead editor, Thomas Low Nichols, had resigned after three months and would forsake daily journalism to become a medical doctor and promote, with his physician wife, health foods, spiritualism, and hydropathy. The two senior partners of the *Aurora*, Anson Herrick and John F. Ropes, attempted to find a niche audience by positioning their new paper against the salacious topics of the penny press: seductions, disappearances, sensational crimes such as embezzlement and murder, and other maleficence perpetrated up and down the social scale. The market "hook" for the *Aurora* was that it would be "a sound, fearless and independent daily paper, which shall at all times and on all occasions advocate and sustain the dignity and interests of our country" (qtd. in Whitman, *The Journalism, Vol. I,* 1). Whitman took to this outlook and orientation avidly and enthusiastically. His employers boasted that Whitman was a "bold, energetic and original writer" who would carry out the "original design" of the paper. In his March 29, 1842, article, "The New York Press," Whitman provided short sketches of twelve city newspapers (including the *Aurora*) and concluded:

> Very few really good papers are published in New York. Most of them are bound up in partisanship or prejudice, and are incapable of taking enlarged and comprehensive views of matters and things. Five sixths of them are directly or indirectly under the control of foreigners; they therefore, though possessing some marks of ability, are not imbued with any wholesome American spirit. They cannot and do not come out with that fiery enthusiasm in the cause of truth and liberty—that vigor of advocacy—that energy and boldness and frankness which will ever mark the apostle of the new system—the system which teaches far different doctrine from the rusty, cankered, time-honored, anti-democratic philosophy that looms up in Europe, and is planting its poisonous seeds too widely among us. (Whitman, *The Journalism, Vol. I,* 82)

But Whitman's embrace of the American spirit often took perplexing turns in the *Aurora*. Throughout the spring of 1843, editorials in rival newspapers and letters to the editor sharply criticized the *Aurora* for being anti-immigrant and for promoting nativism. In his March 30, 1842, article, "Defining Our Position," Whitman quoted directly from a critical letter and replied that the "motives of the *Aurora,* in some of its recent steps, have been much misunderstood" (Whitman, *The Journalism, Vol. I,* 85). Whitman asserted that the anti-American influences resided not in the people coming to the United States, but in the form and circulation of foreign ideas, customs, or notions that found favor and subverted the potency of a democracy where man "can be trusted to govern himself." In this regard, though Whitman claimed to be a universalist against religious bigotry, he was also a proponent of cultural assimilation:

> We would that all the taint of time defiled custom—all the poisonous atmosphere of European philosophy—all the fallacious glitter of a litera-

> ture which, being under the patronage of courts and princes and haughty church, is not fitted for our beloved America—all the aristocratic notions, interwoven so tightly with social customs, as to be almost ineradicable—we would that all this might have no sway in the land. These things are not for such as we. A higher and holier destiny, a more worthy mission, we sincerely hope, belong to us. (Whitman, *The Journalism, Vol. I,* 85)

The occasion for the correspondent's charges against the *Aurora* had to do with the New York public schools and the efforts of Catholic bishop John Joseph Hughes, with support of Whig governor William Seward, to change the system of public school funding in New York City so that parochial schools would receive operational monies. Whitman blamed the "lowest class of foreigners" for disrupting a public meeting on the matter and for bullying and intimidating peaceful citizens and driving school officials from the stage. Whitman characterized these "foreigners" in terms that make us cringe today:

> Bands of filthy wretches, whose very touch was offensive to a decent man; drunken loafers; scoundrels whom the police and criminal courts would be ashamed to receive in their walls; coarse, blustering rowdies; blear eyed and bloated offscouring from the stews, blind alleys and rear lanes; disgusting objects bearing the form of human, but whom the sow in the mire might almost object to as companions—these were they who broke into the midst of a peaceful body of American citizens—struck and insulted the chosen officers of the assemblage, and with shrieks, loud blasphemy, and howlings in their hideous native tongue, prevented the continuance of the customary routine. We saw Irish priests there—sly, false, deceitful villains—looking on and evidently encouraging the gang who created the tumult. (Whitman, *The Journalism, Vol. I,* 57)

In responding to public criticism of this kind of language, Whitman conceded that he used "harsh epithets" in condemning Bishop Hughes and his Irish priests: "but that we know our motives are good, and that our aim is holy; and that therefore we shall be absolved from blame" (Whitman, *The Journalism, Vol. I,* 89). In these self-important terms, it is possible to sense Whitman's anxiety about the volatile state of American democracy during the 1840s, a time when the founding generation had been gone for a generation and universal white male suffrage, itself only a generation old, stood atop whole populations unrepresented in the political contests of the day. Like many Americans, Whitman viewed the growth of new immigrant populations in American cities, the advent of the first industrial revolution, and ongoing sectional tensions with a degree of trepidation. For Whitman, newspapers existed to educate Americans about the right paths for their relatively new republic, and therefore could lay claim to a "holy" aim.

From Whitman's point of view, the school controversy, with its resulting riots and street violence that disturbed the city for a period of weeks, was a severe test of democracy and its principles. His attacks often ran to the conspiratorial and warned of the "Hughes clique" or the "Catholic priests—those hired fomenters of discord and assassins of union" (*New York Aurora*, April 6, 1842). Accordingly, an Irish faction supposedly manipulated Tammany Hall, using the power of their votes to leverage support for the passage of a favorable school bill in Albany that would fund religious inculcation with public dollars and thereby undermine the creation of freethinking citizens. Here Whitman's ecumenicalism faltered against his universalism, and he found himself attacking the faith of immigrants he hoped would assimilate into the "American spirit." Complicating matters was the 1843 New York City mayoral election, where the Irish vote played a key role. When the school bill passed and when the Irish-supported ticket won the city election, Whitman framed the defeat in terms dire to the Republic:

> The indignation of large numbers of our citizens is roused to a pitch altogether ungovernable, against the insults and absolute tramplings upon American citizenship by the Catholics and ignorant Irish. What conduct this indignation will exhibit itself in, it is impossible to tell. Hughes' house is much injured, and in all likelihood the cathedrals would have been attacked and sacked, if the people had not been deterred by the military. (Whitman, *The Journalism, Vol. I*, 115)

When the turmoil finally subsided as Whitman neared the end of his editorship with the *Aurora*, he again responded to the charge that his editorials promoted Native Americanism, as if the tone of them likewise made him uncomfortable:

> Yet with all our antipathy for everything that may tend to assimilate our country to the kingdoms of Europe, we repudiate such doctrines as have characterized the "Native American" party. We would see no man disfranchised, because he happened to be born three thousand miles off. We go for the largest liberty—the widest immunities of the people, as well as the blessings of government. Let us receive these foreigners to our shores, and to our good offices. (Whitman, *The Journalism, Vol. I*, 124)

With the election lost and the fervor cooled, Whitman pragmatically pulled back from the angry and vitriolic rhetoric and charges he had made against Bishop John Hughes and the Catholic priests and returned to basic bromides of democratic principles. Within the ideology of Whitman's Jacksonian inclinations, as the nation expanded geographically and demographically, the base of free voters had to expand continuously in order for the foundations of the Republic to remain strong, or at least strongly Democratic. Practically, a split between native and Irish Democrats opened a political space for rival parties. Retaliations and recriminations, such as disfranchisement, choked off "the largest liberty," and, as much as Whitman mistrusted at this point the American Catholic hierarchy, he recognized that religious liberty and the safety of Catholic Churches were part of the larger democratic equation.

While the Catholic school bill was the prime newsworthy topic during Whitman's short tenure at the *Aurora*, his work there also provided him with column space to develop a distinctive voice and style that delighted in scenes, or "peeps," of activities, and people of the city, all expressed with a conviction that the newspaper could educate the American citizenry.

His reporting strengths were descriptive, out-and-about walks and excursions, strolling down a main thoroughfare like Broadway down to the Battery, or observing the same from a vantage point of the balcony of P. T. Barnum's American Museum. In *Aurora* articles like "Something Worth Perusal" (April 7, 1842) and "Sentiment and a Saunter" (April 13, 1842) Whitman developed an ambulatory style that registered sites, sensations, and the immediate process of thought and reaction in the process and rhythm of walking; in these articles Whitman was an urban loafer before he was loafing on the grass. This style offered infinite variation for the author since the saunterer's attention was selective, but his voice introduced the reader to the infinite variety and universal qualities of the things he heard and experienced (Stacy, *Walt Whitman's Multitudes*, 56–59).

One stroll took Whitman into the park to observe young boys earnestly and competitively playing a game of marbles, and a group of older gentlemen who observed them:

> How ardent the little gamesters are! How pleased at gaining a spherical moiety of clay—and how cast down at losing it! Thus it is. In our greener age, we pursue shadows and toys; in maturity, the toil and the sweat and the fever are for benefits as intangible, and phantom gewgaws, intrinsically

> as valueless as the objects of our youth. ("'Marble Time' in the Park," *New York Aurora,* April 4, 1842)

Whitman also took his readers along for behind-the-scenes "peeps" at the interiors of antebellum New York City. His March 16, 1842, *Aurora* article, "Life in a New York Market" (Whitman, *The Journalism, Vol. I,* 55–56), describes a Saturday night visit to the Grand Street market and the colorful sellers and buyers there and the sights and sounds of a bustling, well-stocked marketplace where commerce made for a rich scene. Another piece from March 18, 1842, describes New York boardinghouses and the diversity of characters found there (Whitman, *The Journalism, Vol. I,* 61–62). Another "peep" took *Aurora* readers inside a Jewish synagogue and described in positive terms the religious rites, the rituals of prayer, and the individual readings from the sacred Torah (Whitman, *The Journalism, Vol. I,* 76–77, 83–84). In the second visit, Whitman described the overall impression of what he heard and saw (even if he did not understand the language or the ritual). His "fancy" transports him to the original land of the Jews:

> We were in the holy city. The places of the haughty nobles—the magnificent temple which the Jews loved as the apple of their eye . . . And along the public thoroughfare came trailingly a solemn group. In the centre was a pale being with a crown of thorns bound round his forehead, and blood trickling down his brow. It was the Holy Savior of Man, bearing the cross upon his shoulder. And as he passed, the mob scouted and reviled him—his very friends thought it scorn to recognize him; all but *one,* a woman, who followed him even to the place of his crucifixion. (Whitman, *The Journalism, Vol. I,* 84)

Another "peep" took Whitman to the House of Refuge, where 200 young boys or juvenile delinquents lived and went to school in a place of tight military discipline. These articles showed the rich variety of life and scenes in New York without the editor being the subject of attention or the sensibility or personality through which all had to pass. The displacement was away from the editor to the reader, to a "you" or "our" or "we."

Whitman also had philosophical and ethical pretensions. Such an article could be occasioned by a death, such as that of the impoverished McDonald Clarke, who had power and promise as a poet, but whose nobility and gentleness, according to Whitman, proved to be the weakness that caused his death. In his last week with the *Aurora* Whitman wrote about children and their innocence (April 16, 1842), "Life and Love" on April 20, "The Ocean" on April 21, and "Dreams" on April 23. At the end of "Life and Love" Whitman observed:

> So let us be more just to our own nature, and to the gifts which the Almighty has made ineradicable within us. Casting our eyes over this beautiful earth, where so much joy and sunshine exist—looking on the human race with the gentle orbs of kindness and philosophy—sending our glance through the cool and verdant lanes, by the sides of the blue rivers, over the crowded city, or among those who dwell on the prairies, or along the green savannahs of the south—and we shall see that everywhere are the seeds of happiness and love. Yet unless they are fostered, they will be entombed forever in the darkness—and their possessors may die and be buried, and never think of them but as baubles and worth no care. (Whitman, *The Journalism, Vol. I*, 133)

These four philosophical pieces can be read as Whitman's attempt to regain balance and a wider, more universal perspective after the narrow sectarian and political battles that erupted in New York in often ugly and violent ways during the debate over public school funding.

The reasons for Whitman's separation from the *Aurora* are unclear, and what scanty evidence exists proves to be contradictory and circumstantial. Both the owners and Whitman recriminated each other bitterly in print. From Whitman's point of view, he left the paper because his contributions to its success were not appreciated or recognized and because the two proprietors introduced disruptions that hampered the daily running of the paper and its meeting a tight production schedule. Nonetheless, his editorship of the *Aurora* resulted in an expansion of circulation by 25 percent to a distribution of 5,000 daily (Bergman, "Introduction," lii). According to Whitman, this was due to his ability to write lively, fresh lead articles and take strong, independent positions that exposed and assailed "a thousand dangerous influences operating among us—influences whose tendency is to assimilate this land in thought, in social customs, and to a degree, in government, with the moth eaten systems of the old worlds" ("We," Whitman, *The Journalism, Vol. I*, April 9, 1842, 106). Besides this aggressive defense of all that was "American," Whitman developed a repertoire of articles that honed his prose and brought some measure of balance to the paper and a day-to-day sense that no matter what the upsets, life would continue in ordinary ways that were interesting and illuminating. He did what Herrick and Ropes hired him to do: expand the newspaper's circulation and take strong and independent stands against the supposedly dangerous influence of European ideas and customs in America, all through original and compelling writing.

The period from April 1842 to March 1846 is one in which Whitman utilized all his newspaper experience and his writing skills to make a living and remain active in the competitive literary marketplace. After leaving the *Aurora*, Whitman edited the *New York Evening Tattler*, wrote for and edited the *Sunday Times*, and contributed articles to the *Sun* and the *Daily Plebian*. In the period 1843–1844 he edited the *New York Statesman* and then the *New-York Democrat* (merged with the *New York Plebian* in October 1844). Two of the papers he edited were publications created for Democratic political campaigns and for the promotion of certain tickets and candidates. These papers quickly disappeared after their purposes were served, and when published, had few of the leading editorials, news features, or stories like those Whitman had written for the *Aurora*.

Unfortunately, few issues of these papers have survived, although references to them or items from them were reprinted in other papers (Bergman, "Introduction," lxi). In addition, Whitman successfully placed articles, poetry, fiction, and sketches in a number of newspapers and in literary magazines before he began his work as chief editor of the daily *Brooklyn Eagle* in early March 1846. He also wrote a series of fifty-five articles for the *Brooklyn Evening Star*, an assignment that signaled his move across the river to Brooklyn, his boyhood home.

Two publications from the early 1840s represent Whitman's development of an article type he later used at the *Eagle* and, ultimately, refined into a complex patriotism that deemed the American republic "essentially the greatest poem" in the first edition of *Leaves of Grass* (1855). "A Ramble up the Third Avenue—The Old House at Kipp's Bay—Landing of the British Troops There in 1776—Washington's Bravery and Escape" in the *Sunday Times* for March 20, 1842 (Whitman, *The Journalism, Vol. I*, 140–142), and "Twenty-Fifth November" in the *Sun* for November 25, 1842 (Whitman, *The Journalism, Vol. I*, 163–164), were ostensibly commemoration and historical pieces in which Whitman visited Revolutionary War battle spots and recalled in vivid detail what decisive moments or battles took place there. Though much of the physical evidence of the war had disappeared as new buildings and roads replaced those standing in 1776, Whitman took the reader to the exact historical spot where the Battle of Long Island took place and in quick sketches painted the scene of military conflict. At Kipp's Bay on Manhattan Island, Whitman's George Washington reacts with an uncharacteristic outburst when his troops flee the oncoming redcoats:

> On this occasion—and it is said to have been, with one exception, the only time he was heard to use profane language during the revolution—the commander-in-chief pulled his chapeau from his head, cast it upon the ground, called the retreating soldiers d----d scoundrels and cowards, and at the same time pulled a pistol from his holsters, and threatened to shoot the first man that passed by him. (Whitman, *The Journalism, Vol. I*, 142)

The *Sun* article for November 25, 1842, lamented the fact that the day of the British evacuation of New York in 1783, which formerly had been recognized with as much enthusiasm as July 4th, was now no longer celebrated, and indeed was almost forgotten. However, the opportunity was still there to walk "this classical ground of the island of Manhattan" and be on the spot where Washington was only fifty yards from the advancing British columns until his "aids [*sic*] pointed out to him his danger and hastened him from the scene" (Whitman, *The Journalism, Vol. I*, 142). For Whitman, commemoration and remembrance offered communion with the past and an opportunity to measure one's commitment to democratic principles against those who risked all for independence and the well-being of the new republic. In this regard, Whitman's journalism echoed contemporary patriotic discourses, but it also offers modern readers the opportunity to uncover the germ of the poet's own brand of patriotism where an idealized United States represents the will of a democratic cosmos (Stacy, "Washington's Tears," 218).

Between the years 1846 and 1848 Whitman again found himself working on a Democratic paper. The *Brooklyn Eagle, and King's County Democrat*, a daily paper with a weekly issue on Wednesdays for circulation on Long Island, was something of a promotion for Whitman. Whereas larger Democratic papers overshadowed the *Aurora* in New York, the *Eagle* represented received Democratic opinion in the burgeoning city of Brooklyn. As editor, Whitman found himself in the middle of a technological revolution that was changing how news was gathered, reported, and distributed.

In 1846 the Magnetic Telegraph Company established a network that included connections between New York, Philadelphia, Baltimore, and Washington, D.C. (Reid 117–127). In at least four *Eagle* articles Whitman referred to specific news that had been received by way of the Magnetic Telegraph Company, such as news about battles in the U.S.-Mexico War or the signing of the Oregon Treaty, which settled a boundary dispute between the United States and Britain. On June 15, 1846, Whitman noted that ratification of the treaty was pending in the Senate, which took place on June 18, 1846. News was moving faster, and events and developments had more currency and even, to some degree, a sense of simultaneity—that is, what was confirmed as happening was continuing to happen; news was approaching up-to-the-minute. With a direct telegraph line between Washington, D.C., and New York City, the newspaper became the medium through which news *happened* since the telegraph's coded messages became print faster in newspapers than in any other print medium. Likewise, as passage across the Atlantic sped up with the use of clipper ships, European and British newspapers arrived sooner and with more frequency. At the *Eagle,* Whitman worked on the cusp of this news and information revolution. Developments in the steam-powered printing press increased the speed of printing threefold in 1830, and by 1837 a press could produce 4,000 papers in an hour (Emery and Emery, 135–143). Reliable, faster printing meant that editors had more time to sift through other newspapers, read the latest telegraphic reports, and find that elusive "hook" for a story or leading article. In his April 19, 1847, article titled "Our New Press" (Whitman, *The Journalism, Vol. II,* 250) Whitman described "our new napier press" as "truly a magnificent piece of workmanship" with its "dull rub-a-dub [shaking] our table from the room below while we write."

Other social and political developments proved as transformative as technology. The U.S.-Mexico War, from April 25, 1846, to February 2, 1848, took place within the time frame of Whitman's *Eagle* editorship and brought the excitement of almost daily direct news from the battlefields and two fronts, public celebrations of major victories with fireworks and massive parades, and questions over the legitimacy of the war and the exacting of territory from Mexico after its defeat, as well as a host of military men who would be likened to Revolutionary heroes in the press. Whitman's position on the U.S.-Mexico War was never in doubt and never varied: the war was, for him, a fortuitous opportunity that offered a higher purpose, namely, the spread of democratic ideals across the continent. On September 2, 1846, less than five months into the war, he wrote:

> That the popular instincts go for an increased "area of freedom," is undeniable. And the popular instincts are right. Our union will stand steadier, the broader and more massive the base on which it stands. It is not the vulgar spirit of conquest and acquisition, either: it is exulting pride in the spread of man's rights, and in the surrounding of their identity with the highest phase of national grandeur, potential strength, and wealth—of physical extent in one compacted nation—athwart which the sun of heaven ever beamed! (Whitman, *The Journalism, Vol. II,* 42)

Over a year later, on December 2, 1847, he wrote:

> We have lofty views of the scope and destiny of our American republic. It is for the interests of mankind that its power and territory should be extended—the farther the better. We claim these lands, thus, by a law superior to parchments and dry diplomatic rules. (Whitman, *The Journalism, Vol. II*, 370)

Those criticizing the United States, such as Horace Greeley's *New York Tribune*, Whitman believed, failed to see how the "very large accessions of fertile territory" will assure the future prosperity of the country (Whitman, *The Journalism, Vol. II*, 370).

Other large political crosscurrents, related to simmering domestic conflicts reopened by the war, ran through the period of Whitman's *Eagle* editorship, the most critical one being the question of the extension of slavery into new lands and whether new states, once established, could decide on the question of slaveholding. Whitman's position was that slavery worked against national interests and was finally unprofitable; slave labor depressed the wages of free laborers and created an economy that undermined the economic viability of small farmers and artisans, those closest to the founders' ideal citizens. In this, Whitman hewed to arguments of the laboring and urban wing of the Democratic Party, which quickly coalesced around free-soil politics in the late 1840s. Likewise, Whitman believed the nation's growth and its development of the largest possible freedoms and opportunities for happiness and well-being were predicated upon the largest possible base of free men able to act with only limited and necessary restraints of law and government, an idealism that echoed the free-market ideology of New York Democrats like William Leggett, whose "Locofocos" challenged Tammany Hall Democrats in the mid-1830s. Furthermore, Whitman believed that both George Washington and Thomas Jefferson foresaw the eventual end to slavery and that the Northwest Ordinance of 1787 exemplified the founders' inclination. Whitman's faith in the "natural death" of slavery proved popular, but finally fantastical. In his November 4, 1847, article titled "Verdict of the Undaunted Democracy of the Empire State in Behalf of the Jeffersonian Ordinance" Whitman wrote:

> They love our party yet; but it must be true to itself, and true to its great duties—true to the memory of the revolutionary fathers who fought for freedom, and not for slavery—true to him, the calm-browed one, and

> the noblest democrat of them all, that, in his original draft of the declaration of American independence, inserted as one prime charge against the king and parliament of Great Britain that they had not taken measures to prevent the extension of slavery in the colonies. Have the ages so rolled backward, and humanity with them, that what we went to war to *stop*, seventy years ago, we shall now keep up a war to *advance*? (Whitman, *The Journalism, Vol. II*, 349)

As the U.S.–Mexico War continued, Whitman became increasingly aware that the issue of the extension of slavery could rend the nation and that efforts like the Wilmot Proviso (passed in the House of Representatives twice, in 1846 and 1847, and defeated in the U.S. Senate twice) to ban slavery in any territory acquired from Mexico could not prevail; in fact, the proviso threatened to divide the Democratic Party itself. The issue split the New York state Democratic Party temporarily in half, as "Barnburners" abandoned the national ticket and its presidential nominee, Lewis Cass (supported by "Hunkers," who hunkered down to maintain party unity), to form the relatively short-lived Free-Soil Party and nominate former president Martin Van Buren. Whitman's *Eagle* editorials during this period read backward in American history to what he saw as the foundational principles and intentions in the Declaration of Independence, the War for Independence, the Northwest Ordinance, Washington's and Jefferson's seeming ambivalence toward slavery, and the political revolution resulting from the two administrations of Andrew Jackson. Whitman set forth his arguments in favor of the Wilmot Proviso with great consistency: an extension of slavery threatened the laboring classes by weakening the economic viability and professional integrity of their work. Broadly, the growth of slavery undermined the principles of freedom and democracy. When animated by the slavery debate, Whitman spoke with fervor and eloquence, even against his own professional interests. His support of the Wilmot Proviso and his free-soil position put him on a collision course with the *Eagle*'s publisher, Isaac Van Anden, and, as a result, Whitman was dismissed in mid-January 1848, perhaps because of his antipathy toward the Democratic nominee, Cass, who rejected the proviso in the name of states' rights. In this case, Whitman's dismissal was purely political, and Whitman, along with thousands of free-soil Democrats, temporarily fell out of good graces with the New York Democratic Party. Though the Free-Soil Party disappeared as a political force after 1852, divisions within the Northern Democratic Party over the slavery issue remained, to be exploited by Whigs like Abraham Lincoln later in the decade.

But the slavery debate was only one of Whitman's interests at the *Eagle.* He wrote about schools, visiting them frequently, and the need for enlightened, well-prepared teachers as well as policies and practices of discipline that respected students and abstained from corporal punishment. He advocated healthy outdoor exercises and games and parks where people could find relaxation and enjoyment of nature. He regularly provided "Literary Notices" of new magazines, books, and other publications that would provide enjoyment, knowledge, worthy moral and social instruction, a sense of history, and an awareness of the world and its great literature. Any reading that aimed at or elevated the lives of people, especially youths and young adults, he highly recommended. Whitman brought issues of public safety and sanitation to his readers' attention, advocating safe and clean streets and water. He frequently wrote about music and operatic performances as well as drama, endorsing American performers and productions, and commended exhibitions of works of art. He argued that Brooklyn needed institutions of culture and science, such as an observatory or theater. These elevating and ennobling resources were especially needed in Brooklyn, a city of working-class people living modestly and practical-mindedly without the flair, excitement, and sharp contrasts available in commercial New York.

Whitman also wrote about poverty and the impoverished and about the exploitation of women workers in New York and Brooklyn. He believed that low pay was the cause of crime, alcohol use, and physical violence. He consistently wrote against protective tariffs as interference with a free and open trade that would bring improvements in employment and wages. These issues resonated with the workers and families of Brooklyn who were hard hit by what became a regular cycle of "panics" and recessions or depressions.

As editor, Whitman was largely responsible for the expanded circulation of what was already a heavily subscribed paper. He worked assiduously to improve the quality and finish of the paper, insisting that the compositors follow his texts exactly (Bergman, "Introduction," lxv). The paper received praise and commendations from other publications, and Whitman frequently wrote about New York sites and events he continued to visit and enjoy, composing some of his earliest pieces on crossing the Brooklyn ferry ("Philosophy of Ferries," Whitman, *The Journalism, Vol. II,* 308). He also tackled international developments and conditions, writing movingly about the starvation in Ireland and supporting Irish relief and contributions. With dismay and sadness, he wrote about the Poles' unsuccessful effort to liberate themselves from the grip of Poland's partitioning occupiers. His interests were always deeply humanistic, with a ready sympathy for the oppressed and unfortunate.

Before his next and last extended editorship, from the spring of 1857 to the summer of 1859 with the *Brooklyn Daily Times,* Whitman went to New Orleans with his brother Jeff and wrote articles for the *New Orleans Crescent,* but within a matter of months he was back in Brooklyn. He became the editor of a Free-Soil Party newspaper, the *Brooklyn Freeman,* in early September 1848 and managed to keep it going for a year even after the free-soil candidates polled 10 percent of the national vote but won no electoral votes in the 1848 election. The party elected two senators and fourteen representatives to the Thirty-First Congress, however, which no doubt provided it with presence and voices and explains Whitman's continuation with the *Freeman* until September 11, 1849. The intense factionalism of the Barnburners and the Hunkers continued to be particularly heated in the state of New York, and did not die down after the 1848 election of former general and Whig candidate Zachary Taylor to the presidency. In the first issue of the *Freeman* Whitman declared his detestation of "Old Hunkerism" and its local representatives:

> Without any real talent, or even a tolerable share of the popular lore, these men have "managed" themselves into office, and into control of the Democratic party here. We have very close at heart the desire to prevent them from ever taking their seats in high places again; and we would resuscitate the Democrats of Brooklyn from their parlaying influence. (qtd. in the *Brooklyn Daily Advertiser,* April 25, 1849)

Whitman may have overestimated the readership for a radical paper like the *Freeman* or the continuing intensity of burning issues once elections were settled. Strictly political newspapers generally had short lives and thrived before elections; papers based on principles, as Whitman's *Freeman,* were even harder to sustain.

When Whitman ended his editorship of the *Brooklyn Freeman* in September 1849, it would be seven years and eight months until he sat in the editor's chair again. He had transformed the *Freeman* into a successful daily paper of the Free-Soil Party orientation and participated avidly in the give-and-take of partisan policies waged in the daily press. Starting in mid-December 1849 he had a brief stint as the principal editor of the *New York Daily News,* but the paper, although well funded and equipped, failed to make it beyond its second full month of publication (Rubin, 224–225). After that, Whitman's connection with newspapers was that of a freelance contributor, and he used his technique of creating a series of articles to sell ten installments of "Letters from a Travelling Bachelor" to the *New York Sunday Dispatch,* which ran from October 14, 1849, to January 6, 1850; "Paragraph Sketches of Brooklynites" and "Church Sketches" to the *Brooklyn Daily Advertiser,* which ran from May 18 to June 6, 1850; his "Letters from Paumanok," which ran in four installments in the *New York Evening Post* in 1851; and his "New York Dissected" series and other articles that appeared in *Life Illustrated* over a period of almost a year in late 1855 through 1856. Other contributions were scattered in a number of different publications in the early 1850s.

During these years Whitman entered the critical phase of his development as a poet, the years that would produce the first two editions of *Leaves of Grass.* He pursued moneymaking enterprises like freelance writing, real estate ventures that involved the buying and selling of houses as well as their construction, job printing, and the sale of books and stationery out of the family house. Once he was out of the day-to-day and hour-by-hour regimen of newspaper editing, Whitman began to open up his horizons and take in a wider variety of experiences and contacts. He frequently stopped by the studios of Brooklyn artists, spent evening hours at the opera and took in the performances of Allessando Bettini and Marietta Alboni, and visited libraries where he could in solitude and silence read the literary works that at his editor's desk he would have had to digest quickly in order to write notices of them.

In "How 'Leaves of Grass' Was Made" (published in the *New York Star* in 1885 and in *Frank Leslie's Popular Monthly* in June 1892, two months after Whitman's death) the poet described his alternation between open-air experiences on the Long Island seashore and the cultural attractions and people of the city, particularly "the singing of the contralto Alboni and Italian opera generally" as "saturating and imbuing everything before I touched the pen to paper on my own account" (Whitman, "How 'Leaves of Grass' Was Made," 732). As a journalist, Whitman had to write for a deadline set by typesetting, proofreading, and the press run. Whitman loved this atmosphere and thrived in it, but once he was out of its grip and out of the public role as editor, he could "best express my own distinctive era and surroundings, America, Democracy" with what "must be an identical body and soul, a personality—which personality, after many considerations and ponderings I deliberately settled should be myself—indeed could not be any other" (Whitman, *November Boughs,* 13).

Here, then, was the essential shift in Whitman's writing life. The journalistic world of a daily newspaper allowed for the personality of an editor, but a personality in the service of circulation and favorable readership, a personality that was acceptable to the proprietor of the paper. Whitman, now a freelancer and nascent poet, committed himself to using his "imaginative faculty" "to give ultimate vivification to facts, to science, and to common lives, endowing them with the glows and glories and final illustriousness which belong to every real thing, and to real things only" (Whitman, *November Boughs*, 7–8).

Though during the next five years Whitman wrote articles for four newspapers and relied on his training and experience as a printer to make a scant living, his most significant work was the writing and printing of *Leaves of Grass* (1855), the preparation of the second edition in 1856, and the promotion of the work, going so far as to write a few positive reviews in which he anonymously introduced himself and his book.

In June 1857, after an almost eight-year hiatus as a newspaper editor, Whitman began his affiliation with the *Brooklyn Daily Times*, an evening paper published six days a week and sold for "six cents a week by carrier or $3.25 a year by mail" ("Walt Whitman as a Journalist," Whitman, *The Journalism, Vol. I*, 435). His work at the *Times*, which spanned two years, was roughly the amount of time he had worked for the *Eagle*. The Panic of 1857 and the resulting economic downturn received attention in the *Times*, and a number of articles documented the hard times of unemployment, the inability of people to pay rents or taxes, and the need for poor relief. Whitman also wrote about practical innovation, especially the railroads as a force of economic development. In this regard, the articles focused heavily on local questions and issues for Brooklyn and the Eastern District of Long Island. He highlighted matters related to sanitation, public health and safety, and the schools and education, and he supported the development of the Ridgewood Reservoir and the Brooklyn Water Works system, which provided the city with fresh, clean water. Whitman also promoted Long Island, continuing his practice of walking into the countryside and describing sites and vistas that were inspiring and restorative. His was a Long Island in transition, as railroads connected its more remote parts, making it more a part of the market economy and changing its largely rural character. Whitman also promoted the development of Brooklyn cultural institutions and continued to write book notices and reviews, always one of his strong suits as an editor, and framed his essays on new books or magazines in terms of their usefulness and educational value, thereby maintaining the reformist theme of his earliest journalism.

Whitman did not limit himself to the local, however. His articles on international developments provided perspectives beyond Brooklyn and reflected his burgeoning interest in places like China, India, and Russia and his continual reading of world history, past and current. A series of articles on the laying of the Atlantic Cable proved noteworthy not only for their celebration of technology and American ingenuity but also for Whitman's conviction that the Atlantic Cable would have transformative moral ramifications on international relations. Almost twenty years later, in "A Passage to India," he included the Atlantic Cable as one of three world-changing modern wonders.

Emory Holloway and Gay Wilson Allen have speculated that Whitman may have alienated or offended the local ministers over his comments on prostitution or his revelation of the dangerous conditions in churches, making them potential fire hazards (Bergman, "Walt Whitman as a Journalist," 436). One scholar even has questioned the extent to which Whitman had editorial control over the content of the *Brooklyn Daily Times* (Loving, 227–232). Whatever the case, Whitman ceased to publish in the *Times* around June 1859, and thereafter his day-to-day contact with the newspaper world ended. Because he did not have a financial stake or investment in any of the large papers he worked for, Whitman could not negotiate conditions of editorial freedom. William Cullen Bryant, of the *New York Evening Post*, and Horace Greeley, of the *Tribune*, could parlay their initial investments into editorial control and then into personal fortunes (Brown, *William Cullen Bryant*; Williams, *Horace Greeley*). But Whitman needed his pay in order to live and could not afford to "buy into" the papers on which he worked.

Although June 1859 marked the end of Whitman's services as an editor to any paper, he remained for almost the rest of his life an active contributor of articles and poetry to a wide array of publications. In the period from 1859 to late 1891 he published just over 130 articles in newspapers and 51 articles in magazines, including seven substantial articles in the prestigious *North American Review*, concluding with "Have We a National Literature?" in March 1891. He published sixty-four poems in newspapers and another forty-five in magazines. From 1863 through 1865 he reported from Washington, D.C., on the nation's capital during the Civil War in nine extended letters to the *New York Times*, and in the same period published war articles of local interest in the *Brooklyn Daily Union* and the *Brooklyn Daily Eagle*.

One of Whitman's most successful types of publications continued to be the progressive and interlinked series. His most extensive (in terms of newspaper space and numbers) was "Brooklyniana: A Series of Local Articles on Past and Present" with No. 1 published in the *Brooklyn Daily Standard* on June 3, 1861, and No. 39 (which really was No. 23) published on November 1, 1862 (in all, there were twenty-two articles, two of the installments with two parts). In March, April, and May 1862 Whitman published seven articles in a series titled "City Photographs," which were featured in the *New York Leader*. Later, in 1874, he developed another series titled "'Tis But Ten Years Since," which ran in consecutive issues of the *New York Weekly Graphic* from January 24 to March 1, 1874. This series commemorated the Civil War veterans and the preservation of the Union.

Whitman's longest association with a publication was with *The Critic: A Fortnightly Review of Literature, the Fine Arts, Music, and the Drama*, published in New York. In the second issue of *The Critic* of January 28, 1881, he published "How I Get Around at 60, and Take Notes. (No. 1)," and five more of this series came out, with No. 6 appearing in the July 15, 1882, issue; each was the lead article. Between January 29, 1881, and February 28, 1891, Whitman published twenty prose pieces and eight poems in this journal, and many of the articles or essays were collected into later volumes of his prose. A number of these publications were reprinted in other publications as well, which did not make him any money but certainly circulated his name as a prose writer and poet.

Whitman's more than thirty years as a contributor and correspondent from 1859 to 1891 illustrate his savvy regarding the publishing market and his ability to write articles that were salable and provided income. He recognized that his knowledge of and passion for New York City and Brooklyn could be turned into features that editors desired. He capitalized on his growing fame and reputation as a poet and became a noted literary historian and critic of American and British poetry and literature. His many book reviews and notices provided him with a knowledge of and familiarity with literature, history, biography, and other areas that few other writers could claim. In his writings he also proved to be a passionate and knowledgeable historian of America from the Revolutionary War to the Civil War, as well as a keen critic of his times.

Whitman's work as a journalist is important for what it reveals about the way his sensibility as a skilled print tradesman established an occupational route that sustained him while at the same time cultivating his literary aspirations. Perhaps more significant, journalism honed Whitman's sense that a piece of writing was a built object as well as the medium for ideas. This sensibility came to fruition in the poet's careful crafting and recrafting of *Leaves of Grass* over thirty years. Whitman imagined an audience of readers with whom he could personally connect both through his words and the book itself. His engagement with the political developments and issues of the day caused him to define and solidify his democratic and moral principles and to align himself with what he believed to be American values established through the American Revolution and the early republic up through the administrations of Andrew Jackson. While party politics often disappointed him, democracy, as a vital and expanding force, never did. The newspaper and, later, *Leaves of Grass* were the media through which democracy was proclaimed.

Whitman's deep faith in the "penny press" was first expressed in his March 26, 1842, *New York Aurora* editorial when he declared that it could "disperse the clouds of ignorance; and make the great body of the people intelligent, capable, and worthy of performing the duties of republican freemen" (Whitman, *The Journalism, Vol. I*, 74). He saw the penny papers as "mighty engines of truth" pitted against the larger newspapers representing the vested interests of the moneyed, aristocratic, and privileged class that sought to stifle or control surging popular democracy. He recognized this development as "our experiment of democratic freedom" that necessitated new doctrines, innovations, and "systems of policy" that would develop the "capacities of men for self-government" and extend citizen self-reliance to a new standard ("Swing Open the Doors!," *Brooklyn Daily Eagle*, July 28, 1846, Whitman, *The Journalism, Vol. I*, 481). Whitman periodically wrote editorials that championed the role of the press in forwarding and securing the full extent of the democratic experiment, and he remonstrated against those newspapers and editors that were bogged down in party politics or self-interested agendas.

In his "The Press—Its Future" editorial for the *Brooklyn Daily Times* issue of July 31, 1857, he wrote: "The introduction of the magnetic telegraph and the invention of lightning presses have made the press *the* institution *par excellence*, of the day. . . . Newspapers have become the mirror of the world, without looking into which, no one can accomplish anything." During his editorship of the *Brooklyn Daily Times*, Whitman wrote over twenty articles on the press and journalists, reflecting his ability to stand back and view the field and profession in which he worked. In his poem "Years of the Modern," from the "Songs of Parting" cluster in the 1881 edition of *Leaves of Grass*, he wrote:

> With the steamship, the electric telegraph, the newspaper, the wholesale
>   engines of war,
> With these, and the world-spreading factories he interlinks all geography,
>   all lands; . . .

The newspaper was a "modern" force and transforming agent that Whitman knew from the inside as editor, as printer, and as freelance contributor.

Whitman's journalism sustained him for over fifteen years, and his versatility in a variety of genres (reportage, narrative, polemic) allowed him to improve the quality and circulation of at least two papers, the *Aurora* and the *Eagle*. He found great satisfaction in the work, though also profound frustrations, generally from the political imperatives placed on him in the highly partisan newspapers of the 1840s and 1850s. He imagined an audience of readers with whom he could personally connect and whom he could influence for the better in a variety of ways, but newspapers finally proved too limited a medium for this connection. He needed total editorial control in a world where editors faced proscriptions from publishers, politics, and the public. While his engagement with the political developments and issues of his times helped him hone his democratic vision and align himself with what he believed to be the spirit of the American Revolution, the penny press of his day and Democratic newspapers in particular proved too limited for his purview. Whitman's editorships ended with resignation or termination (or both), and his freelance work proved too piecemeal and scattered to allow the construction of a sustained voice. Ultimately, Whitman's stalled career in journalism provided a twofold legacy: its opportunities for sustained writing established, as Emerson said, a long foreground for Whitman's vibrant and freewheeling poetry; and, perhaps more important, journalism's limitations pushed Whitman to seek another medium to capture the cosmos with words. In this light, today's readers of Whitman are doubly indebted to his career in journalism.

In one sense, we have always known Whitman's journalism, since so much of *Specimen Days and Collect* is made up of prose that originally appeared in newspapers. In another sense, though, we have only very gradually become aware of the scope, quantity, and chronological sweep of his journalistic writing. The history of the publication of Whitman's pre–Civil War journalism is piecemeal, confusing, and still ongoing. It began in the 1920s, when editors Cleveland Rodgers and John Black published *The Gathering of the Forces* (1920), which made available texts of Whitman's writings for the *Brooklyn Daily Eagle* in 1846 and 1847. Rodgers contributed a lengthy essay titled "Whitman's Life and Work, 1846–1847," which was valuable in establishing the facts and circumstances of Whitman's editorship as well as asserting the importance of his journalism in his development as an American poet and spokesman:

> If this seems long and at times excessive in its praise of what, after all, is only a small part of the work of Walt Whitman, it must be charged to

> my own enthusiasm, stirred by the discovery of so much that is new and inspiring in what Whitman called these "big strong—days—our young days—days of preparation: the gathering of the forces." (Whitman, *Gathering of the Forces*, liii)

While Rodgers and Black presented Whitman's newspaper writings in complete form, nearly faithful to the originals, they removed the editorials and articles from their original chronological sequence, thus blurring historical context. In 1921 Emory Holloway published *The Uncollected Poetry and Prose of Walt Whitman*, which contained some of Whitman's first substantial newspaper pieces, including the 1840 "Sun-Down Papers" from the *Long Island Democrat*, along with some articles from other papers, including his sketches for the *New Orleans Crescent* (1848).

More of Whitman's journalism appeared in the 1930s. Emory Holloway and Vernolian Schwarz edited *I Sit and Look Out: Editorials from The Brooklyn Daily Times* (1932), and Holloway's introduction provided significant facts about Whitman's editorship, commentary on the articles, and an explanation of probable reasons for Whitman leaving the paper. The selections made by Holloway and Schwarz represent only about 10 percent of the writing Whitman did for the *Brooklyn Daily Times* from the spring of 1857 through June 1859, and many of the editorials appear in incomplete and unreliable texts, with silent omissions. Charles I. Glicksberg's *Walt Whitman and the Civil War* (1933) printed "City Photographs," Whitman's 1862 series of articles about New York City that he wrote for the *New York Leader*, along with a number of his *New York Times* Civil War pieces. Then, in 1936, Holloway teamed up with Ralph Adimari to publish *New York Dissected: A Sheaf of Recently Discovered Newspaper Articles by Walt Whitman*, which reprinted all of Whitman's articles of late 1855 and 1856 from *Life Illustrated*, including the series "New York Dissected," which ran in six parts in July and August 1856.

It was not until 1950 that additional collections of the journalism became available, when two books appeared: *Walt Whitman of the New York Aurora: Editor at Twenty-Two*, edited by Joseph Jay Rubin and Charles H. Brown, and Florence Bernstein Freedman's *Walt Whitman Looks at the Schools*, which included articles from the *Brooklyn Evening Star* and the *Brooklyn Daily Eagle*. Except for Joseph Jay Rubin's *The Historic Whitman* (1973), which reprinted the complete run of Whitman's "Letters from a Travelling Bachelor" (ten letters from the 1849–1850 *New York Sunday Dispatch*), the rest of the journalism published and made available for the first time came scattered in various journals, the results of archival detective work by such scholars as William White, who discovered unpublished articles, poems, letters, notes, fragments of printing proofs, and so forth. No other researcher could match the resourcefulness and dogged searching of White, a journalism professor at Wayne State University who, in addition to his many other contributions to Whitman scholarship, published a bibliography of Whitman's journalism in 1969 that laid out clearly just how extensive Whitman's newspaper work was. The importance of the journalism was underscored by the emergence of a body of criticism that began to deal with Whitman's newspaper work, including Robert D. Faner's *Walt Whitman & Opera* (1951), Thomas L. Brasher's *Whitman as Editor of the Brooklyn Daily Eagle* (1970), and Ezra Greenspan's *Walt Whitman and the American Reader* (1990).

In 1998 *The Journalism, Volume I: 1834–1846* appeared, edited by Herbert Bergman, with associate editors Douglas A. Noverr and Edward J. Recchia. *Volume II*, covering 1846–1848, followed in 2003. With these volumes, part of *The Collected Writings of Walt Whitman*, the journalism could for the first time be found in authoritative texts edited to modern textual standards. The early journalism finally began to take its place alongside Whitman's poetry, prose, manuscripts, notebooks, daybooks, and correspondence, which had already been carefully edited by scholars.

This current volume utilizes a four-part topical structure. The first three—"Democracy and Politics," "Moral Suasion," and "The Arts"—reflect Whitman's broad interests over the course of his career as a journalist. The final section, "Come Closer to Me," deserves some explanation. The articles in this section, ranging from 1839 through 1865, illustrate how Whitman sought to develop and convey a personal voice and sense of the immediacy of experience that was more than reportorial and that sought the effect of having the reader at the writer's elbow in a shared experience of observation and sensation. The intended effect was to move the reader closer to Whitman so that between the "I" of the author and the "you" of the reader something personal was shared and exchanged. For Whitman, this was a central need, this seeking of a connection that would become the hallmark of much of his poetry. His ability to create this sense of intimacy between writer and reader was also one of the reasons that he was hired as an editor by newspapers seeking to expand their readership. Whitman was known for his literary style, his ability to bring a fresh, new voice and perspective to a newspaper and make it distinct and individual in a competitive and crowded market. Other newspapers and editors acknowledged his skill at this and his ability to produce results; in fact, two newspapers, the *Aurora* and the *Eagle*, grew impressively in circulation under his editorship.

The editorials and articles are presented here in chronological sequence in each section, and each of the texts is complete, presented exactly as it appeared. The goal is to present the development of Whitman's ideas and positions over the course of his journalistic career (which was his whole public life as a writer), to capture the rich variety of articles he published, to demonstrate his principles and convictions about the United States and Americans, and to suggest his incredible range of interests and knowledge.

This volume includes only a small percentage of the total body of Whitman's journalistic writings, and the focus is on the earlier work from the three newspapers he edited; these are the pieces that were not reprinted or gathered in his later prose works, as was his practice in *Democratic Vistas, and Other Papers*; *November Boughs*; *Specimen Days and Collect*; and *Good-bye My Fancy*, published between 1871 and 1891. In publishing his later journalism in book form, Whitman recognized the important connection it had to his literary reputation. In gathering a broad selection of his earlier journalism in book form, we hope to show how it had an equally important connection to Whitman's development as a writer.

The titles of some articles have been regularized for overall consistency and to facilitate citation. Those titles regularized are the ones that appeared in all bold capitals and were set on the left margins of the columns with the text starting after a dash following the title. These were shorter, non-"leader" articles. All other titles have been reproduced as they appeared.

Works Cited

Bergman, Herbert. "Preface" and "Introduction." In Walt Whitman, *The Journalism, Volume I: 1834–1846*, ed. Herbert Bergman, Douglas A. Noverr, and Edward J. Recchia, xxv–lxx. New York: Peter Lang, 1998.

———. "Walt Whitman as a Journalist, March, 1848–1892." *Journalism Quarterly* 48, no. 3 (Autumn 1971): 431–437.

Brasher, Thomas L. *Whitman as Editor of the Brooklyn Daily Eagle*. Detroit: Wayne State University Press, 1970.

Brown, Charles H. *William Cullen Bryant*. New York: Charles Scribner's Sons, 1971.

Emery, Edwin, and Michael Emery. *The Press and America: An Interpretive History of the Mass Media*. 5th ed. Englewood Cliffs, N.J.: Prentice-Hall, 1984.

Faner, Robert D. *Walt Whitman & Opera*. Philadelphia: University of Pennsylvania Press, 1951.

Greenspan, Ezra. *Walt Whitman and the American Reader*. New York: Cambridge University Press, 1990.

Loving, Jerome. *Walt Whitman: The Song of Himself*. Berkeley: University of California Press, 1999.

Reid, James D. *The Telegraph in America: Its Founders, Promoters and Noted Men*. Reprint ed. New York: Arno Press, 1974.

Rubin, Joseph Jay. *The Historic Whitman*. University Park: Pennsylvania State University Press, 1973.

Stacy, Jason. *Walt Whitman's Multitudes: Labor Reform and Persona in Whitman's Journalism and the First* Leaves of Grass, *1840–1855*. New York: Peter Lang, 2008.

———. "Washington's Tears: Sentimental Anecdote and Walt Whitman's Battle of Long Island." *Walt Whitman Quarterly Review* 27 (2010): 213–226.

White, William. "Walt Whitman's Journalism: A Bibliography." *Walt Whitman Review* 14 (September 1968): 67–141.

Whitman, Walt. *The Gathering of the Forces*. Ed. Cleveland Rodgers and John Black. 2 vols. New York: G. P. Putnam's Sons, 1920.

———. "How 'Leaves of Grass' Was Made." *Frank Leslie's Popular Monthly* (June 1892): 731–735.

———. *I Sit and Look Out: Editorials from the Brooklyn Daily Times by Walt Whitman*. Ed. Emory Holloway and Vernolian Schwarz. New York: Columbia University Press, 1932.

———. *The Journalism, Volume I: 1834–1846,* part of *The Collected Writings of Walt Whitman*. Ed. Herbert Bergman, Douglas A. Noverr, and Edward J. Recchia. New York: Peter Lang, 1998.

———. *The Journalism, Volume II: 1846–1848,* part of *The Collected Writings of Walt Whitman*. Ed. Herbert Bergman, Douglas A. Noverr, and Edward J. Recchia. New York: Peter Lang, 2003.

———. *New York Dissected: A Sheaf of Recently Discovered Newspaper Articles by Walt Whitman*. Ed. Emory Holloway and Ralph Adimari. New York: Rufus Rockwell Wilson, 1936.

———. *November Boughs*. Philadelphia: David McKay, 1888.

———. *The Uncollected Poetry and Prose of Walt Whitman*. Ed. Emory Holloway. 2 vols. Garden City, N.Y.: Doubleday, Page, 1921.

———. *Walt Whitman and the Civil War*. Ed. Charles I. Glicksberg. Philadelphia: University of Pennsylvania Press, 1933.

———. *Walt Whitman of the New York Aurora: Editor at Twenty-Two*. Ed. Joseph Jay Rubin and Charles H. Brown. State College, Pa.: Bald Eagle, 1950.

Williams, Robert C. *Horace Greeley: Champion of American Freedom*. New York: New York University Press, 2006.

I

Democracy and Politics

Parties must remember that the masses of the people are as intelligent as the wire pullers of any faction or clique.

—*SUN*, MARCH 28, 1843

Americanism[1]

New York Aurora

MARCH 23, 1842

It is a lamentable thing that in this country we have so deplorable a passion for whatever is foreign—whatever is fashionable over the water. Each department of taste and science, and even political economy, (strange as it may seem) is imbued with a principle which leads to copying from the English or other Europeans—in their similar department. And we bend in slavish adoration to that which ushers itself in with the stamp of foreign approbation. We dare not question the infallibility of London and Edinburgh critics. A man comes among us with certificates from royal colleges, and baronet professors, and diplomas of employment as court purveyor in whatever his line may be—and our obedient republicans bow themselves humbly to the mandate.

Why should this be? Have we not people among *us* as worthy and as capable, as these European itinerants? Have we not scholars as learned, and philosophers as wise? If we have *not,* it is from the neglect and ingratitude of their own countrymen—who refuse to give them encouragement, or bestow their well earned meed[2] of praise.

But we *have*. Native Americans[3] are numerous among us, who equal in scientific attainments the best and noblest of the old world. The great bar is, that they have been brought up in our midst; they want the enchantment of distance, and the settling test of foreign applause.

The Aurora prides itself on being imbued with an *American* spirit. We look upon emigrants to our republic with friendly and generous eyes; but many things they bring with them might far better be left at home. Brought up to believe in the doctrine of loyalty, and the superstitions of every kind that mark all the countries of Europe, these people find it difficult, when they come to our shores, to throw off the opinions they have worn so long.

Again we say, we have no disposition to look upon foreigners with prejudiced eyes; for we view all the human family with the broad glance of benevolence and love. We say this, not to curry favor with foreigners; that we should disdain. The Aurora has shown that it has no fear or flattery for *them.*

Let the citizens of this great republic be more just to themselves. Let us respect our own capacities, and not hide our lights under bushels.[4]

NOTES

1. Transcribed from scanned original at the Walt Whitman Archive, whitmanarchive.org. This editorial also appears in Walt Whitman, *The Journalism, Volume I: 1834–1846,* part of *The Collected Writings of Walt Whitman,* ed. Herbert Bergman, Douglas A. Noverr, and Edward J. Recchia (New York: Peter Lang, 1998), 65–66.

2. Reward, compensation.

3. In the 1840s "Native American" often signified white, Protestant "native" citizens opposed to Catholic and often Irish immigrants. While Whitman's editorials in the *Aurora* contain many of his most nativist sentiments, explicitly so in other *Aurora* editorials regarding the public funding of Catholic parochial schools, later, in the cluster "Chants Democratic and Native American" from the 1860 edition of *Leaves of Grass,* Whitman used "Native American" in terms more universal than contemporary nativists. In his nativist articles of the spring of 1842, Whitman echoed many of the breathless warnings about the threat of Irish Catholics to American democracy and especially feared politics riven by ethnic and religious allegiances.

4. "Neither do men light a candle, and put it under a bushel, but on a candlestick; and it giveth light unto all that are in the house." Matthew 5:15, KJV.

Organs of the Democracy[1]

New York Aurora

MARCH 29, 1842

It is useless to conceal the fact that the democratic party in New York labor under the disadvantage of having no publication really creditable to them, and really calculated to further their interests. At the present time, the Post,[2] Standard,[3] and New Era,[4] are all at loggerheads. The rock on which they split is the school question; the Standard being plumply in favor of the existing system—the Post also evidently opposed to a change, yet fearful to come out openly—the Era violently arrayed on the side of Hughes and the Catholic priests.[5]

The plain truth of the matter is, it is only by the most strenuous exertions that the New Era has permission to keep out its flag as the organ of Tammany Hall.[6] A large majority of the democratic leaders do not hesitate to express their contempt and dissatisfaction with the Era. They are openly in favor of lopping off from any connection with that stupid print. In this exigency the Era knows that by taking up cudgels for the defence of the Catholic interest, it will have that interest disciplined to its support, as a kind of forlorn hope. The Era undoubtedly thinks, too, that the Tammany leaders will not have the fearlessness decidedly to repudiate the move it has taken—for fear of losing the votes of those under the control of the priests. It remains to be seen whether the whole democratic party are to be led by the nose, by this manoeuvre of a clique of jesuits, and a paper which thus stabs the vitals of the party for the chance of a little advantage to itself.

Not a word has yet been said by the Era, about the nomination of Robert H. Morris as Mayor.[7] The Hughes faction, no doubt, are opposed to that nomination. For our own part, we do not think the city could select a more worthy man than he who at present occupies the mayoralty. He has all the qualifications of experience, ability, and character, that are necessary. As far as we have any preference, therefore, at present, we hope Morris will win the race.[8]

It is wonderful that the democrats do not take summary steps in this business. It is an insult and a disgrace to the party, that a journal presuming to be their organ should thus barter away their honor, and marshall itself under the dictation of a selfish clique of *foreigners*.

The Tammany party want, here in New York, a newspaper bold, manly, able, and *American* in its tenor; a newspaper vigorous and original and fresh. Until they have such a one, the organs at present recognised as theirs, will be no better than dead weight to them. [9]

NOTES

1. Transcribed from scanned original at the Walt Whitman Archive, whitmanarchive.org. This editorial also appears in Walt Whitman, *The Journalism, Volume I: 1834 1846*, part of *The Collected Writings of Walt Whitman*, ed. Herbert Bergman, Douglas A. Noverr, and Edward J. Recchia (New York: Peter Lang, 1998), 79.

2. Alexander Hamilton founded the *New York Evening Post* in 1801; by the 1830s the *Post* published editorials representing the reform interests of editor-in-chief William Cullen Bryant (1794–1878) and editor William Leggett (1801–1839), labor reformer, free-market activist, and founder of the short-lived "Locofoco" faction of the Democratic Party. The Locofocos demanded free trade against economic monopolies and sought to undermine Tammany Hall's control of the Democratic Party in New York City. Whitman, an admirer of Leggett's anti–Tammany Hall iconoclasm, called him "glorious." See Allan Nevins, *The Evening Post: A Century of Journalism* (New York: Boni and Liveright, 1922), 141, 224.

3. The *New York Standard* was edited by John I. Mumford (1791–1863), a prominent merchant, Democratic publisher, and politico who, in addition to his work on the *Standard*, held patronage positions in the Customs House of New York and was a delegate to the Democratic State Convention of 1852. Joseph Alfred Scoville, *The Old Merchants of New York City* (New York: Thomas R. Knox, 1885), 5:194–197.

4. Levi Slamm (1816–1862), editor of the *New Era* in 1842, was a prominent Locofoco activist who followed William Leggett out of the New York Democratic Party in 1835 and proved instrumental in the return of the Locofocos to Tammany Hall in 1838 after the Democrats accepted Leggett's antimonopoly platform. The *Aurora*, in the weeks before Whitman's arrival as editor, described the *New Era* as the "official organ" of Tammany Hall.

5. In 1842 Bishop John Hughes (1797–1864) marshaled the growing power of Irish American immigrants in New York City to force Democratic Party support of public funding for parochial schools. For more on this "school war" of 1842, see Edwin Burrows and Mike Wallace, *Gotham: A History of New York City to 1898* (Oxford: Oxford University Press, 1999), 499; Diane Ravitch, *The Great School Wars: A History of the New York City Public Schools* (Baltimore: Johns Hopkins University Press, 1974), 46–47. For information on Whitman and the Hughes debate, see Jerome Loving, *Walt Whitman: The Song of Himself* (Berkeley: University of California Press, 1999), 63–64; Jason Stacy, *Walt Whit-*

man's Multitudes: Labor Reform and Persona in Whitman's Journalism and the First Leaves of Grass, *1840–1855* (New York: Peter Lang, 2008), 59–67; David Reynolds, *Walt Whitman's America: A Cultural Biography* (New York: Alfred A. Knopf, 1995), 99.

6. Originally named for Tamamend, a mythological chief of the Delaware tribe, the Tammany Society began as a fraternal organization in 1787, but by the early nineteenth century became involved in the politics of New York City in support of the Jeffersonian Republicans. Burrows and Wallace, *Gotham*, 316. By the 1830s Tammany Hall effectively controlled the Democratic Party in New York City and maintained control of the city well into the twentieth century through a complex system of patronage and local ward bosses who often represented a particular immigrant demographic.

7. Robert H. Morris (1808–1855), Democratic mayor of New York 1841–1843.

8. Morris won reelection in 1843.

9. Here Whitman sought to position the *Aurora* as the true voice of Tammany's constituents by painting the *Era* as beholden to a Catholic faction within the party. See Stacy, *Walt Whitman's Multitudes*, 143.

Intelligence of the Working People[1]

Sun

MARCH 28, 1843

There is, in this country, a class of people, very numerous too, who look upon the great mass of the working people as a pack of ignorant know nothings. Such men are to be found in political organizations, in charge of newspapers, and in high stations. We have taken some pains to watch the movements of these people, and see what effect their mean opinions of the working men would have upon their opinions of government, state policy and public affairs. We have obtained much light on this subject, and, after long and close observation, we find that these people are, almost invariably, the admirers of monarchy, the lovers of such a government as would grind the poor into dust, and elevate their own dear selves high above all others. They are so fond of themselves as to be unable to remember that the working man possesses intelligence sufficient to criticize the acts of public servants or conductors of the public press; they think nothing too absurd for the gullibility of the people—the columns of newspapers under their control teem with the most absurd misrepresentation and fraud—packed organizations and emissaries are hired to manufacture public opinion among the knowing ones, with the hope of its spreading throughout the community, the state or the nation—these and a thousand others are the means used by these designing knaves. In the end, however, we have always noticed, that no matter how strong the triumph of error built upon these false notions of the working people may be, its end and overthrow by *these very people* whom it despises, is sure to come the moment the power goes back in the hands of those who conferred it. This fact—proved by history—developed by the every day occurrences of life—should teach political leaders, and all persons who serve the people, to have constantly before them, "*the greatest good to the greatest number*."[2] With this motto, affectionately cherished in all their deliberations for political power, we will guarantee, to those who adopt it, the lasting favor of the people; and to the people in return, we will guarantee a wise government, just laws, protection to life and property, prosperity and happiness.

Parties *must* remember that the masses of the people are as intelligent as the wire pullers[3] of any faction or clique; and that all public measures—their effects upon the public weal, and their bearing upon the rights of the people—are watched with argus eyes[4] by the people: those who forget this principle, whether conductors of the press or of government, may depend upon a fate like that which has cast thousands of their predecessors into the dark abyss of oblivion.

NOTES

1. Transcribed from Walt Whitman, *The Journalism, Volume I: 1834–1846*, part of *The Collected Writings of Walt Whitman*, ed. Herbert Bergman, Douglas A. Noverr, and Edward J. Recchia (New York: Peter Lang, 1998), 171–172.

2. By the early nineteenth century, this proved to be a common adaptation of Jeremy Bentham's axiom that "it is the greatest happiness of the greatest number that is the measure of right and wrong." Jeremy Bentham, *A Fragment on Government*... (London: T. Payne; P. Elmsly; and E. Brooke, 1776), ii.

3. A term of derision toward individuals who manipulated democratic processes to their own ends. For example, "If it were known, for example, that a particular gentleman would, if a candidate for office of governor, lose ten Whig votes in either the county of Wake or Orange [North Carolina], this would be decisive against him, and he would be set aside. But if it were only known that this same individual would lose one or two thousand votes in the West, such knowledge would not shake the determination of these wire-pullers to make him the candidate." T. L. Clingman, "On the Principles of the Whig and Democratic Parties," House of Representatives, March 7, 1844 (Washington, D.C.: Gales and Seatow, 1844), 11.

4. Argus was a legendary Greek giant with 100 eyes.

Texas[1]

New-York Democrat

AUGUST 12, 1844

By a late arrival from Vera Cruz, we learn that the utmost activity prevails in the arrangements for invading Texas—that the 15,000 men authorised for the expedition, are coming in from the various provinces, and that the four millions required to commence the campaign, will be made up as soon as the amount can be collected from the different States among whom it has been apportioned. Under the pretence of repairing the fortifications at St. Juan de Ulloa, and the defences at Vera Cruz, Santa Anna has drawn from England, on security of the mines, two millions worth of powder, ball, cannon, muskets, and ammunitions of war; and several officers connected with the East India army in the late wars, have had permission of the British Government to join the Mexican army destined against Texas. These preparations convince us of the serious intentions of Santa Anna in his designs against Texas. He knows the country has already experienced reverses at the battle of San Jacinto—is determined to retrieve his losses, and soothe his wounded honor—and Texas is not in a condition to repel this formidable invasion, and without aid from the United States, we apprehend the revengeful and sanguinary Mexicans will succeed.[2]

Shall we permit Mexico to recover Texas? The answer every where will be NO! Under no circumstances can the government of the people of the United States allow Texas to revert to Mexico. We are bound by our stipulations with France in the treaty of 1803, to admit Texas into the Union as soon as possible, and to protect her against the encroachments of any power.[3] It is true we made a treaty with Spain in 1819, and surrendered Texas without being aware of the binding obligations of our treaty of 1803, and consequently the cession of Texas to Spain is, in one sense, null and void, and Texas reverts to the United States, if it is still the wish of her people to come into the Union.[4] The injudicious rejection of the treaty by the Senate cannot alter the state of affairs.[5] *Texas is ours*, and the people *will* have it. In spite of secret as well as open opposition, by ill-advised friends and our enemies the federalists[6] and abolitionists,[7] there is a great, and growing, and animated spirit everywhere bursting forth in favor of Texas. In this state it burns with a steady and increased flame, which cannot be extinguished.

Measures, however, must be taken forthwith to arrest the progress of Mexico. It has been asked whether it will be necessary to call Congress together to adopt measures to prevent Texas from falling a prey to her invaders. With the temper and disposition of the present Senate, nothing can be expected. The President has the power to protect the general interests of the country, and can order the forces of the southern division of the army towards the frontiers, and a naval force to rendezvouz at Galveston, to watch the movements of the enemy, and to act definitely whenever the people of Texas shall apply for aid. This is no time to talk of results or apprehensions of a war with Mexico. We are bound to prevent the fall of Texas, if we are wise, and we *will do it* at any hazard.

NOTES

1. This transcription is taken from Walt Whitman, *The Journalism, Volume I: 1834–1846*, part of *The Collected Writings of Walt Whitman*, ed. Herbert Bergman, Douglas A. Noverr, and Edward J. Recchia (New York: Peter Lang, 1998), 196–197. Americans began to settle within the borders of Texas in 1821 when Moses Austin received permission from the Mexican government to bring 300 families, many who were slaveholders, into the Red River region. The population of Anglo-American slaveholders continued to grow in Texas throughout the early 1830s despite the Mexican government's abolishment of slavery and closing of the Texas-U.S. frontier to further Anglo settlement in 1829. When, in 1835, President Antonio Lopez de Santa Anna dissolved the Mexican Congress and instituted a military dictatorship, Texas (along with a number of other Mexican provinces) formed a provisional government, which, when the Mexican army sought to reestablish its authority there, declared Texas an independent republic. After the defeat of the Mexican army at the Battle of San Jacinto (1836), Britain, France, and the United States officially recognized the independent Republic of Texas, which existed between 1836 and 1845, when it was annexed by the United States. K. Jack Bauer, *The Mexican War: 1846–1848* (Lincoln: University of Nebraska Press, 1974), 6–7.

2. Whitman here is fanning the flames of war with Mexico in line with the expansionist platform of the Democratic candidate for president in 1844, James K. Polk. Though the United States did not annex Texas until 1845, since February 1844 the administration of John Tyler had maneuvered American warships in Mexican waters, and Brevet Brigadier General Zachary Taylor had marched an expedition force to the border of Texas, ostensibly in defense of the independent republic. By the time Polk took his oath of office

in March 1845, both houses of Congress had already voted in favor of annexation. Bauer, *Mexican War*, 7–9.

3. Portions of the Red River region in the Republic of Texas lay within the boundaries of the Louisiana Purchase Treaty of 1803.

4. Here Whitman attempts to explain away the Adams-Onís Treaty of 1819, where the United States relinquished all claims to Texas in return for rights to Florida. See Philip Coolidge Brooks, *Diplomacy and the Borderlands: The Adams-Onís Treaty of 1819* (Berkeley: University of California Press, 1939).

5. In April Secretary of State John C. Calhoun negotiated a treaty with the government of Texas for its annexation, though it failed to achieve two-thirds approval in the U.S. Senate.

6. Here Whitman refers to the Whig opponents to annexation by the name of the defunct elitist party of Alexander Hamilton and John Adams.

7. By 1844 the abolitionist press had been active for over a decade and inspired vehement opposition from both Southerners and Northerners. The best known of these publications, William Lloyd Garrison's *Liberator*, had been banned from Southern mail; in 1835 Garrison himself was attacked in Boston by an anti-abolitionist mob. Abolitionists feared that the annexation of Texas would lead to the expansion of slavery beyond the boundaries of the Missouri Compromise (1820).

All Reforms in Government Must Come from the Democratic Impulse![1]

Brooklyn Daily Eagle

APRIL 22, 1846

Is not this true? Look back through the history of our nation, from the close of the Revolutionary war to the present moment, and deny it who can?

Now we would not be considered one of those bigots[2] that think there is no good in humanity, except what resides in some favorite school of faith—We believe in a *general average* of good. We think moreover that a very large portion of that so-called whig party,[3] have much in common with the soundest and truest democracy. But the paramount feature stamped—ingrained, we may call it—in the public career of that party, has hitherto been, is, and doubtless will be, the very opposite of reform. —It is averse to innovation, loves the old rather than the new, and will not favor any "experiment."

—Therefore say we to the people of this island, that if the coming State Convention is to result in any real reform to the Constitution, it must be through the democratic impulse; and to give play for that impulse we must elect the Democratic Delegates. —What dependence is there upon the whigs? If we expect wholesome fruit, do we plant thistle-seeds?[4]

NOTES

1. Transcribed from scanned original, Brooklyn Public Library—Brooklyn Collection. This editorial also appears in Walt Whitman, *The Journalism, Volume I: 1834–1846*, part of *The Collected Writings of Walt Whitman*, ed. Herbert Bergman, Douglas A. Noverr, and Edward J. Recchia (New York: Peter Lang, 1998), 338.

2. Here Whitman applied a contemporary meaning of "bigot," identifying one who is theologically narrow-minded and denominationally exclusive.

3. The American Whig Party had its origins in the fight over the rechartering of the National Bank during the first administration of Andrew Jackson. The name was originally

used by the parliamentary forces that overthrew James II during the Glorious Revolution (1688), and, later, by American revolutionaries. The American Whigs took the name as a way to critique "King Andrew" Jackson and his heavy-handed use of the veto power. See Michael F. Holt, *The Rise and Fall of the American Whig Party: Jacksonian Politics and the Onset of the Civil War* (New York: Oxford University Press, 1999), 27–28. While Democrats often painted Whigs as "an association of narrow-minded, silk-stocking patricians bent on telling other people how to behave," the Whig Party successfully practiced populist campaign techniques in the election of 1840, where the Whig nominee, William Henry Harrison, defeated the incumbent, Martin Van Buren. Holt, 106–107, 190.

4. An important result of the 1846 constitutional convention, among others, was the election of state judges and a twenty-year cycle for proposing a constitutional convention on statewide ballots. New York Constitution (1846), http://www.courts.state.ny.us/history/pdf/Library/1846_constitution.pdf.

Democratic Young Men.[1]

Brooklyn Daily Eagle

MAY 6, 1846

Perhaps no feature of the late victory won by the democratic party[2] in this State is more peculiar, or calls for more special notice, than that part borne in the battle by the democratic *young men*. Indeed in all the late elections of importance, we have noticed the growing and acknowledged influence wielded by this branch of our party. They are rapidly taking precedence of those who are their betters by age. Whether this will be productive of benefits remains to be seen. If we may express our opinion, however, founded on deliberate surveyal of the political history of the past twenty years, we should say it would. Some writer has observed that most of the political reforms of modern times proceed from young men. A little thought will convince any "anxious inquirer" of the truth of this remark.

In our party—the party of progress—it is especially necessary that each successive generation, which is supposed in many respects to be wiser than its immediate predecessor, should lift itself out as much as possible from that which has gone before it, act independently, and with a reliance as much as possible on itself, and its own judgment. Of course the lessons of the past are not to be despised. We may learn much from its experience, its tyranny, its ignorance, and its abominable bigotry. But the past, we often think, brings us more than enough evil to counterbalance its good. We rely too much upon it. We work our course through its example. We are afraid to trust in the fact that we are as men walking in daylight, while they were groping in the dimness of the early dawn—that we therefore are better than the men of old.[3]

The Democratic party, in all its civil disputes, has hitherto seen its more liberal portion come off victorious. The period of victory is merely a question of months. The staid old must in due time die off, and the ardent young must take their places—and the effect of this is, that we cannot hold any conservative opinions long. But the method of a change is worthy of attention. It is unseemingly that members of the same family should "scratch each others' eyes," and allow the most exacerbated feelings of spite to operate in their intercourse. Besides, what good does it do? Abuse neither convinces men, or produces a happy effect on the neighboring spectators.

NOTES

1. Transcribed from scanned original, Brooklyn Public Library—Brooklyn Collection. This editorial also appears in Walt Whitman, *The Journalism, Volume I: 1834–1846*, part of *The Collected Writings of Walt Whitman*, ed. Herbert Bergman, Douglas A. Noverr, and Edward J. Recchia (New York: Peter Lang, 1998), 349–350. This title might have had particular resonance for Whitman's readers as it echoes popular democratic movements of this period like the Young Italy movement (1831) of Giuseppe Mazzini (1805–1872); the Young Hegelians, who inspired Karl Marx (1818–1883); and the Young America movement (1845), which was inspired by labor reformer and Democratic radical William Leggett (1801–1839), *Democratic Review* editor John O'Sullivan (1813–1895), and publisher Evert Duyckinck (1816–1878). The Young America movement promoted democracy, free trade, and unfettered territorial expansion as a means to spread democratic civilization.

2. Whitman probably refers here to the mayoral election of April 1846, when Democrat Andrew H. Mickle (1805–1863) defeated the Whig candidate, Robert Taylor, and the Native Party candidate, William B. Cozzens. Ralph J. Caliendo, *New York City Mayors* (Bloomington, Ind.: Xlibris, 2010), 273.

3. Compare to Henry David Thoreau (1817–1862) in *Walden* (1854): "One generation abandons the enterprises of another like stranded vessels."

Shall we fight it out?[1]

Brooklyn Daily Eagle

MAY 11, 1846[2]

Yes: Mexico must be thoroughly chastised!—We have reached a point, in our intercourse with that country, when prompt and effectual demonstrations of force are enjoined upon us by every dictate of right and policy. The news of yesterday has added the last argument wanted to prove the necessity of an immediate Declaration of War by our government toward its southern neighbor.[3]

We are justified in the face of the world, in having treated Mexico with more forbearance than we have ever yet treated an enemy—for Mexico, though contemptible in many respects, is an enemy deserving a vigorous 'lesson.' We have coaxed, excused, listened with deaf ears to the insolent gasconde[4] of her government, submitted thus far to a most offensive rejection of an Ambassador personifying the American nation,[5] and waited for years without payment of the claims of our injured merchants.[6] We have sought peace through every avenue, and shut our eyes to many things, which, had they come from England or France, the President would not have dared to pass over without stern and speedy resentment. We have dammed up our memory, of what has passed in the South years ago—of the devilish massacres of some of our bravest and noblest sons, the children not of the South alone, but of the North and West—massacres, not only in defiance of ordinary humanity, but in violation of all the rules of war.[7] Who has read the sickening story of those brutal wholesale murders, so useless for any purpose except gratifying the cowardly appetite of a nation of bravos, willing to shoot down men by the hundred in cold blood—without panting for the day when the prayer of that blood should be listened to—when the vengeance of a retributive God should be meted out to those who so ruthlessly and needlessly slaughtered His image?[8]

That day has arrived. We think there can be no doubt of the truth of yesterday's news; and we are sure the people here, ten to one, are for prompt and *effectual* hostilities. Tame newspaper comments, such as appear in the leading democratic print of today,[9] in New York, and the contemptible anti-patriotic criticisms of its contemporary whig organ,[10] do *not* express the sentiments and wishes of *the people*. Let our arms now be carried with a spirit which shall teach the world that, while we are not forward for a quarrel, America knows how to crush, as well as how to expand!

NOTES

1. Transcribed from scanned original, Brooklyn Public Library—Brooklyn Collection. This editorial also appears in Walt Whitman, *The Journalism, Volume I: 1834–1846*, part of *The Collected Writings of Walt Whitman*, ed. Herbert Bergman, Douglas A. Noverr, and Edward J. Recchia (New York: Peter Lang, 1998), 358–359.

2. President Polk gave his war message before Congress on May 11, 1846. The Senate declared war on Mexico on May 13, 1846.

3. On March 28, 1846, General Zachary Taylor (1784–1850) and 3,500 American troops reached the Rio Grande across from the Mexican village of Matamoros. Taylor faced General Francisco Mejia and 3,000 Mexican troops. According to the Mexican government, Taylor and his forces occupied Mexican territory since the province of Texas historically bordered on the Nueces River, about 165 miles to the north. On April 11 General Pedro de Ampudia arrived with 3,000 more troops and threatened to attack Taylor should he refuse to retreat to the Nueces River. Taylor, instead of retreating, interpreted the ultimatum as an act of war and cut off the supply route to the Mexican forces around Matamoros. In reaction, the Mexican forces at Matamoros, now under the command of General Mariano Arista, sent 1,600 cavalry troops across the Rio Grande and ambushed a breakaway force of sixty-three U.S. cavalrymen. President Polk received word of the attack on May 9, 1846, and cited the incident in his war message of May 11, 1846. Robert W. Merry, *A Country of Vast Designs: James K. Polk, the Mexican War, and the Conquest of the American Continent* (New York: Simon & Schuster, 2009), 241–243.

4. Meaning an empty boast or bluster.

5. The Mexican government sent U.S. ambassador John Slidell (1793–1871) home on April 11, 1846, in protest of General Taylor's encampment on the Rio Grande. During the Civil War, Slidell served the Confederate States of America (CSA) in France, where he sought recognition of the CSA. During the *Trent* affair (1861), Slidell was forcibly removed from a British vessel by the U.S. Navy, but was allowed his freedom after Great Britain protested the boarding of a British vessel.

6. Here Whitman echoes Polk's war address of two days previous: "Our commerce with Mexico has been almost annihilated. It was formerly highly beneficial to both nations, but our merchants have been deterred from prosecuting it by the system of outrage and extortion which the Mexican authorities have pursued against them, whilst their appeals

through their own Government for indemnity have been made in vain."

7. Of the U.S. defenders at the Alamo, thirty were from Tennessee, sixteen from Kentucky, and eleven from Texas. Twelve were from Virginia, but no other Southern state had more than seven (South Carolina). Thirteen defenders came from Pennsylvania and five from New York. "The Alamo," http://www.thealamo.org/battle/defenders.php.

8. Here Whitman refers to the battles of Goliad (1835) and the Alamo (1836), where Texas forces were massacred by Mexican troops during the Texas Revolution. Whitman later included a fictionalized description of the massacre at Goliad in *Leaves of Grass* (1855), 40. Walt Whitman Archive, whitmanarchive.org.

9. Perhaps the *New York Evening Post*, which as late as 1845 was against the annexation of Texas. The *New York Herald*, edited by James Gordon Bennett (1795–1872), on the other hand, supported the war. "The Mexican-American War and the Media, 1845–1848," January 30, 1845, http://www.history.vt.edu/MxAmWar/Newspapers/MG/MG1845aJanJune.htm#AAlexGaz.

10. Whitman could be referring here to the *New York Tribune* under Horace Greeley (1811–1872), a leading Whig editor and, later, reform Republican politician.

No Slavery in Oregon.[1]

Brooklyn Daily Eagle

AUGUST 7, 1846

We are well pleased with the decisive vote by which the H. of R.[2] yesterday (6th,) in forming the bill for the Territorial Government of Oregon, voted, 108 to 43, to have *no slavery* there, in the future years![3] Though our cool and sensible men at the North look with infinite contempt of the fanaticism of sundry Northern "abolitionists," there is no denying the pernicious evil of strengthening an institution which Washington[4] and Jefferson[5] condemned, and expressed the most ardent desire to meliorate.[6]—If the "abolitionists," and their foolish encouragers, would only hold their tongues, and let the slow but sure and steady spread of political and moral truth, do its work among the people, all that ought to be done in reference to slavery, *would* be done;—which, by the by, does *not* involve a sudden abrogation of it.[7] *That* would be a great curse to the country, instead of a blessing.

NOTES

1. Transcribed from scanned original, Brooklyn Public Library—Brooklyn Collection. This editorial also appears in Walt Whitman, *The Journalism, Volume II: 1846–1848,* part of *The Collected Writings of Walt Whitman,* ed. Herbert Bergman, Douglas A. Noverr, and Edward J. Recchia (New York: Peter Lang, 2003), 8.

2. The House of Representatives.

3. While James K. Polk campaigned on an expansionist platform in 1844, he proved much less belligerent in the case of the Pacific Northwest than in the Southwest. Within one month of the declaration of war on Mexico by the U.S. Senate, the Polk administration negotiated the Oregon Treaty with Great Britain to settle the northwestern border between Canada and the United States. Since the Republic of Texas, annexed to the United States in 1845, already held slaves, the entrance of the Oregon Territory into the Union as free territory proved a foregone conclusion, especially since it resided north of the southern border of Missouri, the line of demarcation between slave-labor and free-labor states

that fell within the territory of the Louisiana Purchase since the Missouri Compromise of 1820.

4. Though Washington never expressed these sentiments publicly, soon after the Revolution he did so privately in letters published in periodicals and books available to Whitman. For example, from the *Democratic Review*, "it being among my first wishes to see some plan adopted, by which slavery in this country may be abolished by slow, sure, and imperceptible degrees" (George Washington to John F. Mercer, September 9, 1786); and "To set the slaves afloat at once would, I really believe, be productive of much inconvenience and mischief; but by degrees, it certainly might, and assuredly ought, to be effect; and that too by legislative authority" (George Washington to Marquis de LaFayette, May 10, 1786). Both letters appeared in *United States Democratic Review* (November 1843): 558.

5. Thomas Jefferson, in *Notes on the State of Virginia*, claimed that "the spirit of the master is abating, that of the slave rising from the dust, his condition mollifying, the way I hope preparing, under the auspices of heaven, for a total emancipation, and that this is disposed, in order of events, to be with the consent of the masters, rather than by their extirpation." Thomas Jefferson, *Notes on the State of Virginia* (London: John Stockdale, 1787), 272.

6. Here Whitman continues to walk a fine line between nascent free-soil sentiments of his working-class, Democratic constituency (who proved often antipathetic toward both the expansion of slavery and emancipation) and the abolitionist activism of more ardent reformers. Whitman's own New York Democrats nearly split over the Wilmot Proviso, which sought to prevent the spread of the slave labor system to the new territories gained in the U.S.-Mexico War. Whitman himself lost his position at the *Eagle* for his free-soil politics in 1848.

7. This proved a common trope among many Americans who were uncomfortable with the existence of American slavery, but equally ambivalent about emancipation, including George Washington and Thomas Jefferson.

General Taylor.[1]

Brooklyn Daily Eagle

OCTOBER 14, 1846

The more we hear and read of this man, the more we think he in many respects resembles Washington. In moderation, in the most immovable firmness, in caution, in a fatherly regard for his troops,—and, we may add, in a repugnance to carry out the results of war to an extreme of severity against the enemy—it is not too much to say that our Commander on the Rio Grande, emulates the Great Commander of our Revolution. The former prefers—like the latter preferred—to effect positively a measured advantage, rather than grasp after a more brilliant one, and run the risk of losing all, and certainty of losing much; he prefers substance to mere glory—is not ashamed to be generous to a weak foe—seeks to blend in all his acts, a due forbearance—which is so difficult, with the emphatic movements required in our Mexican campaign.

Some of our contemporaries are vexed because Gen. Taylor did not make sharper terms with the Mexicans at Monterey, did not, (we suppose) signalise[2] his victory with more carnage, and glut the cravings of a bloody appetite with a greater infliction of death and disaster.[3] It is a sad commentary on public gratitude for public services that these complaints are so open and cool; for Gen. Taylor 's services might entitle him to a little of that forbearance due even the mistakes of such a man. But that Gen. Taylor has made the least mistake in granting the terms he did grant to Ampudia, it is idle to assert! It is idle—or rather it is presumptuous—for any one, distant from the field of operations, and knowing little of many hidden influences which doubtless had a potent bearing there—to put forward his flippant criticisms on a man who has showed such masterly qualities for his position, as Gen. Taylor has showed. . . . . The official despatches from the conquered head quarters of our army at Monterey hold the following language: "It will be seen that the terms granted the Mexican garrison are less rigorous than those first imposed. The gallant defence of the town, and the fact of a recent change of government in Mexico,[4] believed to be favorable to the interest of peace, induced me to concur with the commission in these terms, which will, I trust, receive the approval of the government. The latter consideration also prompted the convention for a temporary cessation of hostilities. Though scarcely warranted by my instructions, yet the change of affairs since those instructions were issued seemed to warrant this course." It is intimated from Washington that the Government have forthwith sent on orders dissenting from any "cessation"—which, under a specific provision of the capitulation, nullifies the armistice, and leaves matters in that respect as before. . . . . Be that as it may, we honor Gen. Taylor the more that he granted generous terms to a foe in his power—that he preferred all the solid results of a sure and less bloody triumph, to the more brilliant contingency of storming the citadel, of immense slaughter on both sides, and taking a ponderous army prisoners of war.[5] What could he do with prisoners twice the amount of his own force, and in an enemy's country?[6] It would look very showy in print to tell about the deadly struggle, and the triumph that would afterward have followed; but we, for one, prefer the quieter and surer plan which Taylor decided on,—and we honor him that he chose that nobler course—which a commoner hero doubtless, would not have done.

NOTES

1. Transcribed from scanned original, Brooklyn Public Library—Brooklyn Collection. This editorial also appears in Walt Whitman, *The Journalism, Volume II: 1846–1848,* part of *The Collected Writings of Walt Whitman,* ed. Herbert Bergman, Douglas A. Noverr, and Edward J. Recchia (New York: Peter Lang, 2003), 87–88.

2. Spelling in original.

3. Under pressure from President Polk to invade deeper into Mexico, General Taylor marched south and west from the Rio Grande toward the fortified position of the Mexican army at Monterrey. Despite being outnumbered, Taylor took the city on September 24, 1846, with heavy house-to-house fighting in the city, assisted by Texas irregulars who had experience laying siege to fortified houses by propelling timed shells through holes cut with pickaxes in the walls. When Taylor's forces began to drop shells on the central plaza, General Pedro de Ampudia surrendered to American forces. Douglas V. Meed, *The Mexican War, 1846–1848* (Oxford: Osprey Publishing, 2002), 44–45. As terms of surrender, Taylor offered a general armistice that left the Mexican army intact on the assumption that "it would be judicious to act with magnanimity toward a prostrate foe." K. Jack Bauer, *The Mexican War: 1846–1848* (Lincoln: University of Nebraska Press, 1974), 100. Taylor's generous terms angered President Polk, who turned his attention to General Winfield Scott

(1786–1866) because Scott had proposed an ambitious amphibious landing at Vera Cruz and an attack on Mexico City itself. Meed, *Mexican War*, 44.

4. In August 1846 José Mariano Salas (1797–1867) overthrew the government of Mariano Paredes y Arrillaga (1797–1849), who himself had become president only in January 1846 after overthrowing the presidency of José Joaquín de Herrera (1792–1854). Mark Crawford, *Encyclopedia of the Mexican-American War* (Santa Barbara, Calif.: ABC-CLIO, 1999), 139, 209, 244. Taylor seemed to hope that the Salas regime would prove more accommodating to American demands than President Paredes, who had vigorously resisted U.S. encroachments into Mexican territory. Instead, Salas recalled Santa Anna from exile in Cuba. Bauer, *Mexican War*, 279.

5. U.S. forces lost 120 soldiers in the battle. Mexican forces lost 333.

6. Here Whitman tries to justify Taylor's release of Ampudia's forces.

The Queen of England.[1]

Brooklyn Daily Eagle
DECEMBER 5, 1846

A number of persons here—where thrones, the paraphernalia, the trappings of royalty, are looked upon as useless and ridiculous expense, nay, more, as grinding to the people—are fighting a war of words in regard to the rights of women. These, at all events, where royalty exists, can scarcely object to a woman's sway. There seems to be so benignant and kindly an influence exercised over a people by the very *prestige* of a gentle-hearted woman being at the head of the government, that we cannot help applauding the law which allows it. Heaven knows men are rough, selfish, and bloody-minded enough to need ameliorating influences—and this is one of them. . . . . . . When the mildest and most well-wishing brain that ever throbbed beneath the English crown, resolved to set at defiance the tinsel stupidity of the old etiquette of courts, and visit the King of France at the Chateau d' Eu,[2] some seasons since, we felt a satisfaction and a delight, such as are rarely caused in our mind by the deeds of sovereigns—viewing them, as we do, with the eye of a true republican. And it were well for Europe if such visits were made oftener. Well wishers to peace must hope that the Queen will pursue this plan of visiting foreign places; and, if the progress of steam goes on improving for ten years to come as it has improved for ten years past, we could hardly subject ourselves to ridicule by inviting her majesty to come over and spend a week with Brother Jonathan himself![3] Startling as the idea appears to be now, in process of time we may find stranger notions realised.

It is a favorite argument of those who balance the good that Napoleon[4] did against the mighty sum of evil, death and sin, that followed the train of his life and conduct, to say that the simple breaking down of the tight bands that limited one European state from another, and familiarizing the different grades of society with the sight of royalty as a *human thing* were enough of themselves to outweigh all the worse results. There is some truth in this. But if those desirable effects were not dearly bought at the expense of so much treasure, and such an outlay of human life, of keeping a continent in a continued state of anarchy, and arraying army after army against each other for years in succession; if they do so much good to Napoleon's memory as to make philanthropists, in exulting over them, forget his ambition, his selfishness, his shameful desertion of those who loved him truly and fondly when it served his interest to desert them, his placing the glory of France before the lives and rights of all the other nations of the earth; if this be so, what meed[5] of praise shall be given that monarch who goes forth to produce the same beautiful results without the cost of a single life, the provoking of a single malignant thought, or the infliction of a single pain? What Napoleon did amid groans, the smoke of battle and the thunder of cannon, a gentle young woman (we love better to speak of her that way than as a crowned Queen) is doing amid smiles, light hearts, and the glitter of curious gladsome eyes. . . . . .[6] If we were forced to live in a monarchy, we should by all means prefer to be ruled by a Queen!

NOTES

1. Transcribed from scanned original, Brooklyn Public Library—Brooklyn Collection. This editorial also appears in Walt Whitman, *The Journalism, Volume II: 1846–1848*, part of *The Collected Writings of Walt Whitman*, ed. Herbert Bergman, Douglas A. Noverr, and Edward J. Recchia (New York: Peter Lang, 2003), 141–142. Queen Victoria ruled England from 1837 to 1901.

2. Victoria and Albert visited King Louis Philippe at Chateau d' Eu in 1843 and 1845. Michael Nelson, *Queen Victoria and the Discovery of the Riviera* (London: Tauris Parke Paperbacks, 2007), 16; Victoria, Queen of England, *The Letters of Queen Victoria: A Selection from Her Majesty's Correspondence between the Years 1837 and 1861* (New York: Longmans, Green, 1907), 2:51.

3. Brother Jonathan was a common antebellum American stock character who represented an average citizen, or the whole of the country. The image connoted an upright, egalitarian, unaffected republican. Before the Civil War, the names Brother Jonathan and Uncle Sam were often interchangeable, but after the Civil War, the use of Brother Jonathan faded, perhaps because it came to be equated as a particularly Northern character. Winifred Morgan, *An American Icon: Brother Jonathan and American Identity* (Cranbury, N.J.: University of Delaware Press, 1988), 77, 118.

4. Napoleon Bonaparte (1769–1821).

5. A just reward.

6. Here Whitman echoes contemporary feminists like Catharine Beecher (1800–1878),

who advocated women's rights (in education, in Beecher's case) while upholding traditional gender roles: "The proper education of a man decides the welfare of an individual but educate a woman and the interests of a whole family are secured." Catharine Beecher, *A Treatise on Domestic Economy, for the Use of Young Ladies at Home, and at School* (New York: Harper and Brothers, 1845), 36–37.

The UNION Now and Forever![1]

Brooklyn Daily Eagle
FEBRUARY 26, 1847

Does the *Sun*[2] mean really to say that each 'united state' is a separate sovereign in fact, and in its own right? that it could (for that would follow,) withdraw itself at pleasure from the union? that it could do *any thing at all,* in conflict with the supreme power of the constitution and congress? that it is 'independent' any farther than that it has full power to manage its own *local* affairs, and supervise its own *local* institutions? Nay: we think it time that such an extreme heresy (appropriately nestling in the extreme sections of Massachusetts and South Carolina,) should be discountenanced by all true Americans. Especially at this juncture, is the potency of the union to be upheld: for angry voices are already heard even at the capitol, threatening it under certain contingencies . . . . . .[3] Perhaps, however, the difference between the *Sun* and us involves but the explanation of a word. 'Consolidation' (as we suppose) comprises the idea of *compact,* too; and our states are certainly compacted; while just as certainly the greatest and amplest powers of the government are consolidated in congress and the president. But congress and the president can't go a step farther than the constitution allows them—wherein is the palladium of the states' rights.

"The union of these states," says the *Sun,* "consists, therefore, in each state maintaining its own sovereignty and independence, passing its own laws, providing for its own local government; and each state by a constitutional compact becomes united within itself." In such talk as this, though it is quite common, there is evidently a misapplication of terms. If each state *really* possesses 'sovereignty and independence,' each can do what she pleases, irrespective of any limit. But there are many things which the states cannot do. Among other things they have no right to 'nullify'[4] the union.—'E pluribus UNUM' stares such a remark as we have quoted at the commencement of the paragraph, in the face, and puts it down. . . . . . We, perhaps, are as much a 'strict constructionist'[5] as our N.Y. contemporary *can* be—as much in favor of keeping back power from a central point, and having it wielded by the people who are to be directly acted on by it. But we stand by the Constitution, and the Union which stands with *it*—and we say that no dogma or abstraction—no fancied grief or rebellious excitement—no long-drawn inference—shall allow the foundation of a point of danger to that sacred twain.[6]

NOTES

1. Transcribed from scanned original, Brooklyn Public Library—Brooklyn Collection. This editorial also appears in Walt Whitman, *The Journalism, Volume II: 1846–1848,* part of *The Collected Writings of Walt Whitman,* ed. Herbert Bergman, Douglas A. Noverr, and Edward J. Recchia (New York: Peter Lang, 2003), 206–207. The title of this editorial is loosely quoted from Senator Daniel Webster's famous conclusion to a series of debates during the "Nullification Crisis" that pitted federal law and President Andrew Jackson against South Carolina in 1832. Webster's final sentence of the speech reads: "Let their last feeble and lingering glance rather behold the gorgeous ensign of the republic . . . bearing from its motto, no such miserable interrogatory as 'What is all this worth?' nor those other words of delusion and folly, 'Liberty first and Union afterwards'; but everywhere, spread all over in characters of living light, blazing on all its ample folds, as they float over the sea and over the land, and in every wind under the whole heavens, that other sentiment, dear to every true American heart—Liberty *and* Union, now and forever, one and inseparable!" Daniel Webster, *The Speeches of Daniel Webster, and His Masterpieces,* ed. Benjamin Franklin Tefft (Philadelphia: Porter & Coates, 1854), 410–411.

2. The *Sun* was founded by Benjamin Day (1810–1889) in 1833 and sold for one penny, making it one of the earliest newspapers aimed at the working-class population of New York City. Day established the use of newsboys rather than taking subscriptions and sold bundled papers to orphans and the unemployed, who, upon selling a bundle, could keep half of the cost. In 1837 Day sold the *Sun* to Moses Yale Beach (1800–1868), his brother-in-law, who boosted the newspaper's circulation to 38,000, the largest circulation for a daily newspaper at the time. In 1846 Beach was instrumental in organizing the collaboration between New York's largest dailies, the *Sun, Tribune, Herald, Journal of Commerce, Courier and Enquirer,* and *Express,* to pool news sources, especially telegraphy, into the combination that became the Associated Press. Edwin Burrows and Mike Wallace, *Gotham: A History of New York City to 1898* (Oxford: Oxford University Press, 1999), 522, 640, 677.

3. Representative David Wilmot, whose proviso to an appropriations bill for the U.S.-Mexico War stipulated that territories gained in the war be closed to slavery, bitterly reignited the debate between Northern and Southern representatives in Congress, as seen in these remarks of Representative Seaborn Jones, of Georgia, on February 13, 1847: "Stripped of the gaudy coloring which fanaticism and hypocrisy have thrown around

[Wilmot's Proviso], and what is it? That whatever acquisition may be made by the joint labor, the joint peril, and joint treasure of all the States, shall be divided among half of them, and that the remaining half shall possess none of the benefits or advantages accruing from it. . . . [I]t is downright heartless injustice." "A Century of Lawmaking for a New Nation: U.S. Congressional Documents and Debates, 1774–1875," *Congressional Globe*, February 13, 1847, 363, Library of Congress, memory.loc.gov.

4. Whitman's use of the word "nullify" here echoes the political battle between Andrew Jackson and Vice President John C. Calhoun, where Calhoun argued in "South Carolina Exposition and Protest" (1828) that South Carolina had a constitutional right to nullify federal law, in this case, the Tariff of 1828. Jackson reacted with the Force Bill (1833), which authorized presidential enforcement of federal law. A compromise tariff forestalled a showdown between the federal government and South Carolina.

5. One who reads the Constitution narrowly, thereby limiting federal power.

6. Compare to Abraham Lincoln's First Inaugural Address (1861): "I hold that in contemplation of universal law and of the Constitution the Union of these States is perpetual. Perpetuity is implied, if not expressed, in the fundamental law of all national governments. It is safe to assert that no government proper ever had a provision in its organic law for its own termination. Continue to execute all the express provisions of our National Constitution, and the Union will endure forever, it being impossible to destroy it except by some action not provided for in the instrument itself."

Loss of the Wilmot Proviso.[1]

Brooklyn Daily Eagle

MARCH 4, 1847

—Several of the papers are in a fury and gloom because the Wilmot proviso was quashed in the U.S. senate—and because the quashing is concurred in by the house.[2] We, too, desired the enactment of that proviso: but it is by no means vitally important. We look on public opinion as ahead of law in this matter: indeed on such subjects, we have more faith in public opinion than law. The future of the new territory and its organization can safely be left to it. In the mean time, let all hands smooth down and become calmer: we have had too much angry excitement in congress—too many threats and imperious expressions—too many insults to that mother of all our liberty, the republic's union . . . . One thing is assured, beyond a peradventure: the *freemen of the north never will consent to the making of slave states out of the new territory.*[3] And this very defeat of the Wilmot proviso, will but make sterner and more fixed, the determination of all true lovers of our republic.

NOTES

1. Transcribed from scanned original, Brooklyn Public Library—Brooklyn Collection. This editorial also appears in Walt Whitman, *The Journalism, Volume II: 1846–1848*, part of *The Collected Writings of Walt Whitman*, ed. Herbert Bergman, Douglas A. Noverr, and Edward J. Recchia (New York: Peter Lang, 2003), 209–210.

2. In August 1846 the House of Representatives passed, along sectional lines, the appropriation bill with Wilmot's proviso. In the Senate, where the South held greater relative strength, the bill was filibustered. In February 1847 the House of Representatives passed the appropriations bill again with the proviso, but the Senate passed a rival appropriations bill stripped of the proviso, which passed the House when a number of Northern Democrats voted with Southern members of their party. Daniel Walker Howe, *What Hath God Wrought: The Transformation of America, 1815–1848* (Oxford: Oxford University Press,

2007), 767–768; Leonard L. Richards, *The Slave Power: The Free North and Southern Domination, 1780–1860* (Baton Rouge: Louisiana State University Press, 2000), 151–162.

3. In the Treaty of Guadalupe-Hildalgo (1848), which ended the U.S.-Mexico War, Mexico ceded around one million square miles of territory, which included the modern states of California, Nevada, Utah, Arizona, New Mexico, Texas, and a portion of Colorado.

Rights of Southern Freemen As Well As Northern Freemen—Mr. Calhoun's Speech.[1]

Brooklyn Daily Eagle

APRIL 27, 1847

In the speech of Mr. Calhoun[2] delivered at Charleston in March last he says:

> "Indeed, after all that has occurred during the last twelve months, it would be almost idiotic to doubt, that a large majority of both parties in the non-slaveholding states, have come to a fixed determination to appropriate all the territories of the United States, now possessed, or hereafter to be acquired, to themselves, *to the entire exclusion of the slaveholding states.*"

Now is it not strange that a man of the conceded ability of Mr. Calhoun, of his reputed precision of logic and accuracy of expression, should use language like this? "*The entire exclusion of the slaveholding states!*" Mr. Calhoun surely cannot mean what he says. He speaks as though the people of the slaveholding states were all slaveholders. This is any thing but true. In every slaveholding state, we believe, except perhaps South Carolina, a majority of the white freemen are non-slaveholders. Will the exclusion of slavery from the new territory deter *them* from going with their axes and their ploughs into its forests, and making their houses upon its unfurrowed surface? Certainly not. They will go with their free brethren from the north and, not deeming labor degrading, will rear states which will prosper and become mighty under the power of *free* arms and stout hearts. The only persons who will be excluded will be the *aristocracy* of the south—the men who work only with other men's hands. If they cannot condescend to labor, to fell the forests and to plough the fields with their own hands, but must have *slaves* to do what the yeomanry of the north and the majority of white men at the south regard as a proud, virtuous and noble calling—why then they can stay away; and it is difficult to see where the hardship lies of permitting them to do so. If they are willing to regard labor as honorable and to work like the rest of us, they can go into the new territory and find it open to them as it is to the rest who work for a living. But no—they insist that at the outset *freemen shall be excluded* to enable *them* to monopolize the land and cultivate it by their slaves. Let us see if this is not the true state of the case. From the northern and eastern states a constant tide of brave, industrious and energetic *freemen* is flowing to the new territory. Such has been the case for the last fifty years, and such men have founded and matured the great—*nations*, we had almost said—of Ohio, Indiana, Illinois, Michigan, &c. Into those regions have rushed, too, thousands and tens of thousands of free men from the slaveholding states who have been eager to labor where they could do so without degradation. Tens and hundreds of thousands more like them from the east, north *and south*, will be eager to occupy the new territory which may be acquired from Mexico, if they can go and not find themselves the equals only of negro slaves. Where the land is cultivated by slaves it is *not* also cultivated by freemen. It is not in South Carolina and Virginia and the other slave states, respectable (at any rate it is not so practically regarded) for white men to labor on land.

The voice of the north proclaims that *labor must not be degraded*. The young men of the free states must not be shut out from the new domain (where slavery does not now exist) by the *introduction* of an institution which will render their honorable industry no longer respectable.[3] Slavery must not exact *too much* from the democracy of the north. That democracy has been faithful to the "compromises of the constitution" by protecting the institution of slavery (uncongenial as that institution is to all the instincts and sympathies of democracy) within the limits that the constitution found it; and it will be the part of wisdom in its advocates not to weaken its security by further and unreasonable exactions. Instead of a generous recognition of the tolerant spirit with which the north has regarded the institution in the states where it exists, and has conceded almost every thing of power and office and station to the slaveholding states, that spirit is requited much too often by flings and imputations of meanness and of a mercenary spirit, not likely to perpetuate northern forbearance. Witness the following extract from Mr. Calhoun's speech:

> "Fortunately, then, the crusade against our domestic institution does not originate in hostility of interests. If it did, the possibility of arresting the threatened danger, and saving ourselves, short of a disrupture of union, would be altogether hopeless; *so predominant is the regard for interest in those states, over all other considerations."*

Was it a mean or mercenary spirit that has induced the democracy of the north to grant the presidency, with all its power and patronage, to the south, ever since the foundation of the government, with the exception of a single term?[4] On the other hand might we not with truth charge faithlessness and utter cupidity to the south? It has monopolized by an *immense* disproportion the offices of the government. It proved faithless to the democracy of the north in respect to Mr. Van Buren. It is entirely unreliable as to Mr. Wright.[5] Mr. Calhoun is quite right in his conclusion that "it would be almost idiotic to doubt, that a large majority of both parties in the non-slaveholding states have come to a fixed determination" in respect to the new territory—but is wrong in saying that determination is to exclude the people of the slave states. It is to throw the territory open *on equal terms* to the people of the north *and* of the south.

NOTES

1. Transcribed from scanned original, Brooklyn Public Library—Brooklyn Collection. This editorial also appears in Walt Whitman, *The Journalism, Volume II: 1846–1848*, part of *The Collected Writings of Walt Whitman*, ed. Herbert Bergman, Douglas A. Noverr, and Edward J. Recchia (New York: Peter Lang, 2003), 259–260.

2. John C. Calhoun (1782–1850), senator from South Carolina and prominent voice of Southern interests during the generation before the Civil War. Calhoun gave this speech on March 9, 1847, in Charleston.

3. Whitman here echoes David Wilmot's rationale for his proviso against the expansion of slavery to the West: "A great question, affecting the honor and character of the Republic, vital to the interests of the white laboring man, has been jeoparded and endangered. . . . Denunciation and proscription followed all who would not bow down at the shrine of Slavery Propagandism. Northern men, who dared to vindicate the rights of free labor, to speak and vote in favor of the white man and his children, were proscribed by an Administration that owed its existence to the sacrifices and noble efforts of the Democracy in the North. . . . It is time that the white laboring man should know that the Government which he supports by his labor, and defends by his strong arm, is against him in this struggle for his rights." *Appendix to the Congressional Globe*, Slavery in the Territories, Speech of Mr. David Wilmot of Pennsylvania, August 3, 1848, 1076, House Divided: The Civil War Research Engine at Dickinson College, http://hd.housedivided.dickinson.edu.

4. Whitman here refers to presidents who were members of the Democratic Party. Of those, only one was born in the North, Martin Van Buren (1782–1862). Van Buren ran for president on the Wilmot-inspired Free-Soil Party ticket in 1848.

5. Silas Wright (1795–1847) lost his reelection bid for governor of New York in 1846 and

died soon thereafter. Conservative New York Democrats, known as "Hunkers," blamed his sympathy for free-soil Democrats, or "Barnburners," on splitting the party vote and throwing the election to the Whig candidate, John Young. David Reynolds, *Walt Whitman's America: A Cultural Biography* (New York: Alfred A. Knopf, 1995), 116–117; Charles Rufus Skinner, *Governors of New York from 1777–1920* (Albany, N.Y.: J. B. Lyon, 1919), 6.

Some Thoughts about This Matter of the Washington Monument.[1]

Brooklyn Daily Eagle

OCTOBER 18, 1847

—Such enthusiasm was hardly needed to prove how spontaneously the hearts of the American people respond to the name of WASHINGTON—and yet it is very glorious to see the people—thousands and hundreds of thousands of them—eagerly rushing to join in a testimony like the forthcoming monumental procession.[2] But there is one point in which we confess to feel a pain; and that is, the plan of the structure of this monument. In a late visit to the American institute fair, we saw a picture underlined "Washington monument," and were assured by an old gentleman who was receiving in a book subscriptions for the same, that *that* was the plan *fixed* upon by the monument committee. Of that plan, we cannot find terms to speak in sufficient contempt! It is a mixture without uniformity, without apparent design, and certainly without the least appropriateness. One of our New York contemporaries we notice throws doubt on the idea that this *is* the design. *If* it is, it will be a disgrace and a laughing-stock to the whole city and state. . . . . And it is to be remarked that while every one of the papers is crying up the building of a Washington monument in New York—and crying up the procession too—not a single one, (except, we believe, an evening print,) seems to realize either the necessity of having an *appropriate* and most majestic structure; or the surpassing difficulty of planning such a structure. The notion seems to be that *a monument* is to be constructed—that it must cost a great many thousand dollars—and that it must be very big. *We sadly fear that the whole thing will be an entire failure, and that every true artist, and most of our intelligent citizens, will wish the said monument blown up, the moment it is exposed to the public gaze!*[3]

To commemorate such a character as WASHINGTON we want, (we say,) no monument but his country, and his countrymen's hearts! When they forget him, let him be forgotten. It is all well enough to raise proud pieces of showy architecture to your Napoleons, your Walter Scotts, or your Wellingtons—the "great men" of a few ages. But this pure and august being—this MAN without a flaw—asks no pile of brick, stone, and mortar raised! We do not want him brought down to the level of mere common heroes. By the silent shore of the broad Potomac lie WASHINGTON'S mortal ashes; God has his spirit; and his country has his memory. Let his grave be undesecrated by any sacrilegious hand—and let the republic consign the task of preserving his name and fame to no meaner place than its children's bosoms. Is not *that* mausoleum—warmed by vital life-blood which will never forget the sainted hero as long as it flows—better than the cold pomp of marble? Leave such for common men; a higher desert is for WASHINGTON!

Such are our first feelings in the matter. But yet we might acknowledge the propriety of raising a truly grand and appropriate monument to WASHINGTON. It should be as sublime as the purest and highest genius of the ideal could design it—as perfect and durable as mechanism and art could make it; and have *some little* approach, at least, (it *could* have but little,) to the characteristics of the being whom it so boldly assumes to commemorate.

NOTES

1. Transcribed from scanned original, Brooklyn Public Library—Brooklyn Collection. This editorial also appears in Walt Whitman, *The Journalism, Volume II: 1846–1848*, part of *The Collected Writings of Walt Whitman*, ed. Herbert Bergman, Douglas A. Noverr, and Edward J. Recchia (New York: Peter Lang, 2003), 340–341. On October 19, 1847, the anniversary of Cornwallis's surrender at Yorktown, a cornerstone was laid for this monument on Manhattan's Upper East Side in a neighborhood called "Hamilton Square," which was eradicated in 1869 to make way for Central Park. The monument itself was never built, and the cornerstone, measuring five feet square and four feet thick, beneath which was housed a box containing coins, newspapers, a city directory, and a certificate of membership in the Society of Cincinnati signed by George Washington, was never found. "Towering Monument to Washington That New York Began and Then Forgot," *New York Times*, February 18, 1912.

2. The dedication ceremony for the monument was attended by Governor John Young (1802–1852), Mayor William V. Brady (1811–1870), and around 30,000 residents of the city. The poet George Pope Morris (1802–1864) wrote a poem for the occasion that began:

A monument to Washington!
A tablet graven with his name!
Green be the mound it stands upon
And everlasting be his fame.

3. The monument was to display a mixture of neoclassical and gothic revival architectural elements, culminating in a tower with a statue of Washington on top.

Letter from Gen. Cass.[1]

Brooklyn Daily Eagle
JANUARY 3, 1848

THE LATE LETTER OF SENATOR CASS[2]—Gen. Cass has lately been writing a letter on important topics. In it he declares boldly that we should "war to the knife" with Mexico, and that no peace should be agreed upon till an indemnity for all expenses and debts be rendered by the constituted authorities of that country—in which latter idea the country and he are of one opinion. He thinks too that every state must have perfect local control in the management of its affairs, else divisions and bickerings would operate incessantly to split the confederation into sectional fragments. Mr. Cass is opposed to slavery, but he is likewise opposed to any "improper interference" with the government and management of particular states. *Therefore* he could not agree to the principle sought to be established by "the Wilmot Proviso," that in any newly acquired territory the government of the Union should declare, that in such acquired land no slavery should be permitted.

All this might come with a better show of sense, if the legislative power of Congress over all its territories, were not as supreme, while they *are* territories, as the state legislatures over their respective states. While congress is the local government, too, for these territories, it may be viewed merely as a question of policy, of profit and loss, whether to *introduce* negro slavery into those states or not. Is there a sane man who will say that it is profitable so to introduce slavery?

NOTES

1. Transcribed from scanned original, Brooklyn Public Library—Brooklyn Collection. This editorial also appears in Walt Whitman, *The Journalism, Volume II: 1846–1848,* part of *The Collected Writings of Walt Whitman,* ed. Herbert Bergman, Douglas A. Noverr, and Edward J. Recchia (New York: Peter Lang, 2003), 389–390.

2. Lewis Cass (1782–1866), former brigadier general and Democratic presidential

candidate in 1848, faced a Democratic Party split by the Wilmot Proviso and the question of slavery in the territories. In this letter, dated December 24, 1847, to A. O. P. Nicholson, a former Democratic representative from Tennessee, Cass established his conservative position against the Wilmot Proviso on the grounds that it violated local sovereignty and threatened the integrity of the Union. According to Whitman's biographer Jerome Loving, this editorial cost Whitman his editorship of the *Eagle* since the newspaper's owner, Isaac Van Anden, sought to dampen free-soil sentiment in Brooklyn and New York City in the name of party unity. George H. Hickman and Richard Rush, *The Life of General Lewis Cass: With His Letters and Speeches on Various Subjects* (Baltimore: N. Hickman, 1848), 65–70; Jerome Loving, *Walt Whitman: The Song of Himself* (Berkeley: University of California Press, 1999), 111.

Henry C. Murphy[1]

Brooklyn Daily Times

JUNE 3, 1857

We only wish all the appointments of the President and the Senate of the United States were deserving of as perfect commendation, without a single draw-back, as this of Henry C. Murphy to the American Ambassadorship at the Hague.[2] In the present state of things, Mr. Murphy would not only do credit to the United States at that place, but furthermore we say no better appointment could be made for London, Paris, Vienna, or Madrid. We say that America will have no more capable representative abroad any where than this man—and we prophesy that if his life is spared he will justify our words, and that he will yet be employed between his country and a first class foreign court.

Brooklyn knows Mr. Murphy hitherto merely as a successful party caucuser and manager—one of a class plenty north and south, who make of politics a fine game. But he has stuff in him that deserves a better field. In his line, he is a superior man. While still a youth, not more than twenty years old, Henry Murphy was possessed of fine talent. Brooklyn was then but a village. The writer of this remembers well the pleased surprise of young Murphy when he came into the "Long Island Patriot" office, and found himself to be adjudged the writer of the "prize story," for a leading Philadelphia magazine. Seeing some time before the offer by the magazine, Henry had written a tale, "The Reformed," and sent it on to compete with the rest. This was probably his first literary effort, at least of any consequence, and it met with flattering success for so young a person; for as we said, Murphy was at that time hardly more than a boy. Does he not recollect his visits to his friend Samuel E. Clements' office?[3] —Does he not recollect the "carrying on," the cigar-smoking, the animated political discussions, and the canvassing pro and con of some manuscript article intended for the "Patriot"? The writer of this was then a "devil,"[4] only twelve or thirteen years old himself—and Henry Murphy, though not very much older, treated him with great indulgence, good-naturedly overlooking a great many boyish capers.

The penning of these few sentences carries us back to other times—to events and days altogether unknown to the busy and swarming crowds of modern Brooklyn. We can almost think we see the "Old Ferry," and the rude horseboats crossing, and the pilot steering by the ancient tiller. We can almost think we see the rows of great elm trees shading Fulton street, and the unpaved sidewalks with plenty of grass. We would walk down "Love Lane," and stand upon "Clover Hill," and view the bay and river. We cannot resist the inclination to indulge in a few reminiscences.[5]

Brooklyn was, as we have said, but a village, whose affairs were managed by "Trustees." For a long while Gen. Jeremiah Johnson[6] was President of these Trustees—another frequent President was Joseph Sprague.[7] The officials used to meet in a chamber in the "Apprentices Library," corner of Cranberry and Henry streets. The corner stone of this building had been laid by Lafayette.[8] His celebrated visit to America happened just as the foundation of the "Apprentices Library" commenced. Lafayette being at that time invited to Brooklyn, among other places, it was resolved to request him to "lay the corner stone," as it is called. The hero politely acquiesced, and all the school children in Brooklyn marching to the ground (among them the writer of this, at that period six or seven years old,) were helped into places, part of them in the lately excavated cellar. Among those who aided extempore in handing down the children was Lafayette himself; and the writer recollects well the childish pride he experienced in being one of those who were taken in the arms of Lafayette, and reached down by him to a standing place. All this was done that the children could have a good sight of that mysterious something of "laying the corner stone." Doubtless it was thought then that the "Apprentices Library" would go down to future generations as an unequalled specimen of architecture.[9]

The years made rapid changes not only in those children, but in every aspect of Brooklyn. Shortly it became an incorporated city; then the Common Council met in an immense room forming the upper story of "Hall's Buildings," corner of Fulton street and Cranberry. The building was burnt down at the great fire about ten years ago.[10]

While still a village, Brooklyn had, for newspapers, two weeklys—one, the *Long Island Star*, by Col. Alden Spooner,[11] father of E. B. Spooner, the proprietor of the now daily *Evening Star*—the other was called the *Long Island Patriot*, and was for many years conducted by Mr. Birch.[12] After him the paper was owned and edited by Samuel E. Clements, a protege of John T. Bergen,[13] Coe Downing,[14] and Mr. Brasher,[15] and other local magnates of those days—and of him young Murphy was quite a favorite, and was always welcome to the editorial columns. Clements, a "good fellow" personally, was a great, lank, eccentric, hawk-nosed Quaker and Southerner (he often boasted of his Southern blood), and by the influence of his friends got the appointment of Postmaster. One of his performances, when about Brooklyn, created a great excitement—as the reader will understand when we narrate it.

Several gentlemen were very anxious to have the sculptured counterfeit presentment of Elias Hicks,[16] the renowned preacher of "inner light," who had then lately died, at Jericho, L.I. There was a good portrait of Elias, painted by Henry Inman,[17] (that wonderful likeness—We can see it now!)—but the venerable old man was averse to such things, and would never allow a figure to be taken of himself, for a bust. So immediately coincident with the death of Elias, three persons, (of whom Clements, our Brooklyn editor, was one,) agree to go down to Jericho, and by fair or clandestine means, disinter their subject, and take a mould or cast from the face and head! *They did so*. From this mould a permanent one was made, and several busts of Elias were formed, quite perfect, it is said. But soon a quarrel arose, in reference to the division of the anticipated profits from the sale of the bust—for the whole thing was as much intended for a speculation, as to rescue the likeness of Elias, and transmit it to posterity. The quarrel became at length so much exasperated that, either from sullen agreement, or in some crisis of excitement, the moulds and the few busts made from them were all smashed to pieces! Thus ended this singular and in some of its particulars revolting affair.

As we have said, Clements was very tall, (six feet, two,) very thin, with a slow and peculiar gait in walking, long tailed blue coat with gilt buttons, and on his head in summer an enormous broad-brim'd low-crowned leghorn hat. Imagine him promenading the streets (then lanes, with trees,) of Brooklyn—or riding out in his skeleton sulkey.[18] He always kept a horse, generally a pretty fast one; to his country subscribers out in Bushwick, New Lots, Flatlands, &c., carrying round his papers himself. Of a Sunday he used to go to the old Dutch Reformed Church (now in Joralemon street,) to which a narrow lane led up from Fulton street. Then it was an edifice of undressed gray stone, massive, homely, and grand: *now* it is a building patterned from the temple of Minerva, at Athens!

After a short reign, however, Clements got into difficulties, and disappeared west. Wm. Rockwell, (the Judge, who died last summer)[19] followed as editor of the "Patriot"—which continued on with various ups and downs—and a change of name to the "Advocate." At one time Mr. Arnold was its editor.[20]

We suppose Henry C. Murphy—who will herewith have the truth of all these reminiscences recalled to him—tried his hand in writing for this periodical the

"Patriot," frequently. His father, Judge Murphy, lived in the immediate neighborhood, Fulton Street, near High. Henry, when young, was also a well-known member of the best scholastic societies of Brooklyn, especially the Hamilton Literary Association.[21] He was never much of a ready debater.

Some twenty-five years have passed away since then. Twenty-five years! Brooklyn, from a rural village of a few hundred inhabitants, has grown up to be a mighty, rich, and populous city—the third in the United States, and evidently destined to be one of the greatest in the world. Mr. Murphy, early taking to politics, viewing the work therein as an art,—in disposition cautious and conservative, without, (we think,) any profound faith in the people,—was not a man to remain in a subordinate position. He mixed among the managers of the Democratic party of Brooklyn, showed himself apt, keen, a perfect master, one fit to take the reins and handle them in the best way for "the party" as well as himself.

Henry Murphy's first political success was his appointment as Corporation attorney.[22] We have understood that it was in this place he laid the foundation of his fortune—for he is rich. In time, he was nominated and elected Mayor. Then he was chosen to represent the old First Congressional District at the Federal capital. He has also been in Congress a second time. Now he receives from the President a most responsible foreign mission.

Of quiet tone of manners, a thorough gentleman, averse to foppery and tinsel, courteous to all persons, generally taciturn, keen as a razor, not to be hoodwinked, or dazzled, or fooled, or led off from his aim—such are some of the leading mental and social characteristics of the personality of the new Ambassador. To his credit be it added, that his nomination is not the result of any manœuvers or begging solicitations of his own—but is the voluntary offer of the President.

This country deeply needs such men as Henry Murphy to attend to her interests aboard. There is no diplomat, nor collection of diplomats—no camarilla—no schemer—no foreign regime or ministry—none, however circumventive, artful, or carefully disguised—but we would match Henry C. Murphy against them. He is a perfect man of the world, in the most favorable sense; for we believe that with this unsurpassed subtlety and "rapport" with all the various turnings of the mentality of others, Henry Murphy remains, at this day, really possessed of most or all of his youth native good-meaning and interior honor. Torn, scorched, or sweltered, though they may have been in the wrathful hell of party politics—they must be there.[23]

It is rumored that Mr. Murphy has for some time had in view an elaborate literary work, of Historical nature,[24] which, perhaps, will be aided by this appointment—as Irving's Lives of Columbus and His Companions were aided by his sojourn in Madrid.[25] We believe that Henry Murphy could write full as good a History as any of Washington Irving's; and we believe moreover that all relating to the Dutch settlement of New York and Long Island, and the earlier growth of these parts of the State, to be among the most important of themes in American lore—and that they have not yet been treated in any large, profound, or vital spirit, by a writer competent to grasp them. If, as we have heard, these form the subject of the contemplated work, let it come, and let it be worthy of the case it undertakes,—for the theme is a great one. The Dutch, their mark here in America, their literature, grandeur, conscientiousness, immortal spirit of determination—their bloody wars with Spanish tyrants—their maritime daring—and their original knowledge of the principles of political equality, and confederation—These, as descending to America, and making the strongest stamp of all upon America, have yet had no historian, no sayer, or recorder. A grand race, those Dutch![26] those forefathers of this Island, and of Manhattan Island! full as grand as any of the antique races. Yet, so far, known only through some shallow burlesque, full of clown's wit, like Irving's Knickerbocker "history."[27]

Bon voyage to you! Henry C. Murphy—when you start. And may you fulfil[28] our friendly anticipations, and return safe and sound to Brooklyn again.

NOTES

1. Transcribed from a photocopy of original in the papers of Herbert Bergman, East Lansing, Michigan. This editorial partially appears in Walt Whitman, *The Uncollected Poetry and Prose of Walt Whitman*, ed. Emory Holloway (Gloucester, Mass.: Peter Smith, 1972), 2:1–5.

2. Henry Cruse Murphy (1810–1882) was a Brooklyn native and cofounder (and editor) of the *Brooklyn Daily Eagle*, which Whitman edited between 1846 and 1848. Murphy was most prominently a Democratic politician throughout the mid-nineteenth century, serving as mayor of Brooklyn (1842–1843) and congressman (1843–1845, 1847–1857, and 1863–1873). Between 1857 and 1861 he served as minister resident to The Hague. "The End of a Busy Life: Death of Mr. Henry C. Murphy of Brooklyn," *New York Times*, December 2, 1882, nytimes.com. See also Henry Reed Stiles, *A History of the City of Brooklyn, Including the Old Town and Village of Brooklyn, the Town of Bushwick, and the Village and City of Williamsburgh* (Brooklyn, N.Y.: published by subscription, 1870), 3:934.

3. See Jerome Loving, *Walt Whitman: The Song of Himself* (Berkeley: University of California Press, 1999), 33; David Reynolds, *Walt Whitman's America: A Cultural Biography* (New York: Alfred A. Knopf, 1995), 44.

4. A "printer's devil" is an apprentice to a printer. Whitman was Clements's apprentice during 1831 and 1832, making Murphy about twenty-one years old when Whitman met him.

5. This is one of Whitman's earliest printed recollections of the Brooklyn of his boyhood. He was thirty-eight years old when this article was published.

6. Jeremiah Johnson (1765–1852) was a trustee of Brooklyn from 1796 to 1816, and held the position of supervisor of the city for forty years. Johnson raised troops for the U.S.-Mexico War, was rewarded with the military rank of brigadier general, and was given command of Fort Greene in Brooklyn. "Death of General Jeremiah Johnson," *New York Times*, October 23, 1852, nytimes.com.

7. Joseph Sprague (1782–1854), trustee of Brooklyn and president of the village between 1828 and 1831. "Death of an Old Citizen," *New York Times,* December 13, 1854, nytimes.com.

8. Gilbert du Motier, Marquis de Lafayette (1757–1834), French aristocrat and supporter of the American Revolution, during which Lafayette served under George Washington. Lafayette visited the United States in 1825 and, according to a later version of this story, kissed young Whitman, then six years old, upon his visit to Brooklyn.

9. The Apprentices Library eventually became the Brooklyn Museum, though the building that now houses the museum was built in 1898.

10. As Holloway notes, this fire also destroyed the building that housed Whitman's ill-fated attempt at free-soil journalism, the *Brooklyn Freeman*. See Whitman, *Uncollected Poetry and Prose,* 1:3.

11. Whitman apprenticed for Alden Spooner (1783–1848) at the *Star*.

12. Probably George L. Birch, who was recorded as the founder of the *Long Island Patriot* in 1821 in Gabriel Furman, *Notes Geographical and Historical, Relating to the Town of Brooklyn, in Kings County on Long-Island* (Brooklyn, N.Y.: A. Spooner, 1824), 94.

13. John Teunis Bergen (1786–1855) bought the *Long Island Patriot* in 1829. See Leonard Bernardo and Jenifer Weiss, *Brooklyn by Name: How Neighborhoods, Streets, Parks, Bridges and More Got Their Names* (New York: New York University Press, 2006), 59.

14. Coe Downing (1791–1847).

15. Perhaps Philip Brasher, who represented King's County in the New York legislature in 1835. Edwin William, *The New York Annual Register* (New York: J. Leavitt, 1835), 340.

16. Elias Hicks (1748–1840), Quaker minister and leader of the "Hicksite" branch of Quakers after the schism between Hicksites and Orthodox Friends in 1827. See Larry Ingle, *Quakers in Conflict: The Hicksite Reformation* (Knoxville: University of Tennessee Press, 1986). Whitman's parents, Louisa and Walter Sr., were both sympathetic to Hicks's brand of spirit-led worship, though no record exists of either formally joining the Society of Friends. Whitman heard Hicks preach at least once, in 1829, and remembered the event nearly sixty years later in 1888. During the 1880s, Whitman described himself in one instance as "half Quaker." See Walt Whitman, *Complete Poetry and Collected Prose,* ed. Justin

Kaplan (New York: Literary Classics of the United States, 1982), 1232–1233; Donald D. Kummings, *A Companion to Walt Whitman* (Malden, Mass.: Blackwell, 2006), 73.

17. Henry Inman (1801–1846).

18. Or "sulky," named for a rider's desire to ride alone. "A light two-wheeled carriage for a single person." Noah Webster, *Webster's Collegiate Dictionary* (Springfield, Mass.: G. & C. Merriam, 1896), 815.

19. Probably William Rockwell (1804–1856), judge of the Superior Court of Kings County. See Dwight Kilbourn, *Bench and Bar of Litchfield County, Connecticut, 1709–1909: Biographical Sketches of Members, History and Catalogue of the Litchfield Law School, Historical Notes* (Litchfield, Conn.: published by author, 1909), 278.

20. Samuel G. Arnold (1806–1891) published the *Advocate* in partnership with Isaac Van Anden between 1836 and 1838. See Peter Ross, *History of Long Island: From Its Earliest Settlement to the Present Time* (New York: Lewis Publishing, 1903), 3:8. Van Anden owned the *Eagle* during Whitman's tenure as editor between 1846 and 1848, and was probably instrumental in Whitman's removal from that position for his free-soil sympathies.

21. The Hamilton Literary Association, founded in 1830, was a forum for "weekly meetings for debate, and its annual dinners, on which occasions its senior members delight to reunite with the juniors and have a good time together. Many of the first men of Brooklyn have been connected with the brotherhood, and its influence upon all is confessedly excellent." "Twenty-fifth Annual Meeting of the Hamilton Literary Association of Brooklyn," *New York Times*, January 20, 1855, nytimes.com.

22. That is, attorney for the city of Brooklyn.

23. This kind of political puffery could have been part of Whitman's job description as an editor of a Democratic newspaper. Nathaniel Hawthorne, who also depended upon Democratic patronage, wrote a similar piece of hagiography for Franklin Pierce: "The one great secret of General Pierce's popularity is his kind-heartedness. He has a word for all his friends, whether high or low; he has a purse always open to the call of the suffering and oppressed. You can always find him in his place at church on Sundays, and on week-days he is ever ready to assist the poor and unfortunate with his money and his talents." Nathaniel Hawthorne, *The Life of Franklin Pierce* (Boston: Ticknor, Reed and Fields, 1852), 240–241.

24. This was probably Murphy's unpublished "History of Early Maritime Discovery in America," which the *New York Times* described as "not in a sufficiently advanced state to be of practical value" in its obituary of Murphy. "The End of a Busy Life: Death of Mr. Henry C. Murphy of Brooklyn," *New York Times*, December 2, 1882, nytimes.com.

25. Between 1826 and 1829, Washington Irving (1783–1859) served as a diplomat in Spain.

26. Whitman's mother, Louisa Van Velsor, was of Dutch descent.

27. Washington Irving published the satirical *A History of New-York from the Beginning of the World to the End of the Dutch Dynasty, by Diedrich Knickerbocker* in 1809.

28. Spelling in original.

"The Dead Rabbit Democracy"[1]

Brooklyn Daily Times

JULY 8, 1857

And who are they?[2] some one exclaims, at once. We will post you up, dear reader.

Be it known, then, that for some years past our democratic friends in these diggins[3] have been diverging, splitting, forking off, (as those heavenly bodies, the comets, sometimes do,) into two parts. From causes too numerous to mention, the most unscrupulous schemers have so far managed as not to give up possession of the party "station-houses,"[4]—and where the party succeeds, the said schemers have succeeded.

There has been a gradual tendency, (who can deny it?) for many years, of all the most abominable elements of city population, toward the little and large caucuses and regencies of the democracy, doubtless because those elements think they can make the most that way. The hungry hordes of office-seekers, the fighting men, the shysters, the proslavery crowders, the Brookses, the invaders in Kansas, and that strange gathering, the Cincinnati Convention of a year ago, with Mayor Wood, Alderman Wilson, etc., in New York city,—these now stand as "the party." They have compelled the others to do homage to them. And they are "the Dead Rabbit Democracy."

But there is still a passive force in, or alongside of the democratic ranks—not acting with any other. These are the more conscientious men, wishing well to their country, too intelligent to be gulled with the usual claptrap of the kept party organs and spouters—but, from the force of habit, unable to dissever their connection from people who have been their companions so long. This passive force is *not* "the Dead Rabbit Democracy."

Brooklyn is pretty well represented in "the Dead Rabbit Democracy." Its party organ,[5] many of the local managers, and sundry of the office-holders, must be classed in that category. The most marked exception is the Mayor.[6] Evidently he shows no disposition to take his place among the "Dead Rabbits."

Acute reader! you have but to exercise a little of your own penetration and judgment, to tell who "the Dead Rabbit Democracy" really are—and to separate them from the passive force we have alluded to.

The question comes up, these times: Will the "Dead Rabbits" succeed in forcing the whole of their party, the unwilling ones with the rest, to take sides with them? Will they continue to be the organisation, the regulars—all others forced to cave in,—either to withdraw or else sing hosannas to them and their "issues"?[7]

We shall see how this existing question is decided—only adding here that we have no fears for the final result. Adding also, that we do not think the proofs, so far, warrant placing the name of President Buchanan among the mortuary burrowers.[8] Adding also that there is no fit name henceforth for them to be known by but "the Dead Rabbit Democracy."[9] A special inspiration!

NOTES

1. Transcribed from a photocopy of original in the papers of Herbert Bergman, East Lansing, Michigan, with reference to scanned original from the Brooklyn Public Library—Brooklyn Collection. A slightly different version of this editorial also appears in Walt Whitman, *I Sit and Look Out: Editorials from the Brooklyn Daily Times by Walt Whitman*, ed. Emory Holloway and Vernolian Schwarz (New York: Columbia University Press, 1932), 92–94. M. Wynn Thomas notes that this article appears consistent with other articles attributed to Whitman. M. Wynn Thomas, "Representatives and Revolutionists: The New Urban Politics Revisited," in *Whitman East and West: New Contexts for Reading Walt Whitman*, ed. Ed Folsom (Iowa City: University of Iowa Press, 2005), 147.

2. "Dead Rabbits" was the name of an Irish American gang prominent in the 1840s and 1850s in the Five Points district in New York City. On July 4, 1857, a fight between the Dead Rabbits and the nativist Bowery Boys gang allied with the New York City police sparked a riot that left twelve dead and thirty-seven injured, the worst riot since the Astor Place Riot of 1849. Edwin Burrows and Mike Wallace, *Gotham: A History of New York City to 1898* (Oxford: Oxford University Press, 1999), 839. Both the *Evening Post* and the *New York Times* also termed the pro-Irish wing of the New York Democratic Party, led by Tammany Hall, as "Dead Rabbit Democracy." See Whitman, *I Sit and Look Out*, 219; *New York Times*, July 30, 1858, nytimes.com. Whitman made similar critiques of elements of the Democratic Party and Tammany Hall, in particular in his series of articles on the Maclay Bill in the *New York Aurora* (1842).

3. Spelling in original.

4. When Democratic mayor Fernando Wood was stripped of his power, including his control of the police department, by the New York state legislature (controlled by

Republicans), the mayor ordered police officers under his control to remain in their "station houses" while the state's orders were tested in the courts. While many pro-Tammany officers remained at their posts, many others left and were replaced by inexperienced appointees of the state. These green, anti-Tammany officers clashed with pro-Tammany gangs on July 4, 1857, including the Dead Rabbits. See Whitman, *I Sit and Look Out*, 218.

5. According to Holloway, this is the *Brooklyn Daily Eagle*. Whitman lost his position at the *Eagle* in 1848 for his free-soil politics.

6. Samuel S. Powell, Democrat, was mayor of Brooklyn from 1857 to 1860 and during 1872 and 1873.

7. Here Whitman echoes his long-standing antipathy toward Tammany Hall politics and politicians, which reaches back to his nativist articles in the *Aurora* and through his free-soil sentiments expressed in the *Eagle*. In the early 1850s the poet expressed his antipathy toward proslavery Democrats and conservative "Hunkers" in the poems "Song for Certain Congressmen" (*New York Evening Post*, March 2, 1850), "Blood-Money" (*New York Daily Tribune*, March 22, 1850), and "The House of Friends" (*New York Daily Tribune*, June 14, 1850), all of which can be found at the Walt Whitman Archive, whitmanarchive.org.

8. This sentence does not appear in Whitman, *I Sit and Look Out*.

9. Whitman's numerous uses of this term here, coupled with its use in the *Times* and the *Evening Post*, imply an attempt to saddle Tammany Hall with the name of the prominent Irish street gang, which, only a few days earlier, participated in a riot against nativist gangs and police officers.

Prohibition of Colored Persons.[1]

Brooklyn Daily Times

MAY 6, 1858

The new Constitution of Oregon prohibits colored persons, either slave or free, from entering the State—making an exclusively white population. This is objected to by several of the abolition Senators in the U.S. Senate—Mr. Hale and others. Mr. Seward, however, is going to vote in favor of the Constitution.

We shouldn't wonder if this sort of total prohibition of colored persons became quite a common thing in new Western, Northwestern, and even Southwestern States. If so, the whole matter of slavery agitation will assume another phase, different from any phase yet. It will be a conflict between the totality of White Labor, on the one side, and, on the other, the interference and competition of Black Labor, or of bringing in colored persons on any terms.

When the question assumes this shape, will not the popular feeling be in favor of the prohibition? Although at first sight it seems a cruel prohibition, we see, upon examination, much to commend it, and much that will be likely to carry the judgment of the masses of the nation in its favor. The great obstacle to Southern progress and enterprise is well-known to be the fact that White Labor will not demean itself to stand, walk, sit, work, or what not, side by side with the blacks, and on an equality with them. Zealous persons may speak of this as a prejudice, but we think every man has a right to his taste in such things—and the white workingman has in this.

Once get the whole matter presented prominently in that point of view, in new States, and to be decided on those grounds, the question of the abolition of slavery, even in the old Southern States, would arise anew, and would have to be argued in a new way. All the old objections to "abolitionism" would become powerless. Indeed, the arguments would have to be transported—either party to change sides. It would be altogether a contest with reference to the interest of the masses of the Whites, and would have to be settled on the grounds of their benefit.

And can any person of moral or benevolent feelings, then, countenance for a moment, such a plan as the total exclusion of an unfortunate race, merely on account of their color, and because there is a prejudice against them? No, not if there were a shadow of a hope that battling against this prejudice will ever succeed in rooting it out in America. But taking a deep and wide view of the whole question, the answer might perhaps be Yes—strange as it sounds at first.

Who believes that the Whites and Blacks can ever amalgamate in America? Or who wishes it to happen? Nature has set and[2] impossible seal against it. Besides, is not America for the Whites? And is it not better so? As long as the Blacks remain here, how can they become anything like an independent and heroic race? There is no chance for it.

Yet we believe there is enough material in the colored race, if they were in some secure and ample part of the earth, where they would have a chance to develope[3] themselves, to gradually form a race, a nation, that would take no mean rank among the peoples of the world. They would have the good will of all the civilized powers, and they would be compelled to learn to look upon themselves as freemen, capable, self-reliant, mighty. Of course all this, or any thing toward it, can never be attained by the Blacks here in America.

So that prohibitions like that in the new Constitution of Oregon, are not to be dismissed at first sight as arbitrary and unjust. We think the subject will bear much further examination. We even think it not unlikely but it would, when thus examined, meet the approval of the best friends of the blacks, and the farthest-sighted opponents of Slavery. For, we repeat it, once get the slavery question to be argued on, as a question of White Workingmen's Labor against the Servile Labor of Blacks, and how many years would slavery stand in two-thirds of the present Slave States?

NOTES

1. Transcribed from scanned original, Brooklyn Public Library, Brooklyn Collection. Jerome Loving confirms the authenticity of this editorial and points out that Emory Holloway and Vernolian Schwarz left out key sections in their transcription for *I Sit and Look Out*. According to Loving, Holloway and Schwarz's inaccurate transcription made Whitman's arguments in favor of Oregon's whites-only constitution appear to be grounded in a fear of racial amalgamation, when, in fact, Whitman supports the Oregon constitution on the grounds that "he believes . . . the *American people*, will never accept their full integration on any basis." Jerome Loving, *Walt Whitman: The Song of Himself* (Berkeley: Univer-

sity of California Press, 1999), 230–231 [italics in original]. The complete transcription here clearly exhibits Whitman's free-soil, labor-focused ideology regarding the issue of American slavery. There are a number of editorials in the *Brooklyn Daily Times* that relate to Whitman's topic here: "White labor, versus Black labor" (May 23, 1857), "The Colored Folks' Festival" (August 7, 1858), and "A Southerner on Slavery" (November 27, 1858).

2. "And" in original should read "an."

3. Spelling in original.

About China, as Relates to Itself and to Us.[1]

Brooklyn Daily Times
JUNE 12, 1858

The people of California and Oregon, in a way that will probably give the law to the whole of that Pacific empire of which they are a main part, have, by legislative enactment, decided on certain physiological purgings (if we may call them so,) that mark a new era in American Politics. We allude to the laws for the total prohibition of negroes from the vast extent of Oregon,[2] and to the laws lately passed in California, for the exclusion of the Chinese.[3]

We had something to say, some time since, about the Oregon prohibition[4]—and we now propose to give a statement of the California law, and reasons why.

Speaking of such reasons for Chinese exclusion from America, the San Francisco *Bulletin* says:

> We do not want any more of these people here; and there is great danger, unless something be done to check the immigration, that the whole Pacific coast of America will be inundated by them. The Chinese empire differs from every other country on the globe. By its repressive policy, maintained for centuries, it has accumulated upon its vast area a population inconceivably dense. Industry and frugality, pushed to the utmost verge of human endurance, scarcely furnish her teeming millions with food to keep them alive. Every inch of soil has to produce its vegetation. No insect, or vermin, or reptile is so loathsome but is consumed for food.

Year after year people die of starvation in greater numbers in China than would depopulate our State. Sunk into this terrible abyss of physical necessity and want, the moral character of the starving and degraded lower classes is described by recent travellers as being in keeping with their condition. Crimes to[o] horrible to be mentioned in other lands, are there so common and open as not to excite remark. Centuries of idolatry and vice and bestiality have leprousied[5] over their humanity until it is no longer visible. When among them, one doubts that they are men.

Though this is putting the case rather strong, there is foundation enough for it all. Bayard Taylor says of the masses of China people, "Their touch is pollution—it is my deliberate opinion that they are morally the most debased people on the face of the earth."[6]

The San Francisco print goes on to assert:

> Unless some check be given to this Asiatic immigration, it is not altogether a wild speculation to think that these copper colored men may overwhelm the other races on this coast by their numbers—as limitless as were the frogs in Egypt. It is common for some men to affect not to be "afraid of the Chinamen." But we have read somewhere of a great army which was broken up and scattered by myriads of the smallest but most disgusting of insects. Frogs, and locusts, and ants, have all, in the course of time, vanquished the richest countries. Why may not the Chinamen do the same, if they have the numbers?

For it is the opinion in California that plentiful as has been the immigration there from China, it is nothing to what is probably coming, unless prevented by positive laws of exclusion. The reader will understand that the Chinese already swarm in the Golden State, and are looked upon there with much contempt and aversion by the Americans.

It should be added to the above opinions of Bayard Taylor, and of the San Francisco print, that we, without doubt, see the very worst specimens of Chinese, here in America. The "fair Chinese," although numerous and mighty of course in their own land, seldom or never leave it for foreign countries. It is doubtful whether we have ever had a good specimen of them here.

Probably there is no subject more curious, and more enveloped in darkness, than China and the Chinese to-day. They are *not* that dirty and abominable race merely; that is but one of the facts to be told about them. We are to remember that they represent the most ancient forms of civilization, government, and religion, now in force, continued from far remote periods down to the present hour. They occupy a large share of the surface of the early and youthful earth—those regions whence the great historical mass migrations poured out, thousands of years ago, to make, through many and many a century, not only modern history, but much of ancient history.

We are also to remember that, while we write this, the population there in China comprises nearly four hundred millions of human beings—more than one third of all those existing upon the earth. And not this serious fact only is worthy of attention—the literature, manufactures, and all the reminiscences of China, are also worth serious attention.

But China, its government, it exclusiveness, &c, are soon and surely to break up—"the sick man"[7] is going to die. What will come out of it all, no one can tell. New forms must arrange themselves—new growth and new governments. Doubtless a great deal is latent in China—has been repressed there too long.

From our American position on the shores of the Pacific, we cannot but look with deep interest on all these things, and carry out divers speculations upon them. All Asia, middle, northern, and southern—All the countless islands of Polynesia between—are in time to be in more or less intimate connection with us.

NOTES

1. This transcription is made from a photocopy of the original in the papers of Herbert Bergman, East Lansing, Michigan. Holloway and Schwarz, in *I Sit and Look Out*, include this editorial in the "Chronological List of Whitman Editorials" that were "impossible to reprint" because of space constraints. Walt Whitman, *I Sit and Look Out: Editorials from the Brooklyn Daily Times by Walt Whitman*, ed. Emory Holloway and Vernolian Schwarz (New York: Columbia University Press, 1932), 189–196, 232.

2. Oregon had already excluded slavery from its territory. See Whitman's editorial titled "No Slavery in Oregon," *Brooklyn Daily Eagle*, August 7, 1846 (above).

3. This act prohibited "all Chinese or Mongolians from entering the State, unless driven on shore by weather or some accident, in which case they should be immediately sent out of the country." It was ultimately declared unconstitutional by the state's highest court. United States Immigration Commission, "Reports, 1907–1910" (Washington, D.C.: U.S. Government Printing Office, 1911), 67.

4. In "Prohibition of Colored Persons," *Brooklyn Daily Times*, May 6, 1858, Whitman expressed a free-soiler's disdain for the institution of slavery, but some ambivalence toward the equality of African Americans. See Jerome Loving, *Walt Whitman: The Song of Himself* (Berkeley: University of California Press, 1999), 230–231, who also recognizes "Prohibition of Colored Persons" as an editorial by Whitman.

5. Probably "leprosied": "Affected with leprosy, leprous," according to the *OED*.

6. Bayard Taylor (1825–1878) was an author and travel writer. Whitman's quote was taken from *A Visit to India, China, and Japan* (New York: G. P. Putnam, 1854), 354. Taylor continues in this vein: "They constitute the surface-level, and below them there are deeps on deeps of depravity so shocking and horrible, that their character cannot even be hinted." And, "There are some dark shadows in human nature, which we naturally shrink from penetrating, and I made no attempt to collect information of this kind; but there was

enough in the things which I could not avoid seeing and hearing—which are brought almost daily to the notice of every foreign resident—to inspire me with a powerful aversion to the Chinese race."

7. While usually this title is applied to the Ottoman Empire in the nineteenth century, Whitman here uses it to describe China as an aging Asian empire in similarly dire straits. The last Chinese dynasty was overthrown and the Republic of China was founded in 1912.

Untitled[1]

Brooklyn Daily Times
AUGUST 26, 1858

The contest now waging in Illinois, with Senator Douglass,[2] the Administration, and the Republicans, headed by Lincoln and Trumbull[3] as the combatants, is exciting great interest.[4] Of the two, Mr. Lincoln seems to have had the advantage thus far in the war of words.[5] This method of debate in politics, where the antagonists have, each of them, their say before the same audience, is a good one, and ought to be more frequently adopted.

NOTES

1. Transcribed from scanned original, Brooklyn Public Library—Brooklyn Collection. This editorial also appears in Walt Whitman, *I Sit and Look Out: Editorials from the Brooklyn Daily Times by Walt Whitman*, ed. Emory Holloway and Vernolian Schwarz (New York: Columbia University Press, 1932), 96.

2. Stephen A. Douglas (1813–1861) is spelled "Douglass" in the original.

3. Lyman Trumbull (1813–1896) was a prominent Illinois Republican and U.S. senator who, in 1864, authored the Thirteenth Amendment and the Civil Rights Bill, which became the Fourteenth Amendment.

4. Whitman here refers to the Lincoln-Douglas debates during the 1858 Illinois senatorial election. While Lincoln lost the contest, these high-profile debates, primarily over Douglas's controversial Kansas-Nebraska Act (1854), which allowed for popular sovereignty over the issue of slavery in the territories of the Louisiana Purchase, brought Lincoln to national prominence.

5. On August 21 Lincoln and Douglas first met in Ottawa, Illinois, before a crowd of 6,000 spectators. During this first debate, Lincoln framed Douglas's conception of popular sovereignty in terms that appealed to free-soilers like Whitman, who were ambivalent about African American rights but fearful of the spread of slavery, especially of its economic effects on white labor: "I think . . . that [Douglas] and those acting with him, have placed that institution on a new basis, which looks to the perpetuity and nationalization

of slavery. And while it is placed upon this new basis, . . . I believe we shall not have peace upon the question until the opponents of slavery arrest the further spread of it, and place it where the public mind shall rest in the belief that it is in the course of ultimate extinction; or, on the other hand, that its advocates will push it forward until it shall become alike lawful in all the States, old as well as new, North as well as South." Abraham Lincoln, *Abraham Lincoln; Complete Works, Comprising His Speeches, State Papers, and Miscellaneous Writings*, ed. John G. Nicolay and John Hay (New York: Century, 1920), 1:291.

Untitled[1]

Brooklyn Daily Times
MARCH 7, 1859

The New York *Sun* says "there is but one man whom the Democracy can certainly and triumphantly elect to the Presidency in 1860, and that is Douglas of Illinois." They have to choose between two Ds—Douglass[2] and Defeat; and judging from the present temper of the ultra Southerners, they will accept the latter, hoping thereby to precipitate a disruption of the Union.[3]

NOTES

1. Transcribed from scanned original, Brooklyn Public Library—Brooklyn Collection. This editorial also appears in Walt Whitman, *I Sit and Look Out: Editorials from the Brooklyn Daily Times by Walt Whitman*, ed. Emory Holloway and Vernolian Schwarz (New York: Columbia University Press, 1932), 99.

2. Stephen A. Douglas. Spelled "Douglass" in the original.

3. At the Democratic convention in Charleston, South Carolina, Southern Democrats left the convention and nominated their own ticket of proslavery Democrats. This effectively split the Democratic Party into Northern and Southern factions and, along with the advent of the border-states Constitutional Union Party, allowed Abraham Lincoln to win the presidency with 39.8 percent of the popular vote in November 1860. In December 1860 the state of South Carolina seceded from the Union.

II

Moral Suasion

Do they feel no moral responsibility
moving upon their consciences . . . ?

—*SUN*, NOVEMBER 2, 1842

Dickens and Democracy[1]

New York Aurora

APRIL 2, 1842

We yesterday received the April number of the Democratic Review. It contains good reading—rather more than its usual proportion of solid and political articles. The leader is headed "the Reception of Mr. Dickens."[2] We read it with pleasure through three or four pages, when, all of a sudden, how were our eyes startled by seeing the critic join issue with Boz,[3] and attack that writer with a fierceness and openness that might almost be worthy of "the regular army."

The Review says, speaking of Dickens and his novels:

> "There is one striking defect in them, which, in the present undiscriminating applause bestowed on both him and them, we will not omit to notice. We allude to the atrocious exaggeration of his bad characters. There are no such creatures in the world, or in nature. Take Quilp,[4] that hideous and devilish incarnation of the pure abstract of all that is malignant;—what right has Boz to disgust and wound all our moral sensibilities, by giving such a thing a prominent place?"

Then again:

> "True, we cannot close our doors against either him or them, if we would, * * * still, there are no such characters in human nature; and the moral effect of exhibiting such to the imagination is very bad; and a serious drawback on the useful influence of the rest of his writings. * * * The same tone of exaggeration runs indeed through most of his characters."[5]

Lest we should be accused of not treating the critic fairly, we will add, that the general tone of the article in question is highly favorable to Mr. Dickens, and that it expresses the utmost satisfaction with the complimentary course pursued by the Americans toward their great literary guest. We shall now use liberty to make a few remarks about the exceptions taken by the writer in the Review.

Boz appears to be no Utopian. Though such books as his could have been written only by a man whose heart had great store of kindly feelings, confidence in the capability of his fellow men for the attainment of high perfection, genial dispositions—and possessed, also, of a propensity to look on the bright side of life's picture; yet Boz, like the rest of us, knows, no doubt, that there are many wicked men in the world—many beings whose hearts are fearful pest houses, and whose presence is as the taint of some deadly contagion. And it is necessary to exhibit these creatures in their unclothed deformity. Many well meaning, but weak minded people, have an unwholesome delicacy upon this subject. Hold up villainy to public scorn, say we; the wise physician cures no cankers except by cutting with a sharp blade, and a deep stroke.

Is the Review *sure* that "no such characters exist in the world, or in nature," as Dickens' villains? Would to heaven that it could reasonably be sure! Why, almost within the reach of our voice, there is a palpable counterpart to the worst embodiment of evil that the brain of Dickens ever transcribed upon paper! And the being to whom we allude is *worse* than the wickedest character in the Boz novels—inasmuch that the poison he diffuses is gilded, and allowed to pass by common sufferance. A reptile marking his path with slime wherever he goes, and breathing mildew at every thing fresh and fragrant; a midnight ghoul, preying on rottenness and repulsive filth; a creature, hated by his nearest intimates, and bearing the consciousness thereof upon his distorted features, and upon his despicable soul; one whom good men avoid as a blot to his nature—whom all despise, and whom no one blesses—*all this* is James Gordon Bennett.[6] Joined to the craftiness and utterly selfish beastliness of Fagan[7]—the infernal depravity, the gloating, satanic delight in torturing, of Quilp—the dull, callous insensibility to any virtue, of Sikes[8]—this loathsome agent of damnation claims the additional merit of having been spawned, not in an American gutter, but to have ornamented with the presence of his earlier age, some sty, pauper out house, or reeking bagnio,[9] of his native North Britain!

The Democratic Review need not go far, then, to find its own argument overthrown. In truth, the editor of the Review misses the consistency of his own doctrines. It is characteristic, indeed, of a noble mind to look around upon fellow creatures with broad glances of comprehensive love, and generous confidence in their essential capacity for virtue. Yet of him whose opportunity it may be, stern duty requires that he should sometimes paint lofty vice—that he should picture it forth in all its glaring reality—and that he should thus teach how terrible a thing is iniquity, and how wise it is to avoid the paths of evil.

NOTES

1. Transcribed from scanned original at the Walt Whitman Archive, whitmanarchive.org. This editorial also appears in Walt Whitman, *The Journalism, Volume I: 1834–1846*, part of *The Collected Writings of Walt Whitman*, ed. Herbert Bergman, Douglas A. Noverr, and Edward J. Recchia (New York: Peter Lang, 1998), 92–93.

2. The *United States Magazine and Democratic Review*, edited by John O'Sullivan, was in its time the voice of radical Democratic ideology and politics. In 1845 Whitman published "A Dialogue" in the *Democratic Review* (below). A "leader" was typically the first editorial on page 2 of a newspaper and represented the opinions of the editor.

3. Charles Dickens often used the nickname "Boz," short for "Boses," which was a derivation of "Moses." Dickens first used the name in print in *Sketches by Boz* (London: John Macrone, 1837).

4. From *The Old Curiosity Shop*.

5. The complete quote reads: "Still there are no such characters in human life or human nature; and the moral effect of exhibiting such to the imagination is very bad, and a serious drawback on the useful influences of the rest of his writings. The reader learns to believe in the possibility of such total depravity. He meets with persons presenting single aspects of character, or guilty, perhaps, of single acts, resembling the traits of these hideous creations of the magic pen, and is half unfitted to judge them either with that justice due to all or that charity needed alike by all. This same tone of exaggeration runs indeed through most of his characters though, some of the best are free from it ."

6. James Gordon Bennett (1795–1872), editor of the *New York Herald*, pioneered the personality-driven, scandal-seeking penny journalism of the 1830s and 1840s. Bennett's coverage of the murder of Helen Jewett and the investigation thereafter boosted the circulation of the *Herald* to 15,000 copies per day. Edwin Burrows and Mike Wallace, *Gotham: A History of New York City to 1898* (Oxford: Oxford University Press, 1999), 526–527, 539; Patricia Cline Cohen, *The Murder of Helen Jewett: The Life and Death of a Prostitute in Nineteenth-Century New York* (New York: Vintage Books, 1999), 16–19.

7. Spelled "Fagin" in *Oliver Twist* (1838), the adult leader of a gang of criminal boys in the novel.

8. A thief in *Oliver Twist*.

9. Originally a Turkish bathhouse, by the nineteenth century "bagnio" had come to mean a brothel in British English. *OED*.

A Dialogue By Walter Whitman[1]

United States Magazine and Democratic Review
NOVEMBER 1845

What would be thought of a man who, having an ill humor in his blood, should strive to cure himself by only cutting off the festers, the outward signs of it, as they appeared upon the surface? Put criminals for festers and society for the diseased man, and you may get the spirit of that part of our laws which expects to abolish wrong-doing by sheer terror—by cutting off the wicked, and taking no heed of the causes of wickedness. I have lived long enough to know that national folly never deserves contempt; else should I laugh to scorn such an instance of exquisite nonsense!

Our statutes are supposed to speak the settled will and voice of the community. We may imagine, then, a conversation of the following sort to take place—the imposing majesty of the people speaking on the one side, a pallid, shivering convict on the other.

"I have done wrong," says the convict; "in an evil hour a kind of frenzy came over me, and I struck my neighbor a heavy blow, which killed him. Dreading punishment, and the disgrace of my family, I strove to conceal the deed, but it was discovered."

"Then," says society, "you must be killed in return."

"But," rejoins the criminal, "I feel that I am not fit to die. I have not enjoyed life—I have not been happy or good. It is so horrid to look back upon one's evil deeds only. Is there no plan by which I can benefit my fellow-creatures, even at the risk of my own life?"

"None," answers society; "you must be strangled—choked to death. If your passions are so ungovernable that people are in danger from them, we shall hang you."

"Why that?" asks the criminal, his wits sharpened perhaps by his situation. "Can you not put me in some strong prison, where no one will be harmed by me? And if the expense is anything against this, let me work there, and support myself."

"No," responds society, "we shall strangle you; your crime deserves it."

"Have you, then, committed no crimes?" asks the murderer.

"None which the law can touch," answers society. "True, one of us had a mother, a weak-souled creature, that pined away month after month, and at last died, because her dear son was intemperate, and treated her ill. Another, who is the owner of many houses, thrust a sick family into the street because they did not pay their rent, whereof came the deaths of two little children. And another—that particularly well-dressed man—effected the ruin of a young girl, a silly thing who afterward became demented, and drowned herself in the river. One has gained much wealth by cheating his neighbors—but cheating so as not to come within the clutches of any statute. And hundreds are now from day to day practising[2] deliberately the most unmanly and wicked meannesses. We are all frail!"

"And *these* are they who so sternly clamor for my blood!" exclaims the convict in amazement. "Why is it that I alone am to be condemned?"

"That they are bad," rejoins society, "is no defence for you."

"That the multitude have so many faults—that none are perfect," says the criminal, "might at least make them more lenient to me. If my physical temperament subjects me to great passions, which lead me into crime, when wronged too—as I was when I struck that fatal blow—is there not charity enough among you to sympathise with me—to let me not be hung, but safely separated from all that I might harm?"

"There is some reason in what you say," answers society, "but the clergy, who hate the wicked, say that God's own voice has spoken against you. We might, perhaps, be willing to let you off with imprisonment; but Heaven imperatively forbids it, and demands your blood. Besides, that you were wronged, gave you no right to revenge yourself by taking life."

"Do you mean me to understand, then," asks the convict, "that Heaven is more blood-thirsty than you? And if wrong gives no right to revenge, why am I arraigned thus?"

"The case is different," rejoins society. "We are a community—you are but a single individual. You should forgive your enemies."

"And are you not ashamed," asks the culprit, "to forget that as a community which you expect me to remember as a man? While the town clock goes wrong, shall each little private watch be abused for failing to keep the true time? What are communities but congregated individuals? And if you, in the potential force of your high position, deliberately set examples of retribution, how dare you look to me for self-denial, forgiveness, and the meekest and most difficult virtues?"

"I cannot answer such questions," responds society; "but if you propose no punishment for the bad, what safety is there for our citizens' rights and peace, which would then be in continual jeopardy?"

"You cannot," says the other, "call a perpetual jail no punishment. It is a terrible one. And as to your safety, it will be outraged less by mild and benevolent criminal laws than by sanguinary and revengeful ones. They govern the insane better with gentleness than severity. Are not men possessing reason more easily acted on through moral force than men without?"

"But, I repeat it, crimes will then multiply," says society (not having much else to say); "the punishment must be severe, to avoid that. Release the bad from the fear of hanging, and they will murder every day. We must preserve that penalty to prevent this taking of life."

"I was never ignorant of the penalty," answers the criminal; "and yet I murdered, for my blood was up. Of all the homicides committed, not one in a hundred is done by persons unaware of the law. So that you see the terror of death does not deter. The hardened and worst criminals, too, frequently have no such terror, while the more repentant and humanized suffer in it the most vivid agony. At least you could try the experiment of no hanging."

"It might cost too much. Murder would increase," reiterates society.

"Formerly," replies the criminal, "many crimes were punished by death that now are not; and yet those crimes have not increased. Not long since the whipping-post and branding-iron stood by the bar of courts of justice, and were often used, too. Yet their abolition has not multiplied the evils for which they were meted out. This, and much more, fully proves that it is by no means the dread of terrible punishment which prevents crime. And now allow me to ask you a few questions. Why are most modern executions private, so called, instead of public?"

"Because," answers society, "the influence of the spectacle is degrading and anti-humanizing. As far as it goes, it begets a morbid and unhealthy feeling in the masses."

"Suppose all the convicts," goes on the prisoner, "adjudged to die in one of your largest States, were kept together for two whole years and then in the most public part of the land were hung up in a row—say twenty of them together—how would this do?"

"God forbid!" answers society with a start. "The public mind would revolt at so bloody and monstrous a deed. It could not be allowed!"

"Is it anything less horrible," resumes the questioner, "in the deaths being singly and at intervals?"

"I cannot say it is," answers society.

"Allow me to suppose a little more," continues the criminal, "that all the convicts to be hung in the whole republic for two years—say two hundred, and that is a small estimate—were strangled at the same time, in full sight of every man, woman and child—all the remaining population. And suppose this were done periodically every two years. What say you to that?"

"The very thought sickens me," answers society, "and the effect would be more terrible and blighting upon the national morals and the health of the popular heart, than it is any way possible to describe. No unnatural rites of the most barbarous and brutal nations of antiquity ever equalled[3] this; and our name would always deserve to be written literally in characters of blood. The feeling of the sacredness of life would be utterly destroyed among us. Every fine and Christian faculty of our souls would be rooted away. In a few years, this hellish oblation becoming common, the idea of violent death would be the theme of laughter and ribald jesting. In all the conduct and opinions of men, in their every-day business, and in their private meditations, so terrible an institution would some way, in some method of its influence, be seen operating. What! two hundred miserable wretches at once! The tottering old, and the youth not yet arrived at manhood; women, too, and perhaps girls who are hardly more than children! The spot where such a deed should be periodically consummated would surely be cursed forever by God and all goodness. Some awful and poisonous desert it ought to be; though, however awful, it could but faintly image the desert such horrors must make of the heart of man, and the poison it would diffuse on his better nature."

"And if all this appalling influence," says the murderer, "were really operating over you—not concentrated, but cut up in fractions and frittered here and there—just as strong in its general effect, but not brought to a point, as in the case I have imagined—what would you then say?"

"Nay," replies society, with feverish haste, "but the executions are now required to be private."

"Many are not," rejoins the other; "and as to those that are nominally so, where everybody reads newspapers, and every newspaper seeks for graphic accounts of these executions, such things can never be private. What a small proportion of your citizens are eye-witnesses of things done in Congress; yet they are surely not private, for not a word officially spoken in the Halls of the

Capitol, but is through the press made as public as if every American's ear were within hearing distance of the speaker's mouth. The whole spectacle of these two hundred executions is more faithfully seen, and much more deliberately dwelt upon, through the printed narratives, than if people beheld it with their bodily eyes, and then no more. Print preserves it. It passes from hand to hand, and even boys and girls are imbued with its spirit and horrid essence. Your legislators have forbidden public executions; they must go farther. They must forbid the relation of them by tongue, letter, or picture; for your physical sight is not lessened because it is more covert and more widely diffused. Rather, indeed, the reverse. As things are, the masses take it for granted that the system and its results are right. As I have supposed them to be, though the nature would remain the same, the difference of the form would present the monstrous evil in a vivid and utterly new light before men's eyes."

"To all this," says society, "I answer—" *what?* What shall it be, thou particular reader, whose eyes now dwell on my fanciful dialogue? Give it for thyself—and if it be indeed *an answer,* thou hast a logic of most surpassing art.

O, how specious is the shield thrown over wicked actions, by invoking the Great Shape of Society in their defence! How that which is barbarous, false, or selfish for an individual becomes singularly proper when sanctioned by the legislature, or a supposed national policy! How deeds wicked in a man are thus applauded in a number of men!

What makes a murder the awful crime all ages have considered it? The friend and foe of hanging will unite in the reply—Because it destroys that cunning principle of vitality which no human agency can replace—invades the prerogative of God, for God's is the only power that can give life—and offers a horrid copy for the rest of mankind. Lo! thou lover of strangling! with what a keen razor's sharpness does every word of this reply cut asunder the threads of that argument which defends thy cause! The very facts which render murder a frightful crime, render hanging a frightful punishment. To carry out the spirit of such a system, when a man maims another, the law should maim him in return. In the unsettled districts of our western states, it is said that in brutal fights the eyes of the defeated are sometimes torn bleeding from their sockets. The rule which justifies the taking of life, demands gouging out of eyes as a legal penalty too.

I have one point else to touch upon, and then no more. There has, about this point, on the part of those who favor hanging, been such a bold, impudent effrontery—such a cool sneering defiance of all those greater lights which make the glory of this age over the shame of the dark ages—a prostitution so foul of names and influences so awfully sacred—that I tremble this moment with passion, while I treat upon it. I speak of founding the whole breadth and strength of the hanging system, as many do, on the Holy Scriptures. The matter is too extensive to be argued fully, in the skirts of an essay; and I have therefore but one suggestion to offer upon it, though words and ideas rush and swell upon my utterance. When I read in the records of the past how Calvin burned Servetus at Geneva,[4] and found his defence in the Bible—when I peruse the reign of the English Henry 8th, that great champion of Protestantism, who, after the Reformation, tortured people to death, for refusing to acknowledge his spiritual supremacy, and pointed to the Scriptures as his authority—when, through the short reign of Edward 6th, another Protestant sovereign, and of the Bloody Mary, a Catholic one, I find the most barbarous cruelties and martyrdoms inflicted in the name of God and his Sacred Word—I shudder and grow sick with pity. Still I remember the gloomy ignorance of the law of love that prevailed then, and the greater palliations for bigotry and religious folly. I bethink me how good it is that the spirit of such horrors, the blasphemy which prostitutes God's law to be their excuse, and the darkness of superstition which applauded them, have all passed away. But in these days of greater clearness, when clergymen call for sanguinary punishments in the name of the Gospel—when, chased from point to point of human policy, they throw themselves on the supposed necessity of hanging in order to gratify and satisfy Heaven—when, instead of Christian mildness and love, they demand that our laws shall be pervaded by vindictiveness and violence—when the sacrifice of human life is inculcated as in many cases acceptable to Him who they say has even revoked his consent to brute sacrifices—my soul is filled with amazement, indignation and horror, utterly uncontrollable. When I go by a church, I cannot help thinking whether its walls do not sometimes echo, "Strangle and kill in the name of God!" The grasp of a minister's hand, produces a kind of choking sensation; and by some optical fascination, the pulpit is often intercepted from my view by a ghastly gallows frame. "O, Liberty!" said Madame Roland, "What crimes have been committed in thy name!"[5] "O, Bible!" say I, "What follies and monstrous barbarities are defended in *thy* name!"

NOTES

1. Transcribed from Walt Whitman, *The Journalism, Volume I: 1834–1846*, part of *The Collected Writings of Walt Whitman*, ed. Herbert Bergman, Douglas A. Noverr, and Edward

J. Recchia (New York: Peter Lang, 1998), 205–209.

2. Spelling in original.

3. Spelling in original.

4. Michael Servetus (1509–1553), a prominent humanist and theologian, was burned as a heretic.

5. Marie Jeanne Roland (1754–1793), a supporter of the Girondist faction during the French Revolution, supposedly cried these words upon passing a statue of Liberty on her way to the guillotine during the Reign of Terror. See *The Works of Jeanne-Marie Phlipon Roland* (London: J. Johnson, 1800), 53.

The Wrongs of Woman.[1]

Brooklyn Daily Eagle
MARCH 17, 1846

No *true* man can ever be without a deeply seated impulse of love and reverence for woman—a love and reverence not in the abstract merely, as poets talk about in their writings, but actual, and worked into every day thought and conduct. With all its failings, its flippancy, its affectation, and its fickleness—the female character is surpassingly beautiful! What strength of affection it has! What devotion to the sufferer and the unfortunate! And in the phase of motherly love—the crowning glory of the human attributes—what similitude to the immortal kindness of our Saviour himself!

There is a class of cold and monkeyish chatterers who talk by rule in opposition to the female name and nature—who pretend to rail at the sex, and direct the shafts of their puny ridicule against them! They seize on some of those trivial weaknesses of woman—the result, perhaps, of her very virtues, carried to an excess—and find food for their mockery and miserable wit! We have a contempt for all puppies of this sort—and only excuse them because we think their ignorance outweighs their folly. How dare they speak, on principle, against the class of which their own, and every hearer's mother, form part? It is an indirect insult to every young man that listens to them!

We see in the Rochester papers a narrative of "the wrongs of woman," of a worse than ordinary kind—and this narrative it is which has caused the reflections just given. What a heartless brute the husband must have been! But let our readers peruse the story for themselves: Two years ago, a young girl named Hannah E. Williams lived in Boston, and supported herself by dress-making. She became acquainted with a young carpenter, George E. Patterson; their acquaintance ended in love and marriage. Last summer they moved to Rochester—and, according to the testimony there, the husband's conduct ever since has been a series of monstrous cruelties, in a small way, toward the wretched wife. She was sick; but on Tuesday night last, he left Rochester, after having stupefied her with laudanum, and then stripped the rooms and trunks of every thing that could be carried away, even to his own miniature, which she had kept as a memento! Thus deserted, Mrs. Patterson gave way to her grief, which, combined with the former sickness, caused her death.—The latter part of last week she died—a grateful relief to the poor young creature, from a life that had been to her little else than "full of sorrow."[2]

It is customary among certain people to talk about "scolding wives," and all that sort of thing; but women, though they have tongues, have hearts also,—and a wife is almost invariably true to her husband through all kinds of disaster, disgrace, and poverty. We have seen dirty looking criminals before our courts, forsaken it would seem by the whole world—but *the wife* was by their side, and in one face at least, they could see good will and tenderness. Ah, we are too apt—we men—in our imperious way, to fail of our love and respect for woman. The actual *wrong,* all who have any heart will cry out against. But we have sins of omission, as well as commission. We should never forget that the nature of woman, in itself, is always beautifully pure, affectionate, and true—and where those qualities appear not on the surface, they are but hidden by the artificial forms of life, or kept back by the distorted bent of the world's example.

NOTES

1. Transcribed from scanned original, Brooklyn Public Library—Brooklyn Collection. This editorial also appears in Walt Whitman, *The Journalism, Volume I: 1834–1846,* part of *The Collected Writings of Walt Whitman,* ed. Herbert Bergman, Douglas A. Noverr, and Edward J. Recchia (New York: Peter Lang, 1998), 287.

2. Whitman's own sister, Hannah, also had a difficult marriage. Her husband, Charles Louis Heyde, an artist who was commissioned to paint Vermont's state seal in the 1850s, succumbed to alcoholism and was eventually institutionalized. See Jerome Loving, *Walt Whitman: The Song of Himself* (Berkeley: University of California Press, 1999), 385; Vivian Pollak, *The Erotic Whitman* (Berkeley: University of California Press, 2000), 120.

Slavers—and the Slave Trade.[1]

Brooklyn Daily Eagle
MARCH 18, 1846

Public attention, within the last few days has been naturally turned to the slave trade—that most abominable of all man's schemes for making money, without regard to the character of the means used for the purpose. Four vessels have, in about as many days, been brought to the American territory, for being engaged in this monstrous business! It is a disgrace and blot on the character of our republic, and on our boasted humanity![2]

Though we hear less now-a days of this trade—of the atrocious slave hunt—of the crowding of a mass of compact human flesh into little more than its equal of space—we are not to suppose that such horrors have ceased to exist. The great nations of the earth—our own first of all—have passed stringent laws against the slave traffic. But Brazil openly encourages it still.[3] And many citizens of Europe and America pursue it notwithstanding its illegality. Still the negro is torn from his simple hut—from his children, his brethren, his parents, and friends—to be carried far away and made the bondman of a stranger. Still the black-hearted traitors who ply this work, go forth with their armed bands and swoop down on the defenceless villages, and bring their loads of human trophy, chained and gagged, and sell them as so much merchandise!

The slave-ship! How few of our readers know the beginning of the horrors involved in that term! Imagine a vessel of the fourth or fifth class, built more for speed than space, and therefore with narrow accommodations even for a few passengers; a space between decks divided into two compartments three feet three inches from floor to ceiling—one of these compartments sixteen feet by eighteen, the other forty by twenty one—the first holding two hundred and twenty six children and youths of both sexes—the second, *three hundred and thirty six men and women*—and all this in a latitude where the thermometer is at eighty degrees in the shade! Are you sick of the description? O, this is not all, by a good sight. Imagine neither food nor water given these hapless prisoners—except a little of the latter, at long intervals, which they spill in their mad eagerness to get it; many of the women advanced in pregnancy—the motion of the sea sickening those who have never before felt it—dozens of the poor wretches dying, and others already dead, (and they are most to be envied!)—the very air so thick that the lungs cannot perform their office—and all this for filthy lucre! Pah! we are almost a misanthrope to our kind when we think they will do such things!

Of the 900 negroes, (there were doubtless more,) originally on board the *Pons*, not six hundred and fifty remained when she arrived back, and landed her inmates at Monrovia![4] It is enough to make the heart pause its pulsations to read the scene presented at the liberation of these sons of misery.—Most of them were boys, of from twelve to twenty years. What woe must have spread through many a negro mother's heart, from this wicked business!

It is not ours to find an excuse for slaving, in the benighted condition of the African. Has not God seen fit to make him, and leave him so? Nor is it any less our fault because the chiefs of that barbarous land fight with each other, and take slave-prisoners. The whites encourage them, and afford them a market. Were that market destroyed, there would soon be no supply.

We would hardly so insult our countrymen as to suppose that any among them yet countenance a system, only a little portion of whose horrors we have been describing—did not facts prove the contrary. The "middle passage," is yet going on with all its deadly crime and cruelty. The slave-trade yet exists. *Why?* The laws are sharp enough—too sharp. But who ever hears of their being put in force, further than to confiscate the vessel, and perhaps imprison the crews a few days? But the laws should pry out every man who helps the slave-trade—not merely the sailor on the sea, but *the cowardly rich villain, and speculator on the land*—and punish *him*. It cannot be effectually stopped until that is done—and Brazil forced by the black muzzles of American and European men-of-war's cannon, to stop her part of the business too!

NOTES

1. Transcribed from scanned original, Brooklyn Public Library—Brooklyn Collection. This editorial also appears in Walt Whitman, *The Journalism, Volume I: 1834–1846*, part of *The Collected Writings of Walt Whitman*, ed. Herbert Bergman, Douglas A. Noverr, and Edward J. Recchia (New York: Peter Lang, 1998), 288–289.

2. Whitman wrote this article five months before the introduction of Representative

David Wilmot's proviso against the expansion of slavery was added to an appropriations bill for the U.S.-Mexico War. While Whitman is sometimes described as a free-soiler of Wilmot's ilk, therefore situating his antislavery arguments in the context of white working-class rights, this article illuminates Whitman's often overlooked early humanitarian arguments against slavery. For a useful analysis of Whitman's evolving antislavery stance before the publication of *Leaves of Grass*, see Martin Klammer, *Whitman, Slavery, and the Emergence of* Leaves of Grass (University Park: Pennsylvania State University Press, 1995), especially 7–27, where Klammer analyzes Whitman's novel *Franklin Evans; or The Inebriate* (1842).

3. Brazil abolished slavery in 1888.

4. The *Pons*, a ship out of Philadelphia, was captured by the USS *Yorktown* on November 28, 1845, off the coast of Liberia with 900 Africans aboard bound for Brazil. Though the ship contained no Americans on board at the time of its capture, the *Pons* flew an American flag, only to quickly change it to a Brazilian flag upon encountering the *Yorktown*. When the ship was forced to port in Liberia, the captives were released. J. W. Lugenbeel to the American Colonization Society, November 29, 1845, reprinted in *The African Repository* (Washington, D.C.: American Colonization Society, 1846), 22:112; Charles W. Bell to Secretary of Navy George Bancroft, December 16, 1845, reprinted in *The Friend*, May 7, 1846 (Philadelphia: Joseph Kite and Son, 1846), 255.

Legislating for Morality.[1]

Brooklyn Daily Eagle

MARCH 24, 1846

After throwing out about twenty similar bills, in former sessions, the lower house of the legislature of this state have passed the seduction bill to a third reading, and will probably pass the bill itself before long. "Will the Senate dare veto it?"[2] asks a New York print of this morning. We certainly hope they will. That womanly virtue which has no better protection than legislators' statutes, is no kind of virtue at all. We are aware, well enough, that hardly any crime is wickeder than deliberate seduction. There are also many other iniquities, such as filial disobedience, various sorts of cheating, lying, and so on—which are perhaps worse, in their continued commission, than sudden crimes like assaults or thefts. But the former are not fit subjects for the criminal law—nor is seduction. Appeals, we know, are made to the sympathies and feelings of men—but a cool head will acknowledge for such appeals no foundation in truth. We are sure that a law like that at present before the legislature, would, if passed, produce far more harm than good.

NOTES

1. Transcribed from scanned original, Brooklyn Public Library—Brooklyn Collection. This editorial also appears in Walt Whitman, *The Journalism, Volume I: 1834–1846*, part of *The Collected Writings of Walt Whitman*, ed. Herbert Bergman, Douglas A. Noverr, and Edward J. Recchia (New York: Peter Lang, 1998), 301.

2. "Moral Reform in Our Legislature, Correspondence of Our Legislature, March 18, 1846," *New York Tribune*, March 24, 1846.

Is it right to dance?[1]

Brooklyn Daily Eagle

APRIL 17, 1846

Somebody offers a $50 premium for the best tract against *dancing*—to expose the evils of that amusement, and after holding it up to ridicule, put it down to disuse. Three "right reverend fathers of the church," are to read the competing essays, and to decide on the best, about the first of November next, in the good city of Gotham.

Now this may be with sincere motives, but it is all folly. That dancing itself is an agreeable, graceful, wholesome entertainment, nobody will deny. But the objection is against the late hours and thin dresses of fashionable balls—their spiced, indigestible, hot, hearty suppers, and so forth. *There*, we agree with you, sirs! But you may on the same principle offer a premium[2] to disprove the propriety of *eating*. Forty nine persons out of every fifty violate the plainest rules of health, in their diet—and all sorts of foolish customs have been hitched on to man's appetite. The demand of his stomach to be filled whenever empty is made the specious pretext of putting into his blood a thousand noxious ingredients.

Dancing should be pursued differently; and then it would be unobjectionable. We believe among some of the very "tip top" fashionables of New York, it is now not rare to have quadrille parties in the afternoon. The way of dancing through the night till daylight—breathing half a pint of fine dust, and all kinds of impurity—and eating rich food in an unusual quantity—are truly open to the soundest objections. Let balls begin at eight o'clock, and let people who have any idea of comfort, never stay later than twelve!

NOTES

1. Transcribed from scanned original, Brooklyn Public Library—Brooklyn Collection. This editorial also appears in Walt Whitman, *The Journalism, Volume I: 1834–1846*, part of *The Collected Writings of Walt Whitman*, ed. Herbert Bergman, Douglas A. Noverr, and Edward J. Recchia (New York: Peter Lang, 1998), 334.

2. The original reads "premimu."

Hurrah for Choking Human Lives![1]

Brooklyn Daily Eagle

JUNE 24, 1846

The Convention at Albany—amid the many subjects claiming audience of them—will, in due time, debate the right and wrong of the present popular (?) system of legal strangulation.[2] We may expect, then, to see a noble advocacy of reform in this particular; for there are men here who champion that reform, as they hope for God's love!

Trembling for this 'conservative institution' of old times, the advocates of choking the wicked to death, bestir themselves of late, and print articles in their newspapers and magazines, to prove how good it is to strangle—and how grateful the practice to Him who made man in His own image. Monstrous! As if the Holy God, who, they say, wills that there be no more brute sacrifices, can smile upon these manglings and bloody offerings up of the greatest masterpiece, the best-beloved of His works![3]

One of our strangling arguers makes merry at the difficulty, (as he calls it) his opponents have in reconciling their doctrine to certain 'first principles.'—Poor alphabet-learner! Knows he not that writers of the simplest and soundest truths have frequently found it repugnant to descend and prove what is as plain to clear-eyed men as any fact in mathematics—but which obstinate and bigoted people, and reverencers of the example of the past, cannot or will not see? Thus, to a person of large mind, principles are regarded in their application to the widest humanity, in their fitness to the unchanging nature of the heart, and the motives of its action—and not through an artificial medium, tinged by fashion, temporary passion, precedent, and the monotony of things around us.

NOTES

1. Transcribed from scanned original, Brooklyn Public Library—Brooklyn Collection. This editorial also appears in Walt Whitman, *The Journalism, Volume I: 1834–1846,*

part of *The Collected Writings of Walt Whitman*, ed. Herbert Bergman, Douglas A. Noverr, and Edward J. Recchia (New York: Peter Lang, 1998), 435. David Reynolds argues that George Lippard's *The Quaker City* (1845) may have inspired Whitman's ironic celebration of hanging in this article. David Reynolds, *Walt Whitman's America: A Cultural Biography* (New York: Alfred A. Knopf, 1995), 131. From *The Quaker City*: "'Give us but the gibbet,' [the preachers] shrieked. 'Only give us the gibbet and we'll reform the world! Christ said mercy was his rule, we know more about his religion than he did himself, and we cry give us blood! In the name of Moses, in the name of Paul, and John, and Peter, in the name of the Church, in the name of Christ—give us the gibbet, only give us the gibbet!' [. . .] 'Hurrah!' screamed Devil-Bug. 'The gallows is livin' yet! Hurrah!' He sprang from his feet in very glee, and clapped his hands and hurrahed again." George Lippard, *The Quaker City; or, The Monks of Monk Hall. A Romance of Philadelphia Life, Mystery and Crime* (1844; Philadelphia: Leary, Stuart, 1876), 317.

2. Execution by hanging.

3. Whitman here echoes arguments made in "A Dialogue By Walt Whitman," *United States Magazine and Democratic Review*, November 1845 (above).

Radicalism at the West.[1]

Brooklyn Daily Eagle
DECEMBER 30, 1846

Give us, (in many things,) the West, after all! the "fresh, the ever-free"[2] West! . . . . The Constitution of Wisconsin *is* a Constitution. One of the sections is: "All property, real and personal, of the wife, owned by her at the time of her marriage, and also that acquired by her after marriage by gift, devise, descent or otherwise, than from her husband, shall be her separate property. Laws shall be passed providing for the registry of the wife's property, and more clearly defining the rights of the wife thereto, as well as to property held by her with her husband, and for carrying out the provisions of this section."[3] . . . . Another section exempts the homestead of the debtor of the value of one thousand dollars, from any execution or forced sale, for any debt growing out of, or founded upon any contract. This section was adopted in its present form by a vote of 70 to 29. It has created an immense excitement, but all attempts to defeat it on its passage failed, and subsequently the convention has adhered to it with most stringent inflexibility . . . . . . The article on the Judiciary, as finally adopted provides that the judicial power shall be vested in a Supreme Court, Circuit Courts, Courts of Probate, and Justices of the Peace; but for the first five years of state organization and until the Legislature shall otherwise direct, the Circuit Judges shall constitute the Supreme Court. These judges are to be chosen by the people, for the term of five years. Tribunals of conciliation may be established, and their duties prescribed by the Legislature. A tax shall be imposed on all suits commenced in the Supreme or Circuit Courts, and the proceeds applied towards paying the Judges.

NOTES

1. Transcribed from scanned original, Brooklyn Public Library—Brooklyn Collection. Loving suggests that this editorial is by Whitman. Jerome Loving, "Whitman, Walt. *The*

Journalism, volume 2. Ed. Herbert Bergman, Douglas A. Noverr, and Edward J. Recchia [review]," *Walt Whitman Quarterly Review* 22 (Summer 2004): 31–36.

2. Barry Cornwall, "The Sea," in *English Songs, and Other Small Poems, by Barry Cornwall* (London: Bradbury and Evans, 1832), 1. Cornwall was the pseudonym for Bryan Waller Procter (1787–1874). The first stanza of the poem reads:

> The sea! the sea! the open sea!
> The blue, the fresh, the ever free!
> Without a mark, without a bound,
> It runneth the earth's wide regions round;
> It plays with the clouds; it mocks the skies;
> Or like a cradled creature lies.

3. Wisconsin Constitution (1846) Article XIV, Section 1, *Journal of the Convention to Form a Constitution for the State of Wisconsin* (Madison, Wisconsin Territory: Tenny, Holt, and Smith, 1846), 644.

Brooklyn Schools.[1]

Brooklyn Daily Eagle

APRIL 19, 1847

We would extend the spirit of some remarks made in our Saturday's paper, on the management and mismanagement of Brooklyn schools,[2] into an invitation to the proper officers that they take some pains to procure for teachers men of gentlemanly toned minds, of suavity and good temper, and of benevolent dispositions. And we suggest to the teachers themselves, through all departments, male, female, and primary, the diffusion by example of those traits among their pupils. As to children— those little chamelions[3] who take their hue from every thing around them—those little harps that respond in the same spirit, soft and gentle, or wild and discordant, wherewith they are touched—as to children, there are very many who receive the seeds of the most absurd and improper habits from their monitors or teachers at school. Severity and harsh chastisement are like ice to them; and under such cold influence grow no wholesome fruits or beautiful flowers. But gentleness is the sunshine and the summer air.

We like well to know that public attention is *really* widely turned, now-a-days, to the public schools, and to all matters affecting their weal or woe. The monotonous stereotyped phrases about "the advantages of education," are still babbled by some who talk it as parrots talk; but the best part of those who direct society, fully realize the great effects—ascending and descending into all the departments of life and of happiness, of every class and of every age, of the politics, the morals, and even the commerce, of the nation—of the public schools of this land. And when we come to think on the princely munificence ever evinced by the government of the state of New York toward them—the incalculable sums spent upon them, tallied by other sums drawn directly from the people—the fine edifices built for their accommodation, and varied talent employed in sundry ways in ministering to their efficiency—we may well be pardoned for asking, Have all these really produced as much as the richness of the material would warrant? Has there not been a lack of *teachers*, really worthy their noble employment? Have we not jogged on in the path of the past, making the pupil familiar with forms and words instead of essences and things? Such questions are not amiss to be self-put by the members of the Brooklyn board of education, for most of the individuals composing which we have a high respect—too high to think they will ever take it amiss that we endeavor in our humble way to aid the progress of the seminaries of Brooklyn through the frequent remarks and suggestions we make about them, in these columns.

And the time has arrived—we mean to state this item in the most emphatic manner—for *totally banishing the lash, the rod, and the use of blows,* from our schools. Such teachers should be selected as proceed on a principle the reverse of that which requires blows; for we have little faith even in the mild plan unless it come from the voluntary convictions of teachers. And whenever a school is conducted on the *brutal* plan, (we presume there is but one such in Brooklyn,) it seems to us so clear what course the officers should pursue, that we do not think it necessary here even to state it.

NOTES

1. Transcribed from scanned original, Brooklyn Public Library—Brooklyn Collection. This editorial also appears in Walt Whitman, *The Journalism, Volume II: 1846–1848,* part of *The Collected Writings of Walt Whitman,* ed. Herbert Bergman, Douglas A. Noverr, and Edward J. Recchia (New York: Peter Lang, 2003), 249–250.

2. As a young man, Whitman taught at various rural schools on Long Island.

3. Spelling in original with inverted "n," "chamelious."

Brooklyn Morals.—Those Wax Figures.[1]

Brooklyn Daily Eagle

MAY 8, 1847

One or two of the N.Y. papers make merry over a museum, in this city, of wax figures of murder scenes; and say that "such an exhibition would not be tolerated elsewhere than in Brooklyn." We understand that this 'exhibition' is a concomitant of the menagerie which remained here two days last week, and which remains also more or less in two thirds of the villages and cities of the land. Of course Brooklyn has no more to do with the exhibition (a most miserable way of catching visitors) than any other place...... As to the *Star*'s story, copied and commented on, that "the husband of Mrs. Bickford, (Tirrell,) accompanies the show, and exposes the dresses belonging to his wife," —our venerable contemporary, in believing such a marvellous[2] tale, has been as effectually '*done*' as was the verdant vicar of Wakefield[3] by the 'cosmogany' gentleman.—Tirrell was convicted of adultery, and is now serving out his time in the Massachusetts state prison.[4]

The moral character of Brooklyn has been jeopardised,[5] heretofore, by the setting afloat of divers ridiculous stories, which would give the impression abroad that the only events worth noting here were petty police cases, rows, wrangles, indecorous proceedings, and so on. Newspaper writers' fields are, of course, illimitable (except by the limits of propriety and law); and we would be the last to exercise a needless fastidiousness toward them. But do not some of our craft, here in Brooklyn, confine themselves too much within the most belittled part of their duties—descriptions of such events as we allude to above?

NOTES

1. Transcribed from scanned original, Brooklyn Public Library—Brooklyn Collection. Loving suggests that this editorial is Whitman's. Jerome Loving, "Whitman, Walt. *The Journalism, volume* 2. Ed. Herbert Bergman, Douglas A. Noverr, and Edward J. Recchia [review]," *Walt Whitman Quarterly Review* 22 (Summer 2004): 31–36.

2. Spelling in original.

3. The main character of Oliver Goldsmith's (1730–1774) *The Vicar of Wakefield* (1766).

4. Maria A. Bickford was murdered by her lover, Albert J. Tirrell, in Boston in 1845. By 1846 a traveling wax exhibit of the pair featured "the identical dress that was given her by Tirrell" and "the jewelry and other ornaments worn by her in Boston; all of which have been obtained of Mr. James Bickford . . . at a great cost." Qtd. in Daniel A. Cohen, "The Murder of Maria Bickford: Fashion, Passion, and the Birth of a Consumer Culture," *American Studies* 31, no. 2 (1990): 5–30, 19.

5. Spelling in original.

Long Island.—The English and the Dutch.[1]

Brooklyn Daily Eagle

JULY 29, 1847

In the course of certain long and elaborate investigations which we have been led to make, lately in reference to Brooklyn rights, as against the usurpations of New York city,[2] we have come into possession of proof of the following fact, which we have never heard stated—that as far, most undoubtedly, as Long Island is concerned and we believe New York island too, there is no single instance during the Dutch supremacy, of any usurpation, disturbance or quarrel, founded on any injustice in respect to lands, or taking from the Indians unfairly, or swindling one party out of them for the unjust benefit of another party.[3] When the Dutchmen had any propositions to make for land occupied by the Indians, or even claimed by the latter, they called them together, found out their terms, and either agreed to those terms, or left the Indians still in possession.—The consequence was, the two parties were always on friendly terms with each other; and amid the long list of wrongs and cheats which the history of the red men shows that they have received from the whites, it is beautiful to know that from the Dutch, the Quakers, and the Moravians, they have received but honest and kind treatment—and that between those three parties and the aboriginal inhabitants treaties have been observed in good faith, and friendship cordially reciprocated.[4]

-But with the English rule on Manhattan and Long Island, came, on the contrary, the beginning of foul play, of driving the Indians off either by force or fraud, of quarrels, of taking property unjustly; and an innumerable train of similar evils.[5]—The history of the English governors is a history of shameless rapacity, favortism,[6] and petty extortion. Knowing little law, in most cases, but their own caprice, and the rule of force, they violated 'vested rights' with a daring hand; and the Indians, being without either power, active friends in the government, or knowledge, were the victims of these wicked governors.

NOTES

1. Transcribed from scanned original, Brooklyn Public Library—Brooklyn Collection. While not included in the *Collected Writings*, Loving suggests that this editorial is by Whitman. Jerome Loving, "Whitman, Walt. *The Journalism, volume* 2. Ed. Herbert Bergman, Douglas A. Noverr, and Edward J. Recchia [review]," *Walt Whitman Quarterly Review* 22 (Summer 2004): 31–36.

2. On June 29, 1847, the *Eagle* published an editorial criticizing New York City's annual collection of "a large sum of money" from its "water right" to Brooklyn's ports. Whitman called on Brooklynites to "Put on the panoply of justice, and take for your shield the peaceful but powerful weapons of equity and right, and you will prevail" if they would not "be held tributary to New York, . . . your oppressive neighbor."

3. Whitman's maternal grandfather, Cornelius Van Velsor (1760–1826), was of Dutch heritage.

4. Whitman here overlooks early and often vicious conflicts between the Dutch and the Wiechquaesgecks and Hackensacks, a good example of which was the massacre of "scores of men, women and children" in a raid led by Director-General Willem Kieft (1597–1647) under the auspices of the Dutch West India Company in 1642 at Pavonia. At a raid on a native village at Corlear's Hook near Manhattan, the Dutch "brought back to New Amsterdam for display . . . [t]he heads of more than eighty victims." Edwin Burrows and Mike Wallace, *Gotham: A History of New York City to 1898* (Oxford: Oxford University Press, 1999), 38–39. See also Paul Otto, *The Dutch-Munsee Encounter: The Struggle for Sovereignty in the Hudson Valley* (New York: Berghahn Books, 2006).

5. The hyphen at the beginning of this sentence is in the original.

6. Spelling in original.

Public Annoyances and Municipal Negligence.[1]

Brooklyn Daily Eagle

DECEMBER 2, 1847

We have, lately, had many reasons to allude to the negligence of certain municipal officers, and to contractors, in permitting the obstruction of the public streets unnecessarily, and in leaving them so obstructed for a most unreasonable length of time.—Our complaints have not been objected to in a single quarter—nor have those complained of been defended by a single person. In one or two instances, there seems to have been some feeble attempt to do better; but each attempt has expired in its own feebleness. The evils alluded to grow more and more numerous every day. Hardly a morning passes without some one coming into our office and mentioning an additional item of negligence or culpable oversight or public annoyance.

These facts are *not* stated with any wish to injure any of the municipal officers. They are stated *as* facts—notoriously within the knowledge of every man who goes out in our streets. They are loudly cried out against by the citizens. They are not only annoyances in the present, and serious ones, but they are calculated to injure the future prosperity of the city. Besides that, they beget a bad tone in the city government, and form a very bad example for successors. The city pays men, and pays them well, for performing certain duties—and those duties are not performed. Every citizen is forced to aid this payment; and is it any wonder that he should grumble a little when he sees no return?

As instaces[2] that have come under our daily observation—tallied by scores of similar instances in the notice of people residing in other sections of the city—we may mention the tediously drawn out job of repaving that much used part of Fulton street just below the new city hall; and also the building of a public cistern in Prince street. In the former case, the work, which should have been completed in a few days, consumed *months*. In the latter case, it is likely to remain unfinished *all winter*; and not an evening passes without alarm and danger being created in the neighborhood, through some unadvised driver getting in the toils there, or some stranger half breaking his bones. We say that there are *dozens* of such sins of omission and commission: they are known in every part of the city.

Reasons, perhaps, are to be assigned *why* the work is not done more rapidly; but there are no reasons why the proper officers should not see, in the beginning, that there is a proper understanding about its being done in a reasonable time. The executive power of the city is to blame in the premises. The inspector of lamps, &c. is notoriously to blame: his department is out of order continually. What is he appointed for but to see that it is *not* out of order?

NOTES

1. Transcribed from scanned original, Brooklyn Public Library—Brooklyn Collection. Loving suggests that this editorial is by Whitman. Jerome Loving, "Whitman, Walt. *The Journalism, volume* 2. Ed. Herbert Bergman, Douglas A. Noverr, and Edward J. Recchia [review]," *Walt Whitman Quarterly Review* 22 (Summer 2004): 31–36.

2. Instances, "instaces" in original.

"The worth of liberty."[1]

Brooklyn Daily Eagle

DECEMBER 10, 1847

Mr. Giles's lecture on this topic, at the Institute,[2] last night, was one of the most powerfully written and warmly delivered speeches we ever heard.[3] Rarely have the divine proportions of liberty been praised by more eloquent lips: rarely, if ever, has the accursed nature of tyranny and slavery, in all their influences and results, been pourtrayed[4] in words more effective and clear, or in a manner more enthusiastic! The lecturer's picture of a slave, the *thing* without the feelings of a man—*not* a husband, *not* a parent, *not* a wife, *not* a patriot—and impossible to be either, in its proper sense—was burningly fearful and true. It will long live upon our memory, and, we doubt not, in the memories of many a man and woman who heard it...... The invocation to those who have suffered for liberty, was an august specimen of oratory in its highest form—oratory which thrilled to the heart and made the blood tingle! "Let *them* come," said the speaker, "who have fallen on the field of battle. Call back the sunken-hearted, and the weary-souled, in this cause. Call back a million martyrs from their graves. Call the witnesses from the stake, and men and women from the bloody scaffold. Call those who pined in exile, away from their countries and the faces they loved. Make the tombs of the earth, the caverns of the mountains, and the depths of the sea, give up their dead, who championed this great right of man, and fell for it; and add to these still more whose testimony is not recorded, and who wrought and perished in obscurity—and you will have *something* only—but then only a part—of the immeasurable cost of the divinest possession of our race, LIBERTY."[5]

For ourselves, and in the name of all who love freedom and hate oppression, we would thank Mr. Giles for this not merely intellectual treat, but for his noble promulgation of some of the best principles in the spirit of christianity, and that lie at the foundation of our republican government and the rights of all human beings.

NOTES

1. Transcribed from scanned original, Brooklyn Public Library—Brooklyn Collection. Loving suggests that this editorial is by Whitman. Jerome Loving, "Whitman, Walt. *The Journalism, volume* 2. Ed. Herbert Bergman, Douglas A. Noverr, and Edward J. Recchia [review]," *Walt Whitman Quarterly Review* 22 (Summer 2004): 31–36.

2. Ruth Bohan describes the Brooklyn Institute (founded in 1823 as the Apprentices' Library Association) as "the city's leading cultural institution" during the 1840s and 1850s. Ruth Bohan, "'The Gathering of Forces': Walt Whitman and the Arts in Brooklyn," *Mickle Street Review*, No. 12, "Walt Whitman and the Visual Arts" (1990): 15.

3. Jerome Loving considers this lecture by Unitarian minister Henry Giles (1809–1882) to have exerted a profound influence on Whitman's evolving antipathy toward the institution of slavery by "focusing on the slave's humanity instead of the slaveholder's immorality and cruelty." Jerome Loving, *Walt Whitman: The Song of Himself* (Berkeley: University of California Press, 1999), 112.

4. Spelling in original

5. Giles's image of the reawakened dead who perished in the name of freedom calls to mind Whitman's train of phantom Patriots who retreated before the armed parade of Anthony Burns (1834–1862) through the streets of Boston upon Burns's return to slavery. *Leaves of Grass* (1855), 89. Walt Whitman Archive, whitmanarchive.org.

Scenes in a Police Justice's Court Room.[1]

Brooklyn Daily Times
SEPTEMBER 9, 1857.

It was Dickens, we think, who first became known as an author by his graphic delineations of life in the police-courts.[2] And truly there is "ample room and verge enough" in these places for the exercise of the largest powers of wit and pathos and the rarest descriptive talent. Life's drama is played there, on a miniature scale, and tears and laughter succeed each other just as they do on the larger stage. A morning spent in "looking on" at Clarry's, or Feeks', or Cornwell's, or Blachley's, or any of the city police-courts is time well bestowed, even though nothing were sought beyond the amusement of an idle hour.

Justice Cornwell, we believe, disposes of more business in this line than any of his brethren. Let us then look in, for a moment, at his quarters in the City Hall, and see what is going on. It is Monday morning, and there is an unusual number of cases to be gone through with. The room is crowded with spectators, some of them witnesses, some friends of the prisoners; and the atmosphere is close and anything but fragrant. Passing within the railing we come to a large space where the unlucky "arrests" are seated in melancholy array, facing the Justice and Clerk. Strolling about, or lolling in arm-chairs, are the policemen detailed for the Court, and hovering about like birds of prey are the regular legal *habitues*[3] of the place, always on the look-out, with the sharpest kind of a scent, for anything in the shape of a fee, from a second-hand silver watch to a $25 "mint-drop."[4] This class answers to the "Tombs Shysters"[5] of Gotham, but we will do them the justice to say that they are on the whole much more respectable and not half so unscrupulous. They are uniformly fluent in speech and make up in glibness what they lack in legal acquirements. However, no very complicated cases come up in these precincts, so that it does'nt[6] matter greatly. One thing is certain, the business is a paying one for those who "know the ropes" and keep on the right side of the officials.

The prisoners, as they sit ranged in order before the Rhadamanthus[7] on the bench, present every possible variety of size and complexion. There are some half-dozen bull necked, low-browed rowdies who have been arrested for participating in a "free fight" in a porter-house.[8] These have evidently been up before, and care nothing for it. Next them sits a poor, brutalized Irishman, an habitual drunkard, who has been fetched up for beating his wife. The sodden wretch, with blinking, blood-shot[9] eyes and matted hair, sits shaking and shivering with suffering at the unwonted deprivation of his morning dram. Next him sits an old woman denominated in the classic language of the police courts, a "Bummer,"[10] who has just gone off, probably from the same cause, into a fit of what may be either hysterics or incipient delirium. The officer runs and brings a cup of water, and it is good to see that even here the spirit of womanly sympathy and kindness is not quite extinct, for two females who sit immediately behind the poor creature, support her head and bathe it with a pitying care—true women and Good Samaritans they! Beside her a spruce and flashy youth is seated. He has been arrested for passing counterfeit money, and by his cool and self-satisfied air and the grin into which he occasionally breaks, in his whispered conversation with his counsel, it is easy to see that the proof against him is small and that he fully expects to get off, this time, to renew his depredations. Next to this chap, on whose sallow visage "thief" is written in legible characters, are perched two little boys whose ragged shoes, low as the bench is, do not touch the floor. These are fair specimens of the thousands who run about the streets, destitute, uncared for, and who are training for the State Prison and the gallows. The juveniles in question have been brought up for stealing brass and iron fixings from unoccupied houses, a very common theft among the youngsters who figure at these places, and who are encouraged in it by junk-shop keepers. These are the staple of the cases brought up for disposal—assaults and batteries, wife-beatings and small thefts. Most of the business is done in a routine manner and disposed of in double quick time —and the rapidity with which $10 fines are inflicted upon unfortunate "drunks" is only equalled[11] by the rapidity with which they are *not* paid. But sometimes through this dreary, monotonous course of sin and crime, a ray of merriment will break, "something rich" will turn up, and Court and spectators will grin as delightedly as did ever audience in Burton's parquette.[12] Of such a nature, invariably, are the rows among the women, in which scratching and hair-pulling are the most prominent features. Most of these feminine rows occur in "tenant houses" and cheap boarding establishments, and more merriment is sometimes to be extracted from these real-life affairs than from the most screaming farce.

Police Justices ought to be capital judges of human nature, for they certainly see it in all its imaginable varieties. We believe, in fact, that they are so. Whether the constant contemplation of such misery, degradation and wickedness tends to humanize and soften the character,[13] is another question. But however that may be, a visit to one of these places is not without its lessons, and one will be apt to depart, not thanking God that he is "not as these Publicans,"[14] but cherishing a wider charity and a deeper sympathy with the short-comings and frailties of our common humanity.

NOTES

1. Transcribed from scanned original, Brooklyn Public Library—Brooklyn Collection. This editorial also appears in Walt Whitman, *The Uncollected Poetry and Prose of Walt Whitman*, ed. Emory Holloway (Gloucester, Mass.: Peter Smith, 1972), 2:10–13.

2 Charles Dickens, "Criminal Courts," in *Sketches by Boz* (London: John Macrone, 1837), 49–62.

3. Spelling in original; presumably "habitués."

4. A gold coin.

5. "A term applied to a set of men who hang about the Police Courts of New York and other large cities, and practise in them as lawyers, but who, in many cases, have never been admitted to the bar. They are men who have served as policemen, turnkeys, sheriff's officers, or in any capacity by which they have become familiar with criminals and criminal courts." John Russell Bartlett, *Bartlett's Dictionary of Americanisms* (Boston: Little, Brown, 1859), 405. In this case, Whitman refers to individuals who serve in this capacity at The Tombs in Lower Manhattan.

6. "does'nt" in original.

7. A mythological Greek king known for his wisdom who judged the dead in the underworld.

8. A "porter house" served port, liquors, and often steak, according to the *OED*.

9. Hyphen in original.

10. An idler, according to the *OED*.

11. Spelling in original.

12. First performed in 1848 in Baltimore, William Evans Burton's (1804–1860) play *The Toodles* was performed in New York City throughout the 1850s. Thomas Allston Brown, *A History of the New York Stage from 1732 to 1901*, vol. 1 (New York: Dodd, Mead, 1903); Whitman, *Uncollected Poetry and Prose*, 2:12.

13. Holloway inserts "man" for "character."

14. "The Pharisee stood and prayed thus with himself, God, I thank thee, that I am not as other men are, extortioners, unjust, adulterers, or even as this publican." Luke 18:11, KJV.

Why Should Church Property Be Exempt from Taxation?[1]

Brooklyn Daily Times

MAY 26, 1858

In a debate last Monday night, in the Common Council, the points were pretty well presented, as far as the question went, on the matter of taxing a Clergyman's residence, just the same as any body else's residence; and it was decided that the said clergyman must "pay." The decision seems to be a very just one; but we think still more remains to be said.

We must confess we can see no reason why church property, of any kind whatever, should be exempt from the usual taxation. In Brooklyn especially the churches are rich. They have means enough to pay their proportion of the public cost, so onerous upon all the rest—and ought to be ashamed to avoid it. Many of the churches expend large sums in luxuriant decorations for their walls, furniture, &c.; if they can afford this they certainly can afford to pay their taxes.

There is a morbid delicacy about meeting any question where a church is concerned, which it would be as well to put out of the way, and get rid of at once. There are hundreds of benevolent institutions, private schools, &c., that certainly have just as good a claim to be exempt, as religious edifices. Yet no one thinks of demanding exemption for them.

Let steps be taken to procure an alteration of the law, and to put church property on the same level, as to taxation, with any other kind of property.

NOTE

1. Transcribed from a photocopy of original in the papers of Herbert Bergman, East Lansing, Michigan. This editorial is listed in the appendixes of Walt Whitman, *I Sit and Look Out: Editorials from the Brooklyn Daily Times by Walt Whitman*, ed. Emory Holloway and Vernolian Schwarz (New York: Columbia University Press, 1932), 193.

Little Hope Left![1]

Brooklyn Daily Times

JULY 10, 1858

We expressed, at the time of the sailing of the Telegraphic Fleet, our very slight hopes that this gigantic enterprise would be successfully accomplished. The difficulties which surrounded the attempt from its inception, and which were too formidable to be entirely explained away by any process of scientific reasoning on the part of hopeful *savans*—the doubtful result of the trial trip—the unpropitious weather which the fleet has had to encounter, and which has been totally unlike what we had hoped and expected in the month of June—and the non-arrival of the Niagara at her point of destination, all lead us to believe that another failure will be the result of this wonderful undertaking.

Must it be so? Must two continents give up this grand hope of eternal union, the fruition of which was to accomplish such vast things for humanity—which was to be a peacemaker and a world's benefactor—which was to enlarge the circle of knowledge by annihilating time and space until man should become, indeed, but little lower than the angels?

Well, if it is not to be, we have, at all events, made the attempt. We attempt things on a Titanic[2] scale, and if we do not succeed the first time, we "try again." Anything not absolutely, by the invincible laws of Nature impracticable we are bound to accomplish. So if the present attempt and future essays which may be made in our day and generation should prove unsuccessful, our children or our children's children may yet see the great problem solved and rejoice in the benefits it will confer.

NOTES

1. Transcribed from a photocopy of original in the papers of Herbert Bergman, East Lansing, Michigan. This editorial contains similarities in language and interests to three other editorials ascribed to Whitman by Holloway that lead us to believe that it is also

by Whitman: "The Cable Laid!" (August 6, 1858), "Honor to Cyrus W. Field" (August 9, 1858), and "The Two Worlds United" (August 17, 1858). William White also lists this editorial in William White, *Walt Whitman's Journalism: A Bibliography* (Detroit: Wayne State University Press, 1969), 49.

2. "Titanic" here is capitalized in the original, perhaps because the "Titans" were a race of monsters in Greek mythology. Charles Dickens capitalized "Titanic" in a similar context in *Hard Times*: "But they were all broken now, and the rain had ceased, and the moon shone—looking down the high chimneys of Coketown on the deep furnaces below, and casting Titanic shadows of the steam engines at rest, upon the walls where they were lodged."

The Cable Laid![1]

Brooklyn Daily Times
AUGUST 6, 1858

It is useless for us to discuss any local or general topic that in ordinary circumstances would be of interest to the public: just now there is but one topic of conversation, and that is the unlooked for, but magnificent, success of the grand Atlantic Telegraph enterprise.

We, in common with the press throughout the country, anticipated no such good luck as has eventually attended this last attempt to lay the Cable. The news of its successful accomplishment, therefore, published in yesterday's *TIMES*, was a still more joyful surprise to us and to the thousands who had begun to despond as to the ultimate triumph of the vast enterprise, at least in our day.[2]

Yesterday, throughout the country, nothing else was talked of. This one great topic, like Aaron's rod,[3] swallowed up all lesser ones, and wherever the news extended,—from Maine to Georgia, the great heart of the people exulted and their enthusiasm found vent in cheers and in bonfires, in bell-ringing and illuminations. No event of the century has so stirred up the latent enthusiasm of the masses. Each man feels an accession of new power—each man who has the intelligence to comprehend the nature of this vast triumph of human intellect, feels like a new Prometheus[4] who has stolen fire from Heaven to annihilate time and distance and to win for himself the fabled attributes of the immortals.[5]

We cannot begin to estimate, as yet, the vast consequences of this great achievement to humanity and to the world. Should the wires work as is anticipated, and no new misfortune arise to damp our expectations, such momentous results will follow as cannot now be even faintly appreciated. Not only will the Atlantic Cable be a means of communicating intelligence as to the rise or downfall of stocks, not only will it be a material agent for the transmission of late news for the press, but it will have a vast moral effect;—it will be a civilizer and a peace maker—it will be like the dawn of a Millenium day to the troubled nations—it will usher in a Golden Age of peace on earth and good will to man.

It may be that we are too sanguine. It may be that the majority of people, who had given up all hopes of seeing the grand project carried out, and were over despondent, are now too hopeful in their sudden joy and triumph. As yet we have no assurance that the Irish end of the cable has been landed as safely as that yesterday brought on shore at Newfoundland, and for some little time yet, we must wait before considering the great problem decisively solved. Perhaps a few hours may bring us the glorious intelligence which all await with so much anxiety. The first message, which will be transmitted from England to America by the representative head of the old country, Queen Vic., to President Buchanan, will flash across the land from north to south and from east to west on lightning wings and with lightning effect. Let us await the result with hopeful anticipations, and if they are justified by the end, let us ever, hereafter, turn a deaf ear to the croakers, and boldly proclaim that there is no limit to the genius of the century, and to the persevering enterprise of its leading spirits.

P.S.—So far all is well. The Agamemnon has arrived at Valentia Bay, on the coast of Ireland, but in consequence of the absence of telegraphic apparatus for the transmission of anything beyond signals, no messages have yet been received. Nevertheless, it is a triumph as it is.

NOTES

1. Transcribed from a photocopy of original in the papers of Herbert Bergman, East Lansing, Michigan. This editorial is listed in the appendixes of Walt Whitman, *I Sit and Look Out: Editorials from the Brooklyn Daily Times by Walt Whitman*, ed. Emory Holloway and Vernolian Schwarz (New York: Columbia University Press, 1932), 194.

2. From the Associated Press, August 7, 1858: "The Atlantic Telegraph Cable was successfully landed here yesterday morning, and is in perfect order. The *Agamemnon* has landed her end of the Cable and we are now receiving signals from the Telegraph House in Valentia. The United States steamer *Niagara* and her Majesty's steamers *Gorgon* and *Porcupine* leave for St. Johns to-morrow. Due notice will be given when the Atlantic Telegraph Line will be open for public business. Cyrus W. Field." *New York Times*, August 9, 1858, nytimes.com.

3. "For they cast down every man his rod, and they became serpents: but Aaron's rod swallowed up their rods." Exodus 7:12, KJV.

4. Prometheus was a Greek mythological hero who stole fire from the Gods to give to humans.

5. Compare this language to "Little Hope Left!," July 10, 1858: "Must two continents give up this grand hope of eternal union . . . which was to enlarge the circle of knowledge by annihilating time and space until man should become, indeed, but little lower than the angels?"

The Two Worlds United.[1]

Brooklyn Daily Times
AUGUST 17, 1858

At last the great problem is solved. The Old World and the New are united. The great Atlantic Telegraph enterprise, notwithstanding the doubts of the croakers and the sneers of the unbelieving, has gloriously succeeded, and all doubts are forever set at rest as to the practicability of spanning the world with telegraphic wire—of joining Europe, Asia, Africa, America, and Australia together by electric current.

In the midst of this great triumph we cannot help thinking that the Queen's Message, which was received by the President, via Trinity Bay, last evening, and duly passed on to the Capital, was utterly unworthy of the grandeur of the occasion—reminding us more of a mere form of words such as is supplied by a "Complete Letter Writer," than such a grand sentiment as was expected to signalize this most extraordinary event in modern history.[2] The disappointment felt by the people is deep and heartfelt. They[3] were brimming over with excitement and enthusiasm, and the cold, formal message of the lady who is now the representative of English royalty, chilled them with a peculiar sense of its inappropriateness. If the communication had been sent in answer to an invitation to a public dinner or a ball, it could not have been more formal, stiff and disappointing than it is. That this was so, the entire press this morning united in agreeing, and the explanation given this afternoon in another column, though it helps matters along a good deal, is still not exactly what was expected.

The reply of the President is better[4]—commonplace enough, in all conscience—but still sufficiently significant for the occasion, and by the side of Her Majesty's frigid "message" really appears in a most favorable contrast. Upon the whole, it is altogether too good for the "message," both in style and tone. It seems to have been an enormous stretch of condescension on the part of "Victoria Regina" to communicate with the foremost man and chosen head and representative of America at all, even upon an occasion like the present.

Doubtless the people of our America must be highly flattered by the information that Her Majesty felt "the deepest interest" in this great work, which is destined to revolutionize the world, to establish, as the Directors on the other side said, "Peace on earth and good will to man," and to accomplish such mighty results as have not yet been dreamed of by the most sanguine. The chilliness of the dispatch is truly refreshing in this August weather. Perhaps, however, we ourselves have not much to boast of. Neither despatch[5] was quite worthy of the occasion.

But, at all events, our doubts are now set at rest, once and forever, as to the practicability of communicating across the Atlantic. In the grandeur of this greatest achievement of the Nineteenth Century, let us forget everything minor and petty, and think only of the immensity of the work that has been accomplished. Let all honor be paid to the originators of the enterprise who have carried it out to such a triumphant and successful conclusion. Let a generous and large-hearted recognition be made on the part of the public to those who have persevered to the end, amid doubt and danger, amid sneers and suspicion on the part of the conceited doubters who, from the beginning have thrown cold water on the grand undertaking. The great achievement is at all events recognized in its true light by the people of both countries. Over the mighty Atlantic, Saxon extends the hand of amity to Saxon. The two branches of the all-conquering race that is always progressing and extending its power and influence, whether in the icy Artic and Antarctic or in the tropical heats of India—which is the foremost race of all the earth—which is first in war, first in peace, first in all the beautifying and civilizing arts—which holds the destinies of the earth in its control—now are one in fact, as they have all along been in spirit, and as the lightning flashes from shore to shore, they mentally look into each others honest eyes and strike palms together in friendly greeting.[6] Thank Heaven for this great boon to the human race—thank Heaven for this assurance—for it is an assurance—that misunderstandings and wars, and rumors of wars are at an end between the mother country and us. Beneath the Atlantic wave lies a chord of communication which, please God, will vibrate forever with the peaceful messages of commerce, the lightning-winged words of the press, and the thousand anxious queries of individual affection as to the health and happiness of the absent and the loved. We need add no more. The simple fact itself, that time and space are annihilated by man's inventive power and that the whole world may "reason together"[7] without the aid of palpable agencies is so sublime, that all commentary seems impertinent. It is useless for us to speculate as to the ultimate effects of this grand achievement. The two peoples, hereafter to be forever one, will work out the problem for themselves.

1. Transcribed from a photocopy of original in the papers of Herbert Bergman, East Lansing, Michigan. This editorial is listed in the appendixes of Walt Whitman, *I Sit and Look Out: Editorials from the Brooklyn Daily Times by Walt Whitman*, ed. Emory Holloway and Vernolian Schwarz (New York: Columbia University Press, 1932), 194.

2. "The Queen desires to congratulate the President upon the successful completion of this great international work, in which the Queen has taken the deepest interest. The Queen is convinced that the President wil[l] join with her in fervently hoping that the electric cable, which now connects Great Britain with the United States, will prove an additional link between the two places whose friendship is founded upon their common interests and reciprocal esteem. The Queen has much pleasure in thus directly communicating with the President, and in renewing to him her best wishes for the prosperity of the United States." John Mullaly, *The Laying of the Cable, Or the Ocean Telegraph* (New York: D. Appleton, 1858), 300.

3. The original reads "The . . ."

4. "The President cordially reciprocates the congratulations of her Majesty the Queen, on the success of the great international enterprise accomplished by the science, skill, and indomitable energy of the two countries. It is a triumph more glorious because far more useful to mankind, than was ever won by conqueror on the field of battle. May the Atlantic Telegraph, under the blessing of Heaven, prove to be a bond of perpetual peace and friendship between the kindred nations, and an instrument destined by Divine Providence to diffuse religion, civilization, liberty and law throughout the world. In this view, will not all nations of Christendom spontaneously unite in the declaration that it shall be forever neutral, and that its communications shall be held sacred in passing to their places of destination, even in the midst of hostilities?" Mullaly, 300.

5. Spelling in original.

6. Whitman was not above this kind of ethnic triumphalism late in life as well: "The American people, ever sturdy, ever instinctively just, by right of Teutonic descent, have only to perceive any great wrong and the work of redemption is begun for that hour. I heartily approve of the action of the California Vigilance Committee, it is worthy of the promptness and just anger of the Anglo-Saxon race." Horace Traubel and Thomas Harned, *The Complete Prose Works of Walt Whitman* (New York: G. P. Putnam's Sons, 1902), 7:24. See also Heidi Kathleen Kim, "From Language to Empire: Walt Whitman in the Context of Nineteenth-Century Popular Anglo-Saxonism," *Walt Whitman Quarterly Review* 24 (Summer 2006): 1–19.

7. "Come now, and let us reason together, saith the LORD." Isaiah 1:18, KJV.

The Moral Effect of the Atlantic Cable[1]

Brooklyn Daily Times

AUGUST 20, 1858

When Beranger,[2] the French Poet of Freedom, wrote that great lyric of his, calling upon the nations to "join hands" in amity,[3] and with prophetic vision told them of the day when international quarrels should cease and the lion should lie down with the lamb, he must have had some dim foresight, which for aught we know, is vouchsafed to the "bards sublime," of the grand triumph of man's ingenuity and skill which has just set our people wild with joy and excitement.

It is well to pause and enquire into the reasons of this mighty outburst of enthusiasm all over the land. On no former occasion within our recollection has there been anything like it. Time and again there have been great celebrations, on occasions of national interest, but nothing like this before. Never before has there been such a universal jubilee—never before have the people of these States united so unanimously and so ardently in glorifying a grand scientific achievement.

We think that after all, it is not the mere utilitarian gain to come out of the new enterprise that has produced the effect in question. Probably to an immense majority, the Telegraph Cable will not bring one iota of personal benefit, and it can be neither the scientific nor the utilitarian relations of this grand experiment that can account for the exultation with which it has been greeted and the unbounded enthusiasm with which it has everywhere been received. Most probably the moral element in this matter has more to do with the feelings of joy and gratulation that prevail everywhere, than any merely material considerations. It is the sentiment of *union* that makes the popular heart beat and quiver. It is the union of the great Anglo-Saxon race, henceforth forever to be a unit, that makes the States throb with tumultuous emotion and thrills every breast with admiration and triumph.

The popular instinct, now-a-days, says that England and the United States are no longer to keep each other at arms-length. The two countries—or at least, the two peoples—both courageous, enterprising, and ardent, feel that henceforth their old prejudices and rivalries must be set aside. They feel that henceforth it is not in the power of time-serving, capital-making politicians to create bitterness between them. They feel that England and America alone stand faithful and true to the great cause of freedom. They both feel that this Telegraph Cable is not alone a material bond for the transmission of news of the rise and fall of stocks, and of news-gossip generally, but that it will also subserve a higher purpose—that it will link together nations that in heart and feeling are hereafter to be one.

NOTES

1. Transcribed from a photocopy of original in the papers of Herbert Bergman, East Lansing, Michigan. This editorial also appears in Walt Whitman, *I Sit and Look Out: Editorials from the Brooklyn Daily Times by Walt Whitman*, ed. Emory Holloway and Vernolian Schwarz (New York: Columbia University Press, 1932), 159–160.

2. Pierre-Jean de Béranger (1780–1857). According to K. H. Francis, Whitman knew the works of Béranger. K. H. Francis, "Walt Whitman's French," *Modern Language Review* 51 (October 1956): 493–506. According to Horace Traubel and Thomas Harned, an article on Pierre-Jean de Béranger was found among Whitman's papers. Horace Traubel and Thomas Harned, *The Complete Prose Works of Walt Whitman* (New York: G. P. Putnam's Sons, 1902), 7:81.

3. From "The Holy Alliance": "I saw the descending of Peace from afar; / Flowers, corn-blades and gold in her pathway arose; / The air was serene, and the thunders of war / Were quenched at her feet, in a harmless repose; / And she said, "Noble equals in prowess, advance! / Men of England, Spain, Germany, Muscovy, France! / —O, peoples, forgetting all bygone defiance, / Join hands in the bond of a Holy Alliance!"

III

The Arts

America need not look abroad for noble deeds to celebrate, or inspired bards to commend them to the popular heart.

—*DAILY PLEBEIAN*, DECEMBER 4, 1843

Mr. Emerson's Lecture[1]

New York Aurora

MARCH 7, 1842

The transcendentalist had a very full house on Saturday evening. There were a few beautiful maids—but more ugly women, mostly blue stockings[2]; several interesting young men with Byron collars,[3] lawyers, doctors, and parsons; Grahamites[4] and abolitionists; sage editors, a few of whom were taking notes; and all the other species of literati. Greeley[5] was in extacies whenever any thing particularly good was said, which seemed to be once in about five minutes—he would flounce about like[6] a fish out of water, or like a tickled girl—look round, to see those behind him and at his side; all of which very plainly told to those, both far and near, that he knew a thing or two more about these matters than other men.

This lecture was on the "Poetry of the Times."[7] He said that the first man who called another an ass was a poet.[8] Because the business of the poet is expression—the giving utterance to the emotions and sentiments of the soul; and this expression or utterance is best effected[9] by similes and metaphors. But it would do the lecturer great injustice to attempt any thing like a sketch of his ideas. Suffice it to say, the lecture was one of the richest and most beautiful compositions, both for its matter and style, we have ever heard anywhere, at any time.[10]

NOTES

1. Transcribed from scanned original at the Walt Whitman Archive, whitmanarchive.org. This editorial also appears in Walt Whitman, *The Journalism, Volume I: 1834–1846*, part of *The Collected Writings of Walt Whitman*, ed. Herbert Bergman, Douglas A. Noverr, and Edward J. Recchia (New York: Peter Lang, 1998), 44.

2. Whitman uses the term negatively here to describe a woman with intellectual interests.

3. A soft collar supposedly worn by the Romantics. Here Whitman implies a dandified

male with intellectual/poetic aspirations.

4. Followers of Sylvester Graham (1794–1851), who promoted happiness through dietary and sexual discipline.

5. Horace Greeley (1811–1872), editor of the rival *New York Tribune,* was a prominent Whig, and later Republican, reform advocate throughout the mid-nineteenth century. In 1872 Greeley ran for president as a Liberal Republican and lost to Ulysses S. Grant.

6. Original reads "lik" for "like."

7. Ronald Angelo Bosco and Joel Myerson argue that Emerson eventually incorporated elements of this lecture into "Poetry and Imagination" and "Eloquence." Ronald Angelo Bosco and Joel Myerson, eds., *The Selected Lectures of Ralph Waldo Emerson* (Athens: University of Georgia Press, 2005), 83.

8. " [T]he man who first called another man Puppy or Ass was a poet, and saw at the moment the identity of nature through the great difference of aspect. His eye so reached to the thought and will of the wretch he beheld, that he could hear him bark or bray, with a bestial necessity under this false clothing of man." Ibid., 87.

9. "effected" in original.

10. While Whitman mocked members of Emerson's audience in this editorial, in the last sentence he exhibited the respect for Emerson's ideas that later motivated him to send a copy of the first edition of *Leaves of Grass* (1855) to Emerson. Emerson famously responded with a letter that began, "I am not blind to the worth of the wonderful gift of 'Leaves of Grass.' I find it the most extraordinary piece of wit & wisdom that America has yet contributed."

Untitled[1]

New York Aurora

MARCH 8, 1842

"Had you seen him,
Your eyes had witnessed twain, and yet but one—
For in his heart he was an innocent child,
And in his make a man. O, brutal earth,
That ever laugh'dst and jeerd'st, and looked in scorn
Upon this angel, bodied in gross flesh."

—*KIT MARLOWE*[2]

Although it was not our fortune to be acquainted with the Poor Poet, the eccentric and unfortunate McDonald Clarke,[3] whose death last Saturday is the subject of considerable comment in our city press—we felt grieved at the news. He seems to have been a simple, kindly creature—a being whose soul, though marked by little that the crowd admire, was totally free from any taint of vice, or selfishness, or evil passion. From his peculiarities, he was exposed to ridicule of vulgar men, who seldom go beyond externals; yet Clarke possessed all the requisites of a great poet.[4]

Whoever has power, in his writings, to draw bold, startling images, and strange pictures—the power to embody in language, original, and beautiful, and quaint ideas—is a true son of song. Clarke was such an one; not polished, perhaps, but yet one in whose faculties that all important vital spirit of poetry burnt with a fierce brightness. From his being so out of the common channel; from his abruptness, and, if we may so call it, jaggedness, of style—many persons have not taken the trouble to read the fugitive effusions which he, through our paper and others, gave to the world. But they are mostly all imbued with the spiritual flame. We always, on perusing Clarke's pieces, felt, in the chambers of the mind within us, a moving and a responding, as of harp chords, struck by the wind.[5]

He was very poor. Not of the earth, earthy—not engaged in the withering toils of traffic—not a votary at the altar of any golden idol—was he to whose memory we devote this passing tribute. It is a dreary thought—the likelihood that, through the chilness[6] of destitution, this man, his soul swelling with gorgeous and gentle things, was prevented the chance of becoming an ornament to the world, instead of its scoff and laughing stock. It is a dreary thought, too, that poor Clarke's case has its copies so many times repeated among us. What a devil art thou, Poverty! How many high desires—how many aspirations after goodness and truth—how many noble thoughts, loving wishes toward our fellows, beautiful imaginings—thou hast crushed under thy iron heel, without remorse or pause! What majestic beauty thou hast condemned to pine unnoticed in the shade—while sister beauty, with wealth, made drunk the eyes of men! What swelling hearts thou has sent down to the Silent House, after a life of bitterness and strife! What talent, noble as that of famous poets and philosophers—what minds, fit to govern empires, or instruct the world—what souls, glowing in secret with the halo of science—thou dost doom, year after year, to pine in obscurity, or die in despair!

It is well. Clarke was little fitted for elbowing his way amid the mass; let no one grieve that he has passed away. Let us hope that he is in that place which we are fond of believing to be peopled by joy never ceasing, and by resplendent innocence and beauty. On earth, his love, from its oddness and inconsistence with fashion, was laughed to scorn; up Above, it will find itself amid kindred elements.

We understand that papers are up at several places, to receive subscriptions for erecting a monument to the memory of the hapless poet. We commend the object as a deserving one. And, strangely enough several years ago, a scheme was jocosely suggested of an exactly similar purport. Clarke heard of it, and wrote the following which we are permitted to publish. It is singular that this effusion, which was written June 11, 1835, should come in play as it now does:—

THE DEAD POET.

'Tis but barren respect they are paying him now!
    It can flatter but selfish passions, only—
When the laurel *first* blooms on his mouldering brow,
    Genius must mourn that its fate is so lonely.

Human pomp is a pitiful thing—
    But to decorate death is indeed disgusting!
Let the green sprig rise, and the red herb spring
    Where no slab in the wind and rain is rusting!

He was left by these sunrise friends, to droop,
When his doom would have turned on the roll of a dollar!
For a spirit like his, that scorned to stoop,
Could never a selfish interest follow.

But his form must rise, like the sun, in his might,
Blast Envy's fog by its own strong lustre,
Or in silence go down with a clouded light,
Till memory's stars o'er its ashes cluster.

Oh, let him rest in his nameless place—
The few who knew and loved him, know it—
They will guard it from Ostentation's face,
That would shame, not soothe, the sainted Poet.

Majestic marks of crumbling stone,
Are for those whose memory else would perish;
But the human heart is the urn alone,
A poet's pride would wish to cherish!

We hope, however, that no reader will be discouraged from contributing his moiety to the memorial proposed, because of the above sentiments of Clarke. They only prove the more fully his deservedness of the poetic wreath.

We have strung out our notice far beyond what we originally intended for its dimensions.[7] Perhaps, however, the space thus used may not be unprofitably used. It may teach that genius, after all, is a dangerous[8] trait. Its fires, to be sure, sometimes enlighten and beautify, but quite as often scorch, wither, and blast the soul of its possessor. Like Phæton's[9] privilege, the mighty gift conferred, may bring death and ruin.

Peace to thy memory, Afara![10] In
"the sphere which keeps
The disembodied spirits of the dead,"[11]

may the love of angels, and the ravishing splendor of the Country Beautiful, and the communion of gentle spirits, and sweet draughts from the Fountain of all Poetry, blot out every scar of what thou hast suffered here below!

1. Transcribed from scanned original at the Walt Whitman Archive, whitmanarchive.org. This editorial also appears in Walt Whitman, *The Journalism, Volume I: 1834–1846*, part of *The Collected Writings of Walt Whitman*, ed. Herbert Bergman, Douglas A. Noverr, and Edward J. Recchia (New York: Peter Lang, 1998), 46–48.

2. Christopher Marlowe (1564–1593), poet and playwright.

3. McDonald Clarke (1798–1842) was a well-known New York poet in the early nineteenth century. By the 1830s Clarke had cultivated a reputation as the "mad poet of Broadway" who, against the tradition of the gentlemanly amateur poet, survived by selling his poems to newspapers, thereby taking advantage of the rise of the penny press. Andrew C. Higgins, "McDonald Clarke's Adjustment to Market Forces: A Lesson for Walt Whitman," *Mickle Street Review*, No. 15 (2004). The Hudson River School painter and engraver Asher Brown Durand befriended Clarke and provided assistance to him. John Durand, *The Life and Times of A. B. Durand* (New York: C. Scribner's Sons, 1894), 87–90. Clarke supposedly copied the aesthetic of Lord Byron, married an actress who left him after a short time, and died in an asylum before his forty-fifth birthday. "The Mad Poet," *New York Times*, November 12, 1893, nytimes.com.

4. Contemporary newspapers described Clarke in no less admiring terms, but highlighted his "madness" and tragic, romantic personality: "McDonald Clarke is a strange, an incomprehensible being! To do him justice is no easy matter; and to say that he possesses a world of talent, is not to utter an extravagant expression.—Few men have given to the world happier strains of genuine poetry, than McDonald Clarke, and yet poor fellow, his muse is such an unbridled jade, that she can never do him any good." *New York Evening Journal*, August 14, 1833, fultonhistory.com.

5. Whitman's description here gives some clue as to his later ideal of himself as a poet. Another contemporary source warns young men about Clarke's talent: "[T]he fate of McDonald Clarke is sufficient warning to young men of genius! . . . Why toil upward to the 'destiny of an American poet,' unless they wish to be crazy, drunken, ragged and starving, and finally have a beautiful sepulcher in Greenwood Cemetery?" *New World*, October 5, 1844, fultonhistory.com. In the *Sunday Times*, Whitman mentioned visiting McDonald's grave on a visit to Greenwood Cemetery on May 5, 1844 (below).

6. Spelling in original.

7. In original, the sentence contains no period.

8. Spelled "dangeroHs" in original

9. In Greek mythology, Phæton was the son of Helois, god of the sun. Phæton attempted to drive his father's chariot that pulled the sun and was killed by Zeus.

10. "Afara; a poem" (1829) by Clarke either generally came to be one of his monikers or was used particularly so by Whitman and the *Aurora*. The day before this editorial was published, an *Aurora* article on Clarke's funeral, perhaps by Whitman, was titled "'Afara' is no more!"

11. William Cullen Bryant (1794–1878), "The Future Life."

Italian Opera in New Orleans[1]

New York Aurora

APRIL 15, 1842

We perceive by the New Orleans papers that "Somnambula"[2] has been brought out there, and that Mrs. Sutton has produced quite a sensation in the principal character. The "corps" has been playing for some time in that capital—but hitherto, from some underhand intrigue, Mrs. Sutton was kept in the back ground. —*Morning Herald.*

The above piece of stupid humbug is, of course, from Bennett's pen.[3] No other paper in the country but his ever attempted to soft soap La Signora Fatoni Sutton[4] as she desired him to style her—into a *prima donna*. Only read the puff direct, and the stupidity is obvious. First, he says she has made quite a sensation, and, secondly, that by some underhand intrigue, she was kept in the back ground. Was there ever such inconsistency? The fact is, La Signora *Fat*-oni is only a second rate singer, and about a third rate musician. She had a fair chance at the Park, in Norma, and could not succeed in drawing even the expenses. As a concert singer, she was thrown into the shade by Borghese, and yet she had the temerity to go to Havana and New Orleans to test the public favor with that accomplished artist.

We hope they will keep La Signora Fatoni at the south, for here we have some real musical and dramatic talent which is quite unavailable. At the present time we have Mr. and Mrs. Seguin, and Manvers,[5] wanting an engagement at the Park. We have Miss Ayres[6] and Miss Horn,[7] with Chapman,[8] Lambert,[9] Tom Placide,[10] John Sefton,[11] T. D. Rice,[12] and several others. Next week we shall have Forrest and Clifton[13] here, so that we do hope our fair, fat, and forty friend, La Signora, as she loves to be called, will stay away until we send for her, and that will be a long while first. Nobody but Bennett ever tried to persuade the people that Mrs. Sutton could sing—but heaven spare us from ever seeing her attempt to act again!

NOTES

1. Transcribed from scanned original at the Walt Whitman Archive, www.whitmanarchive.org. This editorial also appears in Walt Whitman, *The Journalism, Volume I: 1834–1846*, part of *The Collected Writings of Walt Whitman*, ed. Herbert Bergman, Douglas A. Noverr, and Edward J. Recchia (New York: Peter Lang, 1998), 120.

2. "La Sonnambula" ("The Sleepwalker") was composed by Vincenzo Bellini (1801–1835) in 1831 and performed at the Park Theater, New York, in 1835. See Vera Brodsky Lawrence, *Strong on Music: The New York Scene in the Days of George Templeton Strong* (Chicago: University of Chicago Press, 1995), 1:36.

3. James Gordon Bennett (1795–1872) helped initiate the print culture of the penny paper with the *New York Herald* in 1835. Bennett set the standard for these prurient and racy publications with his firsthand description of the corpse of Helen Jewett, a prostitute who was murdered by one of her clients, Richard Robinson, in 1836, which Bennett followed with coverage of the trial of Robinson and his acquittal. See Patricia Cline Cohen, *The Murder of Helen Jewett: The Life and Death of a Prostitute in Nineteenth-Century New York* (New York: Vintage Books, 1999), 16–19.

4. Sutton first performed her husband's English translation and adaptation of Bellini's opera *Norma* on February 25, 1842, at the Park Theater. One reviewer described her performance as "cloying and sickening," though Sutton performed *Norma* twelve times in New York City. Brodsky Lawrence, 1:133.

5. Probably Anne Seguin, Edward Seguin, and Charles Manvers, who starred in Bellini's *Norma* at the Park Theater in April 1841. Joseph Norton Ireland, *Records of the New York Stage, from 1750–1860* (New York: T. H. Morrell, 1867), 372.

6. Probably English actress Jane Ayres, described in *Records of the New York Stage* as a "blithe, good-humored, buxom English girl, who played chambermaids . . . and rural damsels with great archness and spirit." Ibid., 231.

7. Perhaps English actress Kate Horn, who first appeared in *Sudden Thoughts*, a farce, in October 1840. *Records of the New York Stage* described Horn as "so well satisfied with the impression made by her personal charms, that she took no pains to prove that she possessed talent of any kind." Ibid., 45.

8. Probably English actor W. B. Chapman, or his nephew, Henry Chapman, who appeared on stage together during the 1840s. Ibid., 460.

9. Lambert was an English actor who appeared in farces like *Shocking Events* of September 1838, where he played Griffinhoof and "surpassed all buffos then known to our stage." Ibid., 275.

10. Placide was described in *Actors as They Are* as a "Frenchman," who "is one of the most careful of actors. Every part he takes he studies thoroughly in the ideal, the words, and action and the costume." O. A. Roorbach, *Actors as They Are: A Series of Sketches of the Most Eminent Performers Now on Stage* (New York: O. A. Roorbach, 1856), 76.

11. John Sefton became famous in the role of Jemmy Twitcher in *The Golden Farmer, or Jemmy Twitcher in England* (1835). Sefton continued to play this role throughout the 1840s. The character of Twitcher first appeared in *The Beggar's Opera* (1727) by John Gay.

12. T. D. Rice was a minstrel who gained popularity in the 1830s with the song "Jim Crow," which "attained a popularity unequaled by anything of the kind before or since." In the late 1820s Rice had acted in comedies with mixed success until he "commenced his negro singing and burlesque operatic performances," which "'wheeled [him] about' from poverty to fame and fortune." Ireland, 55–56.

13. Edwin Forrest (1806–1872), known for his passionate and unrestrained style, was popular among the Northeast's working class and Irish immigrants. The Astor Place Riots of 1849 took place after a long rivalry between Forrest and British actor William Charles Macready, a favorite among the upper class in New York City, for the claim of the best Shakespearean. Josephine Clifton (1813–1847) often played opposite Forrest. After her death it became public that Forrest and Clifton had had an affair, and the subsequent scandal precipitated his divorce in 1850. Don B. Wilmeth, *The Cambridge Guide to American Theater* (Cambridge: Cambridge University Press, 2007), 172.

The Hutchinson Family[1]

Daily Plebeian

DECEMBER 4, 1843

The accomplished minstrels of our own soil give their parting concert at Niblo's this evening. In listening to the enchanting strains in which they sing the triumphs of American thought, we feel they are doing a good work. They are nationalizing our sentiments and making us feel that America need not look abroad for noble deeds to celebrate, or inspired bards to commend them to the popular heart. This is precisely what we want—national melodies, and if it may be (and this gifted family shows us we have the material) native performers who can make them more acceptable than the choicest airs of foreign importation. "Genius is of no country,"[2] but we want something that is all our own, fearless, republican, outspoken and free—the musical embodiment of the American character—and the commencement of this we see in the enthusiastic reception invariably accorded to these children of the Granite State.

NOTES

1. Transcribed from Walt Whitman, *The Journalism, Volume I: 1834–1846*, part of *The Collected Writings of Walt Whitman*, ed. Herbert Bergman, Douglas A. Noverr, and Edward J. Recchia (New York: Peter Lang, 1998), 176. The Hutchinson Family Singers were popular abolitionist singers. See Scott Gac, *Singing for Freedom: The Hutchinson Family Singers and the Nineteenth-Century Culture of Reform* (New Haven, Conn.: Yale University Press, 2007).

2. From Charles Churchill, "The Rosciad" (1761). The couplet reads, "Genius is of no country, her pure ray / Spreads all abroad as gen'ral as the day." Charles Churchill, *The Rosciad* (London: W. Flexney, 1761), 4.

American Music, New and True![1]

Brooklyn Evening Star
NOVEMBER 5, 1845

For the first time we, on Monday night, heard something in the way of American music, which overpowered us with delightful amazement.—We allude to the performances of the Cheney family at Niblo's Saloon. They certainly, to our taste, excel all the much vaunted foreign artists, not excepting Templeton,[2] whom we saw there. Simple, fresh, and beautiful, we hope no spirit of imitation will ever induce them to engraft any 'foreign airs' upon their 'native graces.' We want this sort of starting point from which to mould something new and true in American music; and if we are not greatly mistaken the spirit of the Hutchinsons' and the Cheneys' singing will be followed by a spreading and an imitation that will entirely supplant, as far as this country is concerned, the affected, super-sentimental kid-gloved, quavering, flourishing, die-away-in-demnition-faintness[3] style of music which comes to us from Italy and France.

The writer has a good deal to say of the Cheneys, which he will say through other channels—and a few words also *to* them. They are the first ones he has seen or heard who appear worthy the aid and praise of those in the refinement of taste ask for something to put *freshness, newness* and *freedom* in this department of American art. They will hear from him again.

Of the performances on Monday evening, the best was 'The Irish Mother's Lament,' the next best 'Nature's Nobleman.' The 'Farewell to Naxos,' and the 'Vermonters' Song,' were also beautiful exceedingly, and received the deserved compliment of an encore. The piece called 'There was a sound of revelry by night,' was executed with considerable artistic merit, and evinced a capacity which, applied to something else—to pieces of American description and locality for instance—would have been highly acceptable. But we sincerely advise the Cheneys to repeat it no more.

In conclusion, we hope these talented brothers and sister, whatever their temporary success at the outset, will adhere rigidly to the utmost simplicity, and infuse nothing but sound American feeling in their songs—assuring them that they will succeed before long in a manner that will both bring them fame and fill their pockets.

W.

NOTES

1. Transcribed from Walt Whitman, *The Journalism, Volume I: 1834–1846*, part of *The Collected Writings of Walt Whitman*, ed. Herbert Bergman, Douglas A. Noverr, and Edward J. Recchia (New York: Peter Lang, 1998), 233–234.

2. Probably Scottish tenor John Templeton (1802–1886). Vera Brodsky Lawrence, *Strong on Music: The New York Scene in the Days of George Templeton Strong* (Chicago: University of Chicago Press, 1995), 1:317, 410. In relating a critical review of Templeton in his journal, George Templeton Strong (1820–1875) wrote, "[T]he low level of his performance was just as well . . . considering the vulgarity of Templeton's audience." *Mirror*, February 17, 1846.

3. The *OED* defines "demnition" as a "euphemistic pronunciation of damnation."

Heart-Music and Art-Music[1]

Brooklyn Evening Star

NOVEMBER 14, 1845

Our former favorable remarks about the Cheneys' singing, proved last night to have been fully warranted. We formed one of a tolerably numerous audience then convened at the Institute,—and we must say, that the taste which could listen to such melody without the purest pleasure, belongs to one of a class whereof the great Penetrator of Passions, has said—"Let no such man be trusted."[2] In these days of humbug and tinsel, when the fashionable world, (or rather those of it who have the least enjoyment and the most frippery,) runs affectedly after art burlesqued and draped in motley—visits, languishes at, and applauds that which it cannot understand, merely because it is the mode—it is really refreshing to see and hear these Cheneys, excellent children of nature as they are, and with what art they have polished to that perfection which looks like nature.

If whatever touches the heart is better than what is merely addressed to the ear—if elegant simplicity in manner is more judicious than the dancing-school bows and curtsies, and insane smiles, and kissing of the tips of kid gloves *a la Pico*—if songs whose words you can hear and understand are preferable to a mass of unintelligible stuff, (for who makes out even the libretto of English opera as now given on the stage?) which, for all the sense you get of it, might as well be Choctaw or Arabic—if sensible sweetness is better than sweetness all distorted by unnatural nonsense—then does the Cheneys' singing possess unrivalled desert.

"Beautiful Day," and "The Irish Mother's Lament," as given by the sister, were exquisitely beautiful. This young lady has a voice which, in softness, and that rare indescribable swelling quality so powerful an adjunct in pathetic song, we never before heard the equal of. This we deliberately say, with the notes of the popular *prima donna*, Miss Delcy,[3] yet ringing in our ears, and after hearing Mrs. Wood,[4] Mrs. Sequin,[5] Borghese,[6] Pico,[7] and the various vocal talent called in to aid Ole Bull[8] and De Meyer[9] at their concerts. Not the least merit of Miss Cheney, like

Abby Hutchinson,[10] is her unaffected, simple manner—her awkwardness, we may almost call it—which we advise her to cherish, and take no pains to get rid of.

If we may presume on such a liberty, we would in conclusion say a word to Brooklyn audiences:—How strangely stiff and formal they are! How chary of their applause! Or rather how chary of their hands—for our brain has not yet got over that jarring discord produced by kicking and stamping with heavy boots and thumping with canes! Let us whisper in their ear, that kicks are poor tokens of kindness, and no thorough-bred person now-a-days, ever expresses approbation with his *feet*. Your *hands*—give your hands, ladies and gentlemen, where your hearts prompt you to give anything. And during the intervals of the performance, be not afraid of talking, laughing, looking and moving. You are not having daguerreotypes taken, nor acting silent statues—and it comes over one like a chill to see so many persons perched, as it were, on their propriety, and every word in a low whisper.

W.

NOTES

1. Transcribed from Walt Whitman, *The Journalism, Volume I: 1834–1846*, part of *The Collected Writings of Walt Whitman*, ed. Herbert Bergman, Douglas A. Noverr, and Edward J. Recchia (New York: Peter Lang, 1998), 235–236.

2. From Shakespeare's *The Merchant of Venice*, Act 5, Scene 1: "The man that hath no music in himself, / Nor is not moved with concord of sweet sounds, / Is fit for treasons, stratagems and spoils; / The motions of his spirit are dull as night / And his affections dark as Erebus: / Let no such man be trusted. Mark the music."

3. Probably Catherine Delcy, an English singer who performed at the Park Theater in September 1845. Vera Brodsky Lawrence, *Strong on Music: The New York Scene in the Days of George Templeton Strong* (Chicago: University of Chicago Press, 1995), 1:335.

4. Probably Mary Ann Wood, who appeared at the Park Theater as early as 1835. Ibid., 36.

5. Anne Sequin first appears in Whitman's editorial "Italian Opera in New Orleans" in the *New York Aurora*, April 15, 1842 (above).

6. Probably Eufrasia Borghese, an Italian prima donna who first performed in New York in 1841 and was "in reality . . . Juliette-Euphrasine . . . a native of France." Brodsky Lawrence, 1:138.

7. Rosina Pico, who performed in New York throughout the 1830s and 1840s. Ibid., 266, 327, 347.

8. Ole Bornemann Bull (1810–1880), Norwegian composer and violinist. Einar Ingvlad Haugen, *Ole Bull: Norway's Romantic Musician and Cosmopolitan Patriot* (Madison: University of Wisconsin Press, 1993).

9. Leopold De Meyer (1816–1883), Austrian pianist.

10. Of the Hutchinson Family singers.

Art-Singing and Heart-Singing*[1]

Broadway Journal
NOVEMBER 29, 1845

GREAT is the power of Music over a people! As for us of America, we have long enough followed obedient and child-like in the track of the Old World. We have received her tenors and her buffos, her operatic troupes and her vocalists, of all grades and complexions; listened to and applauded the songs made for a different state of society—made, perhaps, by royal genius, but made to please royal ears likewise; and it is time that such listening and receiving should cease. The subtlest spirit of a nation is expressed through its music—and the music acts reciprocally upon the nation's very soul. Its effects may not be seen in a day, or a year, and yet these effects are potent invisibly. They enter into religious feelings—they tinge the manners and morals—they are active even in the choice of legislators and high magistrates. Tariffs can be varied to fit circumstances—bad laws obliterated and good ones formed—those enactments which relate to commerce or national policy, built up or taken away, stretched or contracted, to suit the will of the government for the time being. But no human power can thoroughly suppress the spirit which lives in national lyrics, and sounds in the favorite melodies sung by high and low.[2]

There are two kinds of singing—heart-singing and art-singing. That which touches the souls and sympathies of other communities may have no effect here—unless it appeals to the throbbings of the great heart of humanity itself—pictures love, hope, or mirth in their comprehensive aspect. But nearly every nation has its peculiarities and its idioms, which make its best intellectual efforts dearest to itself alone, so that hardly any thing which comes to us in the music and songs of the Old World, is strictly good and fitting to our own nation.

With all honor and glory to the land of the olive and the vine, fair-skied Italy—with no turning up of noses at Germany, France, or England—we humbly demand whether we have not run after their beauties long enough.

"At last we have found it!" exclaimed we, some nights since, at the conclusion of the performance by the Cheney Family, in Niblo's Saloon.[3] At last we have found, and heard, and seen something original and beautiful in the way of American musical execution. Never having been present at any of the Hutchinsons' Concerts,[4] (the Cheneys, we are told, are after the same token,) the elegant simplicity of this style took us completely by surprise, and our gratification was inexpressible. This, said we in our heart, is the true method which must become popular in the United States—which must supplant the stale, second-hand, foreign method, with its flourishes, its ridiculous sentimentality, its anti-republican spirit, and its sycophantic influence, tainting the young taste of the republic.

The Cheney young men are such brown-faced, stout-shouldered fellows as you will see in almost any American church, in a country village, of a Sunday. The girl is strangely simple, even awkward, in her ways. Or it may possibly be that she disdains the usual clap-trap of smiles, hand-kissing, and dancing-school bends. To our taste, there is something refreshing about all this. We are absolutely sick to nausea of the patent-leather, curled-hair, "japonicadom" style.[5] The Cheneys are as much ahead of it as real teeth are ahead of artificial ones—even those which Dodge, (nature-rival as he is,) sent to the late Fair.[6] We beg these young Yankees to keep their manners plain alway.[7] The sight of them, as they are, puts one in mind of health and fresh air in the country, at sunrise—the dewy, earthy fragrance that comes up then in the moisture, and touches the nostrils more gratefully than all the perfumes of the most ingenious[8] chemist.

These hints we throw out rather as suggestive of a train of thought to other and more deliberate thinkers than we—and not as the criticisms of a musical connoisseur. If they have pith in them, we have not much doubt others will carry them out. If not, we at least know they are written in that true wish benefitting the subject spoken of, which should characterize all such essays.

Walter Whitman.

*The author desires us to say, for him, that he pretends to no scientific knowledge of music. He merely claims to appreciate so much of it (a sadly disdained department, just now) as affects, in the language of the deacons, "the natural heart of man."[9] It is scarcely necessary to add that we agree with our correspondent throughout. Ed. B. J.[10]

1. Transcribed from scanned original at "Walt Whitman at the Lilly," Indiana University, dlib.indiana.edu/omeka/lilly. This editorial also appears in Walt Whitman, *The Journalism, Volume I: 1834–1846*, part of *The Collected Writings of Walt Whitman*, ed. Herbert Bergman, Douglas A. Noverr, and Edward J. Recchia (New York: Peter Lang, 1998), 202–203.

2. Whitman here echoed sentiments of the Young America movement, which commingled free-market economics, territorial expansionism, and calls for a particularly American art. See Edward Widmer, *Young America: The Flowering of Democracy in New York City* (Oxford: Oxford University Press, 2000), especially 81–86.

3. An advertisement in the October 12, 1845, *New York Herald* described a Cheney Family performance at the New York Society Library as "selected from the best American, English and German compositions. They will also introduce several new pieces composed and arranged expressly for them."

4. This appears to contradict Whitman's reviews from December 4, 1843, in the *Daily Plebeian* and an article in the *Brooklyn Evening Star* from November 5, 1845. However, in the *Daily Plebeian* article Whitman did not exactly say that he heard the Hutchinson Family sing and made no references to specific songs, which, of course, he did in his November 5, 1845, *Brooklyn Evening Star* article on the performance of the Cheney Family at Niblo's Saloon. It is also possible that Whitman may have heard the Hutchinsons in a rehearsal or a shorter performance but not in a full concert, as he did with the Cheney Family. The other possibility is that the December 4, 1843, article is not by Whitman, though we know that the November 5, 1845, *Brooklyn Evening Standard* article was by him (as well as this article from the *Broadway Journal*). In our opinion, when Whitman says that he had never been present at any of the Hutchinsons' concerts, he was stating the truth, which is borne out by the manner in which the December 4, 1843, *Daily Plebeian* article was written.

5. A "japonica" is a red-flowered shrub with yellow fruit native to Japan. "Japonicadom" appears to be a term coined by Nathaniel Parker Willis (1806–1867), a prominent journalist, editor, and author. Willis defined "japonicadom" as "the class up town who usually wear in their hair the expensive exotic commonly called a japonica." Nathaniel Parker Willis, *The Prose Works* (Philadelphia: Carey and Hart, 1849), 767.

6. Probably J. Smith Dodge, a dentist who patented "Mode for Inserting Artificial Teeth" in 1844. *Dental Headlight* 5, no. 1 (January 1, 1884): 137.

7. Spelling in original.

8. The colon appears after the "n" in the original.

9. A common theological concept of human nature separated from its spiritual elements. In this case, "natural heart" speaks to the elemental and sentimental or passionate. For example, "The Bible ascribes to the natural heart of man a character utterly incompatible with the existence of religion." Lyman Beecher, "The Native Character of Man," *Native Preacher*, New York 2, no. 1 (June 1827): 4.

10. Edgar Allan Poe was editor of the *Broadway Journal* when this article was published. Whitman later recalled Poe as "very cordial, in a quiet way, appear'd well in person, dress, &c. I have a distinct and pleasing remembrance of his looks, voice, manner and matter; very kindly and human, but subdued, perhaps a little jaded." Walt Whitman, *Complete Prose Works* (New York: D. Appleton), 1909, 17, www.whitmanarchive.org.

How Literature Is Paid Here[1]

Brooklyn Evening Star

FEBRUARY 5, 1846

The writers of America are more miserably paid than their class are in any other part of the world. And this will continue to be the case so long as we have no international copyright. At this time there is hardly any encouragement at all for the literary profession in the way of book-writing. Most of our authors are frittering away their brains for an occasional five dollar bill from the magazine publishers.

A new tack in the publishing department, however, may not unlikely be the precedent for depriving them of even this forlorn hope. The Tribune, speaking of the resuscitation of the New York Review under more *promising* auspices, wittily says, it is intended *not to pay* for contributions to the Review. If this is a good notion, it might easily be extended so as to make the pages of the Review a source of profit to the publishers—as there are plenty of great geniuses in obscurity who would cheerfully pay a dollar or two per page for the privilege of seeing themselves in print. One of our 'National Bards'[2] pays three cents per line for having his effusions to the American Flag and so forth printed in the Sunday papers.

NOTES

1. Transcribed from Walt Whitman, *The Journalism, Volume I: 1834–1846*, part of *The Collected Writings of Walt Whitman*, ed. Herbert Bergman, Douglas A. Noverr, and Edward J. Recchia (New York: Peter Lang, 1998), 252.

2. It is difficult to know whom Whitman refers to here, but this appears to be one of the earliest examples of Whitman's thinking of an author embodying the nation, a concept that would shape his poetic voice in *Leaves of Grass.* Whitman was perhaps inspired to use "bard" in these terms by Isaac D'Israeli's *Amenities of Literature, Sketches and Characters of English Literature* (1841), which he reviewed positively in "Honor to Literature!," *Brooklyn Daily Eagle*, March 9, 1847 (below). On Shakespeare, D'Israeli writes, "Shakespeare now stands alone the national bard." Isaac D'Israeli (1766–1848) was the father of Prime Minister Benjamin D'Israeli (1804–1881).

New Publications.[1]

Brooklyn Daily Eagle
MARCH 9, 1846

JOURNEY TO ARARAT: *By Dr. Frederick Parrot.* Harper and Brothers, New York.[2]

The great interest attaching to ARARAT on account of its scriptural associations, will necessarily secure to this work a very wide circulation—yet not on this account alone is it one of value. The journey (performed in 1829, under the patronage of the Russian Emperor) was a long and difficult one, through regions and among people at present but little known—and as the whole enterprise was undertaken and carried out by intelligent, scientific persons, of undoubted veracity, the results of their researches, as here given, are interesting and important in more respects than one. A minute description is given of Ararat and vicinity.

The book is handsomely bound in muslin—contains about 400 pages—and is enriched with a valuable map and a number of fine wood engravings.

THE FAIRY BOOK: *Illustrated with Eighty Elegant Engravings.* Harper & Brothers.

Ten thousand children, we are sure, will thank the Messrs. Harper from the bottom of their little hearts, for presenting them with this beautiful book—or rather, which is pretty much the same thing, for giving their kind parents an opportunity to present it to them. Here are "The Children in the Wood," "The Sleeping Beauty," and twenty-five other capital stories, twelve of which have been translated expressly for this work—to say nothing of the pretty pictures, or the large, clear type, and snow-white paper. Price, with illustrated paper cover, 50 cts.—with handsome cloth do, 75 cts.

The "Illustrated Bible" of the Harpers is rapidly approaching a completion. The last number fully equals any of its predecessors in point of beauty.

THE WIGWAM AND THE CABIN: *By W. Gilmore Simms.* Second Series. Wiley & Putnam, New York.[3]

Simms is unquestionably one of the most attractive writers of the age; and yet some of his characters—to our mind at least—are in exceedingly bad taste. It *may* be all well enough to introduce a "foul rabble of lewd spirits," in order to show that "Virtue can triumph even in the worst estates,"[4] but it is our impression that ladies and gentlemen of refinement—to say nothing of heads of families—would rather take the maxim upon trust than have it exemplified to them or their children through the medium of a picture so very coarse and indelicate in its details, as that drawn by Mr. Simms in his "Caloya." The last chapter of this story is rendered particularly objectionable by the introduction of a revolting drunken scene[5]—and the tale as a whole is certainly calculated to reflect no credit upon American literature, either at home or abroad.

There are several other tales in this volume, of an unexceptionable and highly entertaining character.

NOTES

1. Transcribed from scanned original, Brooklyn Public Library—Brooklyn Collection. This editorial also appears in Walt Whitman, *The Journalism, Volume I: 1834–1846*, part of *The Collected Writings of Walt Whitman*, ed. Herbert Bergman, Douglas A. Noverr, and Edward J. Recchia (New York: Peter Lang, 1998), 272.

2. Frederick Parrot supposedly made the first recorded ascent of Mount Ararat in 1829. "Across Asia on a Bicycle: A Pause at the Mountain of the Ark," *Century Illustrated Monthly Magazine* 48 (June 1894), 183.

3. William Gilmore Simms (1806–1870). According to Poe, "The fiction of Mr. Simms gave indication . . . of genius, and that of no common order." Edgar Allan Poe, *The Complete Works of Edgar Allan Poe: Criticisms* (New York: G. P. Putnam's Sons, 1902), 8:289.

4. W. Gilmore Simms, *The Wigwam and the Cabin* (New York: Wiley and Putnam, 1845), 1.

5. From the chapter Whitman referred to, "'Nigger is d--n dog!' cried the savage, his hiccoughs sufficiently overcome by his rage to allow him a tolerable clear utterance at last. As he spoke the blow was given full at the head of the driver. Mingo threw up his left hand to ward off the stroke, but was only partially successful in doing so. The keen steel smote the hand, divided the tendon between the fore-finger and thumb, and fell with considerable force upon the forehead. 'Oh you d--n black red-skin, you kill mossa best nigger!' shrieked the driver, who fancied, in the first moment of his pain, that his accounts were finally closed with the world." Ibid., 190.

Polishing the "Common People."[1]

Brooklyn Daily Eagle

MARCH 12, 1846

It is a frequent remark that we Americans do not give enough encouragement to the fine arts. Perhaps this is unavoidable; for in the course of our national existence—the subduing of wild territories—the prosecution of two heavy wars, and the general turmoil incident to the first fifty years in the life of a great empire, we have had little time to attend to the finer and more polished enjoyments of existence. Such luxuries do not come, by any means, the first in the course of a people's efforts, either.—They are the fruit of time—long in ripening.

Yet we could wish the spreading of a sort of democratical artistic atmosphere, among the inhabitants of our republic, even now. This may be helped onward cheaply and conveniently in many ways. It is well known what a refining effect the cultivation of music has on the masses. Much good might also be done by the more frequent diffusion of tasty prints, cheap casts of statuary, and so on. The influence of flowers, too, is not beneath the attention of those who would have elegance of manners a frequent thing among the people. Who is so poor that he or she cannot possess a few flower pots, and pretty shrubs? Small as some may imagine such business to be, it is potent for good and deserves commendation. And as to prints, there are innumerable ones that can be purchased for a small sum, good enough for any man's parlor. What influence would Dick's[2] engraving of the "Last Supper," alone, produce, if hung up in the daily presence of the families of our land? With the divine face and expression of the Guileless Man beaming down upon them, who could let meanness, selfishness, and passion, get such frequent mastery of reason? With the accursed token of Judas, (the master part of the artist, in our opinion) and the pure gentleness of St. John, placed side by side, what beneficial preference might result from the contrast? Such results, we know, escape the minds of men who judge hastily and superficially; but we are assured the invisible sway of even a picture, has sometimes controlling influence over a man's character and future life.

We love all that ameliorates or softens the feelings and customs. We have often thought, and indeed it is undeniable, that the great difference in the impressions which various communities make on foreigners travelling among them, is altogether caused by the possession or deficiency of these little graces of action and appearance. It must be confessed that we in America, among the general population, have very, very few of these graces. Yet the average intellect and education of the American people is ahead of all other parts of the world. We suggest whether we are not much in fault for entertaining such a contempt toward these "little things," as many will call them.

Let every family have some flowers, some choice prints, and some sculpture casts. And as it is the peculiar province of woman to achieve these graceful and polished adornments of life, we submit our remarks and suggestions especially to them.

NOTES

1. Transcribed from scanned original, Brooklyn Public Library—Brooklyn Collection. This editorial also appears in Walt Whitman, *The Journalism, Volume I: 1834–1846,* part of *The Collected Writings of Walt Whitman,* ed. Herbert Bergman, Douglas A. Noverr, and Edward J. Recchia (New York: Peter Lang, 1998), 279–280.

2. Scottish-born engraver Alexander L. Dick (1805–1855) immigrated to the United States in 1833 and began an engraving business in New York City. Most engravings bearing Dick's name were the work of journeymen employed by him. David McNeely Stauffer and Mantle Fielding, *American Engravers Upon Copper and Steel* (New York: Burt Franklin, 1907), 65.

Music for the "natural ear."[1]

Brooklyn Daily Eagle

APRIL 3, 1846

After all—after hearing the trills, the agonized squalls, the lackadaisical drawlings, the sharp ear-piercing shrieks, the gurgling death-rattles, the painful leaps from the fearfullest eminences to a depth so profound that we for a while hardly expect the tongue to scramble up again—after sitting in the full blaze of the pit of the Italian opera at Palmo's[2] and nigh "the Borghese,"[3] and "the Pico,"[4] time and again—after the cracked voice of Templeton,[5] the most consummate of humbugs, the tiger-like piano execution of De Meyer,[6] and all the long train of Italian artificiality—we turn (we are quite ashamed to confess it) with a vivider relish than ever to that kind of music which seems intended for "the natural man"—Whether it be that our palate rejects, in its homeliness, the niceties of spiced cookery, or that the simple wholesome is better in music, as it is in diet—at all events, give us a good heart-song before the "fashionable article," any day!

We went last night to hear the concert of the 'home branch' of the Hutchinson family[7] at Gothic Hall in this city. A correspondent informs us that the male part of the present band consists of Messrs. Zephaniah,[8] Caleb[9] and Joshua Hutchinson,[10] own brothers of the "family" now in England.[11] The young lady is Miss Ann W. Marvell, their cousin. "Cousin Ann" is just about the age of Abby Hutchinson,[12] and in manners and appearance much the same. A gentleman by the name of Buxton[13] accompanies the others and plays the accordeon[14] to perfection. When at home, he resides in the same town. They give another concert next week.

Among the songs last night "Excelsior"[15] was given with probably the perfectest feeling. (Who can read that strange deep poetry—

The shades of night were falling fast
As through an Alpine village passed
A youth, who bore midst snow and ice,

A banner with this strange device—
"Excelsior."

—without feeling that Longfellow is indeed a true son of song?) "The May Queen," "The Grave of Bonaparte," "Over the Mountain and Over the Moor," were also presented in a handsome manner.[16] We welcome these meritorious young singers, and hope they will find both fame and profit in their future journeyings.

We have now several American vocal bands that in *true* music really surpass almost any of the vaunted *artificial* performers from aboard: there are the Hutchinsons, the Cheneys,[17] the Harmoneons,[18] the Baker family,[19] and the Ethiopian serenaders[20]—all of them well trained, and full of both natural and artistic capacity.

NOTES

1. Transcribed from scanned original, Brooklyn Public Library—Brooklyn Collection. This editorial also appears in Walt Whitman, *The Journalism, Volume I: 1834–1846*, part of *The Collected Writings of Walt Whitman*, ed. Herbert Bergman, Douglas A. Noverr, and Edward J. Recchia (New York: Peter Lang, 1998), 316.

2. Palmo's, on Chambers Street, opened in 1844.

3. Eufrasia Borghese. See note above.

4. Rosina Pico. See note above. Whitman praised Pico on February 13, 1847, in the *Eagle*: "In the first scene of the second act come a few strains of peculiar beauty, which are sung by Pico in that rich and liquid style so much her own." Brooklyn Public Library—Brooklyn Collection.

5. John Templeton. See note above.

6. Leopold De Meyer. See note above.

7. See "The Hutchinson Family," *Daily Plebeian*, December 4, 1843 (above).

8. Zephaniah Hutchinson (1810–1853). The Hutchinson Family, *Excelsior: Journals of the Hutchinson Family Singers, 1842–1846*, ed. Dale Cockrell (Hillsdale, N.Y.: Pendragon Press, 1989), 10.

9. Caleb Hutchinson (1811–1854). Ibid., 193.

10. Joshua Hutchinson (1811–1883). Ibid., 11.

11. The Hutchinsons traveled to England with Frederick Douglass in 1845. Scott Gac, *Singing for Freedom: The Hutchinson Family Singers and the Nineteenth-Century Culture of Reform* (New Haven, Conn.: Yale University Press, 2007), 211.

12. Abby Hutchinson (1829–1892). The Hutchinson Family, *Excelsior*, 11.

13. Probably a relative since the Hutchinson siblings had a great aunt named Sarah Buxton (1751–1828). Ibid.

14. Accordion, "accordeon" in original.

15. In a program from a performance in 1844, the Hutchinsons described this song, originally a poem by Longfellow, as representing "the continued aspirations of Genius. Its motto—'Excelsior,' (still higher) is a word in an unknown tongue. Disregarding the every day comforts of life, the allurements of love, and the warnings of experience, it presses forward on its solitary path. Even in death it holds fast its device, and a voice from the air proclaims the progress of the soul in a higher sphere." Qtd. in Gac, 3.

16. While Whitman in this editorial situated the Hutchinsons on the side of unaffected "heart music," the Hutchinsons were best known by contemporaries for their overtly religious messages and morally uplifting influence. For example, a July 1846 review in the *Musical Gazette* (Boston) began this way: "The occasion of this assemblage of all ranks and classes was indeed a simple one, viewed by itself, but its concomitants furnish matter for deep thought to all who care for their fellow citizens and for the moral and religious elevation of mankind generally." *Musical Gazette* 1, no. 13 (July 13, 1846): 97.

17. See "American Music, New and True!" *Brooklyn Evening Star*, November 5, 1845 (above).

18. The Harmoneons were a Boston minstrel group who appeared in "white face" as the "Albino Family" during the first half of their performances, painting their faces white and donning flaxen wigs. This double-minstrelsy was supposed to showcase the different styles of the races in a humorous way, even down to dividing their printed programs accordingly, with "Citizens" and "Ethiopians" in each half. Dale Cockrell argues that the Harmoneans' white-face performances were burlesques of family singing groups like the Hutchinsons. Dale Cockrell, *Demons of Disorder: Early Blackface Minstrels and Their World* (Cambridge: Cambridge University Press, 1997), 153. See also Charles D. Martin, *The White African American Body: A Cultural and Literary Exploration* (New Brunswick, N.J.: Rutgers University Press, 2002), 89.

19. A New Hampshire singing family. Karin Pendle, *Women & Music: A History* (Bloomington: Indiana University Press, 2001), 203.

20. A minstrel troupe popular before the Civil War.

Government patronage of men of letters.[1]

Brooklyn Daily Eagle
APRIL 6, 1846

WELL DONE.—In the last list of appointments confirmed by the Senate, published in the *Union,* thousands of readers will notice with peculiar gratification that of HAWTHORNE—the gentle Hawthorne—as Surveyor of the port of Salem, Mass. It is a credit of which any administration may be proud, to have the opportunity of thus conferring a portion of its official patronage upon such recipients. The Author of "*Twice Told Tales,*" the Elia[2] of our country returns more honor than he receives, in his acceptance of such a favor. This is the only mode in which our system of government permits the patronage of literature and men of letters, and we only regret that where it can be done with due regard still had to political character, it is not more often resorted to for that purpose. Hawthorne is and has always been a Democrat, while never engaged in active politics;[3] so that we have his name too, one of the brightest in the young annals in our national literature, to grace the party which, notwithstanding Whig pretensions to all the talents and all the education, has already numbered in its ranks the first Poet,[4] the first Historian,[5] the first Novelist, and the First Tragedian,[6] our country has produced. How do the Whigs explain this "singular coincidence." —*News, this morning.*

Most heartily do we respond the sentiment of pleasure which our contemporary feels at this appointment! Though we do not know Hawthorne personally, yet we know him in some sort, and take it upon us to say that he will perform the duties of his office, whatever they may be, in an efficient manner, and to answer all the requirements of propriety.—But the recognizing of the principle, is the thing—the principle that literary men are prominently eligible to civil appointments.[7] In this case it has been applied strongly; for Hawthorne is a quiet shrinking person, and little fitted to make his way through the blustering crowd. We hope the government will act upon the same principle again and again, until it gets to be fixed as one of the settled rules for its action.

"But," says one, "why have mere writers any higher claims for such favor, than those of other professions?"

For the following reasons: Literary men of the highest grade, (particularly those who are guided altogether by their ideas of right, and scorn to bend the knee, "that thrift may follow fawning")[8] in a large majority of cases are wretchedly poor, and though fame sometimes comes, yet profit rarely does. They serve the world, as it were, without fee and without reward—for there is no higher and more useful service to humanity, than that of boldly advocating great truths, or elevating intellectual taste. What office, what money, what gift in the power of government, could have compensated Channing[9] for the great anchor he has built for mental independence in America? What pay *could* pay Bryant[10] for those words of glory and truth, richly ushered as the old English language can parallel? What sum in the treasury might balance the account America never has settled with Fulton? And there are now dozens of struggling literary men—not Channings, of course, or Bryants, or Fultons—but with ardent and truthful minds, who have a far closer claim on the government for nomination to office, than all the political demagogues and fishers that ever existed! Such men, *the country is indebted to*. We talk about a gift from a rich millionaire, to some benevolent institution—a granting one hundred or five hundred dollars—as though humanity were bound in everlasting gratitude to such a philanthropist: but what is equal to the far spread and deeply penetrating influence of intellect, coined in images of beauty or truth, and diffused among all the people, to be incorporated in their characters, and to elevate and improve them, and increase their means of pure enjoyment?

We wish the writers of America, through their various avenues of utterance, would dwell oftener and more pointedly on this theme. Daily and hourly we are working—some of us spending health and life itself in the labor—for the cause of mere politicians, of men who make a *trade* of what in its purity is, or ought to be, nobler than any of the other professions. Though much of this is necessary and unavoidable—and though a very large portion of political candidates are men who may be worked for, and spoken for, with a hearty good will, by the truest writer—yet it were not amiss, amid the immense demands of the state for servants and service, to remember, also, those who have as honest a right to her smiles, as any else!

NOTES

1. Transcribed from scanned original, Brooklyn Public Library—Brooklyn Collection. This editorial also appears in Walt Whitman, *The Journalism, Volume I: 1834–1846*, part of

The Collected Writings of Walt Whitman, ed. Herbert Bergman, Douglas A. Noverr, and Edward J. Recchia (New York: Peter Lang, 1998), 321–323.

2. A pseudonym for Charles Lamb (1775–1834), popular British essayist.

3. Hawthorne wrote a political biography of Franklin Pierce during the election of 1852. Nathaniel Hawthorne, *The Life of Franklin Pierce* (Boston: Ticknor, Reed and Fields, 1852).

4. Probably William Cullen Bryant (1794–1878), who edited the *New York Evening-Post* from 1828 to 1878.

5. Perhaps George Bancroft (1800–1891), who, incidentally, appointed Hawthorne to his post in the Boston Customs House in 1839 before Hawthorne worked at the Salem Customs House. Richard H. Millington, *The Cambridge Companion to Nathaniel Hawthorne* (Cambridge: Cambridge University Press, 2004), xvi, 53, 62.

6. Probably Edwin Forrest (1806–1872), who was famous for his passionate portrayals of Othello, Lear, Macbeth, and Hamlet, as well as the characters Metamora in *Metamora; or, The Last of the Wampanoags* (1829) and Spartacus in *The Gladiator* (1836). Forrest's rivalry with British actor William Macready ignited the Astor Place Riot of 1849.

7. In 1865 Whitman was hired by the Bureau of Indian Affairs as a clerk and was fired six months later when Secretary of the Interior James Harlan discovered that the author of *Leaves of Grass* worked in his department. Whitman then, with the help of supporters in the administration, moved to the Attorney General's Office. J. R. LeMaster and Donald D. Kummings, eds., *Walt Whitman: An Encyclopedia* (New York: Garland, 1998).

8. From *Hamlet*, Act 3, Scene 2: "Nay, do not think I flatter; / For what advancement may I hope from thee / That no revenue hast but thy good spirits, / To feed and clothe thee? Why should the poor be flatter'd? / No, let the candied tongue lick absurd pomp, / And crook the pregnant hinges of the knee / Where thrift may follow fawning."

9. William Ellery Channing (1780–1842), Unitarian theologian.

10. William Cullen Bryant.

Literary News, Notices, &c., Works of Art, &c.[1]

Brooklyn Daily Eagle

APRIL 15, 1846

Typee.[2]—A strange, graceful, most readable book this. It seems to be a compound of the "Seward's Narrative,"[3] and "Guidentio de Lucca,"[4] style and reading. As a book to hold in one's hand and pore dreamily over of a summer day, it is unsurpassed.—(Wiley & Putnam 161 Broadway.)

Titmarsh's Journal.—Every body who has read, (and laughed at withal) the "Yellowplush Correspondence,"[5] knows the forte of this writer. It is a gay, rollicky, slap dash book. (Wiley & Putnam.)

Dick's Astronomy.[6]—A mere newspaper notice could not begin to do this fine work justice. For those beginning the noble study on which it treats, the book is better than any now published. (Harpers, 82 Cliff street.)

Whewell's Morality.[7]—This work, with that just noticed and *Darwin's voyage of a Naturalist,*[8] form part of HARPER'S NEW MISCELLANY, an elegant issue of works at 50 cents a volume, bound in extra muslin, gilt, and printed on good paper. The plan has some improvements on the old "Family Library," with all the good points of that celebrated series. Of Whewell's work the best critics speak in high terms; and of the 'Naturalist' it only needs a slight inspection, to decide most favorably. It is most comprehensive; the author sailed to various parts of the world, and this book is the well-written result of his researches into Geology, Botany, and Orinthology—and his observation of Insects, Fishes, Marine peculiarities, &c. &c.

Thiodolf.[9]—A book from the German of Foque—and with all the intellectual depth and poetical grace of the German. Wiley & Putnam, the publishers, do well to bring out works of this kind—although publishers in general are chary[10] of them.

Littell's Living Age.—Here is contained the culled flowers and the picked fruits of English periodical literature. There is always matter for thought and analysis in the 'Age.' It is published weekly, price 12 1/2 cts. (Taylor & Co., 2 Astor House, N.Y.)

Titian's Venus.—A soft beautiful voluptuous painting—but the exhibitors should not have the bad taste to shoulder it on Titian.[11] Of course, if that artist had any thing to do with it, this is a copy—though it is a very good one.

NOTES

1. Transcribed from scanned original, Brooklyn Public Library—Brooklyn Collection. This editorial also appears in Walt Whitman, *The Journalism, Volume I: 1834–1846,* part of *The Collected Writings of Walt Whitman,* ed. Herbert Bergman, Douglas A. Noverr, and Edward J. Recchia (New York: Peter Lang, 1998), 330–331.

2. *Typee* was Herman Melville's (1819–1891) first book. The full title was *Typee: A Peep at Polynesian Life.*

3. *Sir Edward Seward's Narrative of His Shipwreck, and Consequent Discovery of Certain Islands in the Caribbean Sea: With a Detail of Many Extraordinary and Highly Interesting Events in His Life, from the Year 1733 to 1749, As Written in His Own Diary,* ed. William Ogilvie and Jane Porter (London: Longman, Rees, Orme, Brown, and Green, 1831).

4. Simon Berington, *The Memoirs of Sigr Gaudentio Di Lucca: Taken from His Confession and Examination Before the Fathers of the Inquisition at Bologna in Italy* (London: T. Cooper, 1737). Bergman notes that the first edition appeared in the United States in 1796 and is classified under "imaginary voyages" and "Utopias" in Mansell's *National Union Catalog* of pre-1956 imprints. Whitman, *The Journalism, Vol. I,* 525.

5. William Makepeace Thackeray (1811–1863) wrote a series of humorous stories under the pseudonyms Charles James Yellowplush and Michael Angelo Titmarsh, among others.

6. Probably Scottish astronomer Thomas Dick (1774–1857), *The Practical Astronomer* (New York: Harper, 1846). Dick argued for a "plurality of worlds" and the existence of extraterrestrials. The *Biographical Encyclopedia of Astronomers* describes Dick's theories as "infused with cosmic mysticism that was nonetheless based on a firm grasp of astronomical principles." Virginia Trimble et al., *The Encyclopedia of Astronomers* (New York: Springer, 2007), 296.

7. William Whewell (1794–1866) was a well-known British scientist and public intellectual. According to the *Stanford Encyclopedia of Philosophy,* http://plato.stanford.edu/index.html, Whewell invented the word "scientist" and formulated a moral theory that argued that conscience was the result of natural reason applied to ethical dilemmas, and therefore an integrated part (rather than a separate faculty) of the human psyche.

8. Charles Darwin (1809–1882), *Journal of Researches into the Natural History and Geology of the Countries Visited during the Voyage of H.M.S. Beagle Round the World: Under the Command of Capt. Fitz Roy* (London: John Murray, 1845).

9. Friedrich Heinrich Karl La Motte-Fouque, *Thiodolf the Icelander* (New York: Wiley & Putnam, 1845).

10. Cautious.

11. Tiziano Vecellio (1490–1576).

Dramatics; and the true secret of Acting.[1]

Brooklyn Daily Eagle
AUGUST 20, 1846

The philosophy of acting resides entirely in the feeling and passions—to touch them, wake them, and calm them. No man can be a good actor without this power—and the more he has it, the greater he is upon the stage. This is stating the thing in its simplest form . . . . Now there are two ways of exercising such a sway over the passions of an audience—the usual way; which is boisterous, stormy physical, and repugnant to truth and taste; and another way, that actors rarely condescend to take, which consists in an invariable adherence to Nature, and is entirely mental, and works from within to the outward, instead of being altogether outward. The mental style was Macready's in his best days; he touched the heart, the soul, the feelings, the inner blood and nerves of his audience. The ordinary actor struts and rants away, and his furious declamation begets a kind of reciprocal excitement among those who hear him, it is true—but there is as much difference between it and the result produced by the true actor, as between mind and body.[2]

Though we never acted upon the stage, we know well enough, from the analogy of things, that the best way in the world to represent grief, remorse, love, or any given passion, is to feel them at the time, and throw the feeling as far as possible into word and act. This is a rare art, we admit; but no man or woman can be really great on the stage who has it not. The strange and subtle sympathy which runs like an electric chain through human hearts collected together, responds only to the touch of the true fire. We have known the time when an actual awe and dread crept over a large body assembled in the theater, when Macready merely appeared, walking down the stage, a king. He was a king—not because he had a tinsel gilded crown, and the counterfeit robe, but because he then dilated his heart with the attributes of majesty, and they looked forth from his eyes, and appeared in his walk. Such a power was worth a thousand vociferous plaudits for giving words of anger or defiance in tones to split the very roof! Mrs. Siddons,[3] in characters where a moving passion was maternal grief, wept hot scalding[4] real tears! Kean's eyes,[5] in Richard,[6] used to burn almost lurid with hate and wicked wishes! . . . . What agitation caused in a spectator's mind merely by loud lungs, can equal in intensity the result of one little touch of real feeling of this kind? Sock and Buskin![7] let us whisper in your ear (if any one of you reads this paragraph) the whole secret of penetrating your hearers' hearts: throw into your own identity (due labor and perseverance will give you the art of doing so at will) the character you are to represent. This, under the guidance of discretion and good taste, is all that is necessary to make the best of performers. Discard the assistance of *mere* physical applications. You have hammered away long enough at the ear—condescend, at last, to affect the heart.

—We went over last evening (19th) to the Park theater, to see how they were getting along—the old management and most of the old stock company, in a new commencement. The piece was the Nervous Man;[8] and the best played part in it, by far, was Mr. Barrett's[9] Mr. Aspen. It was indeed a treat to see such a bit of art as that—true to nature, not over-done, point-device in every thing. Mr. Collins[10] (the star) has an agreeable way with him, and a person may well sit and take pleasure from his performance; but there are many players in the stock cos. in New York, quite as well as he. Mrs. Vernon,[11] (Lady Leech) of course, did what she had to do, to admiration! She is not surpassed by any actress on the boards in her line; and is one of the public's (and our) dear old favorites . . . . The house was well filled last night, and we should think the management was putting money in its purse.[12]

NOTES

1. Transcribed from scanned original, Brooklyn Public Library—Brooklyn Collection. This editorial also appears in Walt Whitman, *The Journalism, Volume II: 1846–1848*, part of *The Collected Writings of Walt Whitman*, ed. Herbert Bergman, Douglas A. Noverr, and Edward J. Recchia (New York: Peter Lang, 2003), 24–25.

2. Whitman's reference to British actor William Macready lends some nuance to the nativist aesthetics he presented in editorials like "The Hutchinson Family" (December 4, 1843), "American Music, New and True!" (November 5, 1845), "Heart-Music and Art-Music" (November 14, 1845), "Art-Singing and Heart-Singing" (November 29, 1845), "Music for the 'natural ear'" (April 3, 1846), and "About Acting" (August 14, 1846). In his critique of the actor who "struts and rants away," Whitman may have been explicitly criticizing the popular American actor Edwin Forrest, who by the mid-1840s was engaged

in a public feud with William Macready, which had explicitly nativist overtones. For an analysis of Whitman's complicated aesthetic nationalism in this editorial, see Jason Stacy, *Walt Whitman's Multitudes: Labor Reform and Persona in Whitman's Journalism and the First* Leaves of Grass*, 1840–1855* (New York: Peter Lang, 2008), 80–81.

3. British actress Sarah Siddons (1755–1831).

4. Original reads "scaling."

5. British actor Edmund Kean (1787–1833).

6. In *Richard III*.

7. Representing comedy and tragedy.

8. William Bayle Bernard (1807–1875). William Bayle Bernard, *The Nervous Man: A Farce, in Two Acts* (London: J. Duncombe, 1833).

9. British actor George Barrett (1794–1860), described in the *New York Times* as "[i] n tragedy he was simply endurable, but in the opposite line was so perfectly at home that he soon came to be regarded as our very best light comedian." "Recollections of the Park Theater," *New York Times*, September 29, 1872, nytimes.com.

10. John Collins (1811–1874) was an Irish-born actor. *The Nervous Man* was his first appearance on the U.S. stage. Joseph Norton Ireland, *Records of the New York Stage, from 1750–1860* (New York: T. H. Morrell, 1867), 464.

11. British actress Jane Vernon (1796–1869).

12. Original reads "it purse." Perhaps an allusion to Iago in *Othello*, Act 1, Scene 2: "Put money in thy / purse; follow thou the wars; defeat thy favor with / an usurped beard; I say, put money in thy purse."

Miserable State of the State.—Why Can't We Have Something Worth the Name of American Drama?[1]

Brooklyn Daily Eagle

FEBRUARY 8, 1847

Of all '*low*' places where vulgarity (not only on the stage, but in front of it) is in the ascendant, and bad-taste carries the day with hardly a pleasant point to mitigate its coarseness, the New York theatres—except the Park—may be put down (as an Emeralder[2] might say,) at the top of the heap! We don't like to make these sweeping assertions in general—but the habit of such places as the Bowery, the Chatham, and the Olympic theaters, is really beyond all toleration; and if the N. Y. prints who give dramatic notices, were not the slaves of the paid puff system, they surely would sooner or later be 'down' on those miserable burlesques of the histrionic art.[3] Yet not one single independent dramatic critic seems to be among many talented writers for the N. Y. press. Or rather, we should say, not one single upright critic is permitted to utter candidly his opinions of the theatricals of the metropolis; for we would not insult the good taste of the intelligent literary men connected with the press over the river, so much as to suppose that their eyes and ears do not make the same complaint to them as ours make to us in the matter alluded to.

We have excepted the Park theatre in the charge of vulgarity, because the audiences there are always intelligent, and there is a dash of superiority thrown over the performances. But commendation can go not much further. Indeed it is not a little strange that in a great place like New York, acknowledged as the leading city of the western hemisphere, there should be no absolutely *good* theatre. The Park, once in a great while, gives a fine play, performed by meritorious actors and actresses. The Park is still very far, however, from being what we might reasonably expect in the principal dramatic establishment of the metropolis. It is but a third-rate imitation of the best London theatres. It gives us the cast off dramas, and the unengaged players of Great Britain; and of these dramas and players, like garments which come second hand from gentleman to valet, every thing fits awkwardly. Though now and then there is ground for satisfaction, the average is such as men of refinement cannot applaud at all. A play arranged to suit an English audience, and to jibe with English localities, feelings, and domestic customs, can rarely be represented in America, without considerable alteration. This destroys its uniformity, and generally deprives it of all life and spirit. One of the curses of the Park, and indeed of nearly all theatres now, is the *star* system. Some actor or actress flits about the country, playing a week here and a week there, bringing as his or her greatest recommendation, that of *novelty*—and very often indeed having no other.—In all the intervals between the appearance of these much trumpetted[4] people, the theatre is quite deserted, though the plays and playing are often far better than during some star engagement. We have seen a fine old English drama, with Miss *Cushman* and her sister—Mrs. *Vernon*,[5] *Placide*,[6] *Fisher*,[7] and several others whose betters in their departments could hardly be found—we have seen such a beautiful[8] piece, well put upon the stage, and played to a forlorn looking audience, thinly scattered here and there through pit and box—while the very next week, crowds would crush each other to get a sight of some flippant well-puffed star, of no real merit, and playing a character written (for the play consists of nothing but *one*, in such cases) by nobody knows whom—probably an ephemeral manufacturer of literature, with as little talent as his employer.

If some bold man would take the theatre in hand in this country, and resolutely set his face against the starring system, as a system,—some *American* it must be, and not moulded[9] in the opinions and long established ways of the English stage,—if he should take high ground, revolutionize the drama, and discard much that is not fitted to present tastes and modern ideas,—engage and encourage American talent, (a term made somewhat nauseous by the use it has served for charletans,[10] but still a good term,) look above merely the gratification of the vulgar and of those who love glittering scenery—give us American plays too, matter fitted to American opinions and institutions—our belief is he would do the republic service, and himself too, in the long round.

NOTES

1. Transcribed from scanned original, Brooklyn Public Library—Brooklyn Collection. This editorial also appears in Walt Whitman, *The Journalism, Volume II: 1846–1848*, part of *The Collected Writings of Walt Whitman*, ed. Herbert Bergman, Douglas A. Noverr, and Edward J. Recchia (New York: Peter Lang, 2003), 189–190.

2. A person from Ireland.

3. For a description of antebellum theaters, see Lawrence W. Levine, *Highbrow/ Lowbrow: The Emergence of Cultural Hierarchy in America* (Cambridge, Mass.: Harvard University Press, 1988).

4. Spelling in original.

5. Probably Ida Vernon, actress.

6. Henry Placide (1799–1870), comedian.

7. Perhaps Clara Fisher (1811–1898), British-born actress.

8. "beautifu-" in original.

9 Spelling in original.

10. Spelling in original, but with inverted "n," "charletaus."

Honor to Literature![1]

Brooklyn Daily Eagle

MARCH 9, 1847

In the old hemisphere, there are some world-famed piles of yet-entire architecture, which—though passed upon by 'public opinion' as complete—were intended by their projectors to form but parts of a still more stupendous design. We could not help thinking, as analogous to the structures we have mentioned, the book D'Israeli's *Amenities of literature*[2]—that standard even of our bookish time; (Harpers pub., fourth Am. edition.) It seems to have been—indeed was—the intention of the author to have made a complete history of literature—and the after circumstances which prevented the fulfilment[3] of that intention, painful enough in themselves, are far more painful when it is considered what the world has lost through them. But even what the world has lost, makes perhaps more valuable what is left of the treasure . . . . The 'Amenities' commence with the dawn of the intellectual light in Britain, as far as anything about it is known—with the Druidical institutions.—And the after pages show the deep research of the writer—his enthusiastic love of his subject—his faculty of order, too—for the whole chain is in consistent and harmonious connection. While reading the book, one cannot help being struck with How[4] much the world is indebted to literature, and literary men! how nearly all that has advanced humanity has been advanced by them! how *they* have been the conservators of that depth of virtue which consists not in abstractions, but in realities! how the fires of good impulses which seemed to have gone out, in many and many an age in the past, have secretly been cherished by them, and opened again at the first fair chance! how the pleasant things of life have been scattered, and the sorrows of life ameliorated, and the roughness of life smoothed, and manliness encouraged, and meanness rebuked, by them! Through the long dreary stretch of periods which the lover of his race fain would turn from, the silver rein of literature alone, and what it carries with it, sparkle like a brook athwart a barren moor . . . . Such reflections teaches this book: and if it had not, though it has, manifold merits, that would entitle it to the good will of all who duly appreciate and 'revere the humanities.'

NOTES

1. Transcribed from scanned original, Brooklyn Public Library—Brooklyn Collection. This editorial also appears in Walt Whitman, *The Journalism, Volume II: 1846–1848*, part of *The Collected Writings of Walt Whitman*, ed. Herbert Bergman, Douglas A. Noverr, and Edward J. Recchia (New York: Peter Lang, 2003), 219.

2. Isaac D'Israeli (1766–1848) was the father of Prime Minister Benjamin D'Israeli (1804–1881). Isaac D'Israeli described *Amenities of Literature: Sketches and Characters of English Literature* (1841) as a "philosophy of books, where their subjects, their tendency, and their immediate and gradual influence over people discover their actual condition." Disraeli's description of the relationship between an author and nation sounded like a precursor to Whitman's own. Disraeli: "Authors are the creators or the creatures of opinion; the great form an epoch, the many reflect their age. With them the transient becomes permanent, the suppressed lies open, and they are the truest representatives of their nation for those very passions with which they are themselves infected." Whitman: "Of all mankind the great poet is the equable man. . . . He bestows on every object or quality its fit proportions neither more nor less. He is the arbiter of the diverse and he is the key. He is the equalizer of his age and land. . . . Without effort and without exposing in the least how it is done the greatest poet brings the spirit of any or all events and passions and scenes and persons some more and some less to bear on your individual character as you hear or read. . . . The soul of the largest and wealthiest and proudest nation may well go half-way to meet that of its poets. . . . If the one is true the other is true. The proof of a poet is that his country absorbs him as affectionately as he has absorbed it." Isaac D'Israeli, *Amenities of Literature: Sketches and Characters of English Literature* (New York: J. & H. G. Langley, 1841), iii–iv; Walt Whitman, *Leaves of Grass* (1855), whitmanarchive.org.

3. Spelling in original.

4. In original, "how" is capitalized and is preceded by a comma.

Something About Art and Brooklyn Artists— A correspondent furnishes us with the following[1]

New York Evening Post

FEBRUARY 1, 1851

Though the collection of paintings of the Brooklyn Art Union[2] now open, includes none approaching to the highest order of merit, it is nevertheless a very agreeable collection, and contains some works of taste and talent. The association is composed mostly of young artists, who have the matter in their own hands, and, by means of judges, committees, and so forth, decide upon the pictures to be purchased, the prices to be paid, and the different other means of encouraging the painters, as well as advancing the prosperity of the "establishment." This thing of encouragement, 'specially of encouragement to the younger race of artists, commends the Brooklyn Art Union to the good will and patronage of the public. A great reason why the very large majority of our painters are distressingly feeble, is, the absence of enough of such encouragement. How would the cause of education stand now, were it not for the powerful favor which is extended to it from so many quarters, apart from those who are directly interested?

Nor is it too much to say, that nearly the same reasons which exist to compel this favor and sustenance in behalf of public education, will, if carried out, give some portion of the like wafting influences, to refined art. If we are bound, as we are by general acknowledgement, to furnish a fair education to all the children of the people, why not go a step further, and do something to add grace to that education—a polish to the raw jaggedness of the common school routine? Nearly all intelligent boys and girls have much of the artist in them, and it were beautiful to give them an opportunity of developing it in one of the fine arts.

At any rate, it seems to me that some organization of power to speak with decision, and to bring light out of the present darkness, is very much needed. For there are at the present moment ten thousand so-called artists, young and old, in this country, many of whom are working in the dark, as it were, and without aim. They want a strong hand over them. Here is a case for the imperial scepter, even in America. It is only a lucky few who can go abroad. From that few are probably left out the very ones who ought to go; and it is sometimes questioned whether those who go, are afterward any the better.

What a glorious result it would give, to form of these thousands a close phalanx, ardent, radical and progressive. Now they are like the bundle of sticks in the fable, and, as one by one, have no strength. Then, would not the advancing years foster the growth of a grand and true art here, fresh and youthful, worthy this republic, and this greatest of the ages? Would we not, at last, smile in return, at the pitying smile with which the old art of Europe has hitherto, and not unjustly, regarded ours?

These thousands of young men, idly as the business world too generally regards them—and despondingly as the severe taste is fain to turn oft times from their work—are in the main, composed of the nobler specimens of our race. With warm, impulsive souls, instinctively generous and genial, boon companions, wild and thoughtless often, but mean and sneaking never—such are these rapidly increasing ones. Unlike the orthodox sons and daughters of the world in many things, yet it is a picturesque unlikeness. For it need not argue an absolute miracle, if a man differ from the present dead uniformity of "society" in appearance and opinion, and still retain his grace and morals. A sunny blessing, then, say I, on the young artist race! for the thrift and shrewdness that make dollars, are not every thing that we should bow to, or yearn for, or put before our children as the be all and the end all of human ambition.

But I commenced with little else than the intention of saying a few words about some of the younger painters, in Brooklyn.

One of the most promising of these is Walter Libbey;[3] the reader may have noticed some of his pictures in the exhibitions of the Academy, or the New York Art Union. One, lately finished, of a boy playing the flute, is a charming production and would do credit to a master. I don't know where to look for a picture more *naïve,* or with more spirit or grace. The young musician has stopped, by the way-side, and, putting down his basket, seats himself on a bank. He has a brown wool hat, ornamented with a feather; rolled-up shirt sleeves, a flowing red cravat on his neck, and a narrow leather belt buckled round his waist—a handsome, healthy country boy. The face, the position of the hands holding the flute, the expression of the features, are exquisitely fine. I have looked several long looks at this picture, at different times, and each one with added pleasure and admiration. The scene in the background, clear and sunny, is yet subdued as a subordinate part—a servant to the main purpose; and it is a beautiful scene, too. The basket, half of which you see, the light resting here and there on the wide withes; the folds of the trousers, and their shadowed creases made by the open legs; on all these, the work shows the true artist. There is richness of coloring, tamed to that hue of purplish gray, which we see in the summer in the open air. There is no hardness, and the eye is not pained by the sharpness of outline which mars many otherwise fine pictures. In the scene of the background, and in all the accessories, there is a delicious melting in, so to speak, of object with object; an effect that is frequent enough in nature, though painters seem to disdain following it, even where it is demanded.

I returned, the other day, after looking at Mount's[4] last work—I think his best—of a Long Island negro, the winner of a goose at a raffle; and though it certainly is a fine and spirited thing, if I were to choose between the two, the one to hang up in my room for my own gratification, I should take the boy with his flute. This, too, to my notion, has a character of Americanism about it. Abroad, a similar subject would show the boy as handsome, perhaps, but he would be a young boor, and nothing more. The stamp of class is, in this way, upon all the fine scenes of the European painters, where the subjects are of a proper kind; while in this boy of Walter Libbey's, there is nothing to prevent his becoming a President, or even an editor of a leading newspaper.

Mount's negro may be said to have a character of Americanism, too; but I must be pardoned for saying, that I never could, and never will, admire the exemplifying of our national attributes with Ethiopian minstrelsy,[5] or Yankee Hill[6] characters upon the stage, as the best and highest we can do in that way.

We have, in Brooklyn, some more young artists—with others, of more established fame—of whom I should like to offer a few words, at another time; for my talk has already been strung out beyond the proper limits.

W. W.

NOTES

1. Transcribed from scanned original at fultonhistory.com. In the original version of this editorial, all of the paragraphs are in quotes. This editorial also appears in Walt Whitman, *The Uncollected Poetry and Prose of Walt Whitman*, ed. Emory Holloway (Gloucester, Mass.: Peter Smith, 1972), 1:236–238.

2. Modeled on New York's American Art-Union (1839), Cincinnati's Western Art-Union (1847), and the Philadelphia Art-Union (1848), the Brooklyn Art-Union was funded by subscribers to whom art was distributed by lottery and thereby provided a free

gallery for the populace. After the American Art-Union was declared a form of illegal gambling by the New York Court of Appeals in 1851, the Brooklyn Art-Union was disbanded. Natalie Spassky, *American Paintings in the Metropolitan Museum of Art* (New York: Metropolitan Museum of Art, 1985), 2:xix; Ruth Bohan, *Looking into Walt Whitman: American Art, 1850–1920* (University Park: Pennsylvania State University Press, 2006), 19, 216.

3. Ruth Bohan describes Walter Libbey (1827–1852) as "a minor genre painter who is today virtually unknown." Bohan, 17.

4. Bohan compares the sketches of William Sydney Mount (1807–1868) to "Whitman's own habit of filling a series of small notebooks with abbreviated verbal commentaries on his daily experiences." Ibid.

5. Compare to Whitman's admiration for "The Harmoneans" in "Music for the 'natural ear,'" *Brooklyn Daily Eagle*, April 3, 1846 (above).

6. George "Yankee" Hill (1809–1849), comedian, performed stock New England characters. See Whitman, *Uncollected Poetry and Prose*, 1:157, note 8.

Arts and Artists

Remarks of Walt Whitman, Before the Brooklyn Art Union, on the Evening of March 31, 1851[1]

Brooklyn Daily Advertizer

APRIL 3, 1851

AMONG such a people as the Americans, viewing most things with an eye to pecuniary profit—more for acquiring than for enjoying or well developing what they acquire—ambitious of the physical rather than the intellectual; a race to whom matter of fact is everything, and the ideal nothing—a nation of whom the steam engine is no bad symbol—he does a good work who, pausing in the way, calls to the feverish crowd that in the life we live upon this beautiful earth, there may, after all, be something vaster and better than dress and the table, and business and politics.

There was an idle Persian hundreds of years ago who wrote poems; and he was accosted by one who believed more in thrift.—"Of what use are you?" inquired the supercilious son of traffic. The poet turning plucked a rose and said, "Of what use is this?" "To be beautiful, to perfume the air," answered the man of gains. "And I," responded the poet, "am of use to perceive its beauty and to smell its perfume."

It is the glorious province of Art, and of all Artists worthy the name, to disentangle from whatever obstructs it, and nourish in the heart of man, the germ of the perception of the truly great, the beautiful and the simple.

When God, according to the myth, finished Heaven and Earth—when the lustre of His effulgent light pierced the cold and terrible darkness that had for cycles of ages covered the face of the deep—when the waters gathered themselves together into one place and made the sea—and the dry land appeared with its mountains and its infinite variety of valley, shore and plain—when in the sweetness of that primal time the unspeakable splendor of the sunrise first glowed on the bosom of the earth—when the stars hung at night afar off in this most excellent canopy, the air, pure, solemn, eternal—when the waters and the earth obeyed the command to bring forth abundantly, the beasts of the field, the birds of the air and the fishes of the sea—and when, at last, the superb perfection, Man, appeared, epitome of all the rest, fashioned after the Father and Creator of all—then God looked forth and saw everything that he had made, and pronounced it good. Good because ever reproductive of its first beauty, finish and freshness. For just as the Lord left it remains yet the beauty of His work. It is now spring. Already the sun has warmed the blood of this old yet ever youthful earth and the early trees are budding and the early flowers beginning to bloom:

> There is not lost, one of Earth's charms
> Upon her bosom yet
> After the flight of untold centuries,
> The freshness of her far beginning lies
> And still shall lie.[2]

With this freshness—with this that the Lord called good—the Artist has to do.—And it is a beautiful truth that all men contain something of the artist in them. And perhaps it is sometimes the case that the greatest artists live and die, the world and themselves alike ignorant what they possess. Who would not mourn that an ample palace of surpassingly graceful architecture, filled with luxuries and gorgeously embellished with fair pictures and sculpture, should stand cold and still and vacant, and never be known and enjoyed by its owner? Would such a fact as this cause your sadness? Then be sad. For there is a palace, to which the courts of the most sumptuous kings are but a frivolous patch, and, though it is always waiting for them, not one in thousands of its owners ever enters there with any genuine sense of its grandeur and glory.

To the artist, I say, has been given the command to go forth into all the world and preach the gospel of beauty. The perfect man is the perfect artist, and it cannot be otherwise.[3] For in the much that has been said of Nature and Art there is mostly the absurd error of considering the two as distinct. Rousseau, himself, in reality one of the most genuine artists, starting from his false point, ran into his beautiful encomiums upon nature and his foolish sarcasms upon art. To think of what happened when that restless and daring spirit ceased to animate one of the noblest apostles of democracy, is itself answer enough to all he ever said in condemnation of art. The shadows from the west were growing longer, as Rousseau, at the close of a beautiful summer day, felt death upon him. "Let me behold once more the glorious setting sun," was his last request. With his eyes turned toward the more than imperial pomp and with the soft and pure harmonies of nature around him, his wild and sorrowful life came to an end, and he departed peacefully and happily. Do you think Rousseau would have passionately enjoyed the sunset, those clouds, the beauty, and the natural graces there, had such things as art and artists never existed? Was not his death made happier than his life, by what he so often ridiculed in life?

Nay, may not death itself, through the prevalence of a more artistic feeling among the people, be shorn of many of its frightful and ghastly features? In the temple of the Greeks, Death and his brother Sleep, were depicted as beautiful youths reposing in the arms of Night. At other times Death was represented as a graceful form, with calm but drooping eyes, his feet crossed and his arms leaning on an inverted torch. Such were the soothing and solemnly placed influences which true art, identical with a perception of the beauty that there is in all the ordinations as well as all the works of Nature, cast over the last fearful thrill of those olden days. Was it not better so? Or is it better to have before us the idea of our dissolution, typified by the spectral horror upon the pale horse, by a grinning skeleton or a mouldering skull?

The beautiful artist principle sanctifies that community which is pervaded by it. A halo surrounds forever that nation. —There have been nations more warlike than the Greeks. Germany has been and is more intellectual. Inventions, physical comforts, wealth and enterprize[4] are prodigiously greater in all civilized nations now than they were among the countrymen of Alcibiades[5] and Plato.[6] But never was there such an artistic race.

At a neighboring city, the other evening was given, by a lecturer, a beautiful description of this character, making it a model that few in these days would think of successfully copying. The Greek form, he described as perfect, the mind well cultivated as to those things which are useful and pleasing; the man, as familiar with the history of his country, not seeking office for his emoluments or dignity, believing that no office confers dignity upon him who bears it, but that the true dignity of office arises from the character of the man who holds it, and the manner in which he administers it. He is not elated with honors or discomposed with ill success,—pursues his course with firmness, yet with moderation; and seeks not honors or profit for the services rendered his country, which he loves better than himself. He is neither penurious nor extravagant; does not court the rich nor stand aloof from the poor. He can appreciate excellence whether clothed in the apparel of the affluent or of the indigent; is no respector of persons, remembering that manly worth cannot be monopolized by any circle of society. He can mingle in festive scenes, and seek in them the feasts of *reason* as well as the flow of soul; his entertainments are prepared for the intellect as well as the physical appetite. The lyre and song, the harp and recital of heroic verse—sculpture, painting, music, poetry, as well as grave philosophical discourse—each in its turn becomes the channel of a refined and elevated pleasure. As a soldier, he acts upon the principle that, "thrice is he armed who has his quarrel just,"[7] and appeals to force only when negotiations fail, but then with terrific energy. He counts no sacrifice too great for his country. Dying, his proudest boast is, that "no Athenian, through his means, ever had cause to put on mourning."[8]

Yes, distracted by frippery, cant, and vulgar selfishness— sick even of the "intelligence of the age"—it refreshes the soul to bring up again one of that glorious and manly and beautiful nation, with his sandals, his flowing drapery, his noble and natural attitudes and the serene composure of his features. Imagination loves to dwell there, revels there, and will not turn away. There the artist appetite is gratified; and there all ages have loved to turn as to one of the most perfect ideals of man.

The orthodox specimen of the man of the present time, approved of public opinion and the tailor, stands he under the glance of art as stately? His contempt for all there is in the world, except money can be made of it; his utter vacuity of anything more important to him as a man than success in "business,"—his religion what is written down in the books, or preached to him as he sits in his rich pew, by one whom he pays a round sum, and thinks it a bargain,—his only interest in affairs of state, getting offices or jobs for himself or someone who pays him—so much for some points of his character.

Then see him in all the perfection of fashionable tailordom—the tight boot with the high heel; the trousers, big at the ankle, on some rule inverting the ordinary ones of grace; the long large cuffs, and thick stiff collar of his coat—the swallow-tailed coat, on which dancing masters are inexorable; the neck swathed in many bands, giving support to the modern high and pointed shirt collar, that fearful sight to an approaching enemy—the modern shirt collar, bold as Columbus, stretching off into the unknown distance—and then to crown all, the fashionable hat, before which language has nothing to say, because sight is the only thing that can begin to do it justice—and we have indeed a model for the sculptor. Think of it; a piece of Italian marble, chiselled[9] away till it gets to the shape of all this, hat included, and then put safely under storage as our contribution to the future ages, taste for our artistical proportion, grace, and harmony of form.

I think of few heroic actions which cannot be traced to the artistical impulse. He who does great deeds, does them from his sensitiveness to moral beauty.

Such men are not merely artists, they are artistic material. Washington in some great crisis, Lawrence in the bloody deck of the *Chesapeake*, Mary Stewart at the block, Kossuth in captivity and Mazzini in exile,—all great rebels and innovators, especially if their intellectual majesty bears itself out with calmness amid popular odium or circumstances of cruelty and an infliction of suffering, exhibit the highest phases of the artistic spirit. A sublime moral beauty is present to them, and they realize them. It may be almost said to emanate from them. The painter, the sculptor, the poet express heroic beauty better in description; for description is their trade, and they have learned it. But the others *are* heroic beauty, the best beloved of art.

Talk not so much, then, young artist, of the great old masters, who but painted and chiselled.[10] Study not only their productions. There is a still better, higher school for him who would kindle his fire with coal from the altar of the loftiest and purest art. It is the school of all grand actions and grand virtues, of heroism, of the death of captives and martyrs—of all the mighty deeds written in the pages of history—deeds of daring, and enthusiasm, and devotion, and fortitude. Read well the death of Socrates, and of a greater than Socrates. Read how slaves have battled against their oppressors—how the bullets of tyrants have, since the first king ruled, never been able to put down the unquenchable thirst of man for his rights.[11]

In the sunny peninsula where Art was transplanted from Greece and, generations afterward, flourished into new life, we even now see the growth that is to be expected among a people pervaded by love and appreciation of beauty. In Naples, in Rome, in Venice, that ardor for liberty which is a constituent part of all well developed artists and without which a man cannot be such, has had a struggle—a hot and baffled one. The inexplicable destinies have shaped it so. The dead lie in their graves; but their august and beautiful enthusiasm is not dead:—

Those corpses of young men,
Those martyrs that hung from the gibbets,
Those hearts pierced by the gray lead,
Cold and motionless as they seem,
Live elsewhere with undying vitality;
They live in other young men, O kings,
They live in brothers again ready to defy you;
They were purified by death,
They were taught and exalted.

Not a grave of those slaughtered ones,
But is growing its seed of freedom,
In its turn to bear seed,
Which the winds shall carry afar and re-sow,
And the rain nourish.
Not a disembodied spirit
Can the weapons of tyrants let loose,
But it shall stalk invisibly over the earth,
Whispering, counseling, cautioning.[12]

I conclude here.—As there can be no true Artist, without a glowing thought for freedom, so freedom pays the artist back again many fold, and under her umbrage Art must sooner or later tower to its loftiest and most perfect proportions.

NOTES

1. This editorial also appears in Walt Whitman, *The Uncollected Poetry and Prose of Walt Whitman*, ed. Emory Holloway (Gloucester, Mass.: Peter Smith, 1972), 1:241–247, from which this transcription is taken.

2. From William Cullen Bryant's "Forest Hymn."

3. Holloway notes Whitman's indebtedness to Ralph Waldo Emerson's essays "The American Scholar" and "The Divinity School Address." Whitman, *Uncollected Poetry and Prose*, 1: 243.

4. Spelling in original.

5. Alcibiades (450–404) was a youthful student of Socrates and, later, an Athenian politician who temporarily joined the Spartan cause during the Peloponnesian War.

6. Plato (424–347), a student of Socrates and later founder of the Academy, composed the most well known Socratic dialogues.

7. "What stronger breastplate than a heart untainted! / Thrice is he armed that hath his quarrel just, / And he but naked, though lock'd up in steel / Whose conscience with injustice is corrupted." William Shakespeare, *Henry VI* pt. 2, Act 3, Scene 2.

8. "[Pericles] had listened, however, all the while, and attended to all, and, speaking out among them, said that he wondered they should commend and take notice of things which were as much owing to fortune as to anything else . . . and, at the same time, should not speak or make mention of that which was the most excellent and greatest thing of all. 'For,' said he, 'no Athenian, through my means, ever wore mourning.'" Plutarch, *Lives*, vol. 1, "Pericles," trans. John Dryden (Philadelphia: John D. Morris, 1895), 329.

9. Spelling in original.

10. Spelling in original.

11. Whitman portrayed the poet in similar terms in the preface to his first edition of *Leaves of Grass* (1855): "The power to destroy or remould is freely used by him but never the power of attack. What is past is past. If he does not expose superior models and prove himself by every step he takes he is not what is wanted. The presence of the greatest poet conquers . . . not parleying or struggling or any prepared attempts. Now he has passed that way see after him! there is not left any vestige of despair or misanthropy or cunning or exclusiveness or the ignominy of a nativity or color or delusion of hell or the necessity of hell . . . . and no man thenceforward shall be degraded for ignorance or weakness or sin." From the Walt Whitman Archive, whitmanarchive.org.

12. From Whitman's poem "Resurgemus," published in the *New-York Daily Tribune* in June 1850. Walt Whitman Archive, whitmanarchive.org.

Walt Whitman a Brooklyn Boy. Leaves of Grass: (A Volume of Poems Just Published.)[1]

Brooklyn Daily Times

SEPTEMBER 29, 1855

To give judgment on real poems, one needs an account of the poet himself. Very devilish to some, and very divine to some, will appear these new poems, the Leaves of Grass: an attempt, as they are, of a live, naive, masculine, tenderly affectionate, rowdyish, contemplative, sensual, moral, susceptible and imperious person, to cast into literature not only his own grit and arrogance, but his own flesh and form, undraped, regardless of foreign models, regardless of modesty or law, and ignorant or silently scornful, as at first appears, of all except his own presence and experience, and all outside of the fiercely loved land of his birth and the birth of his parents, and their parents for several generations before him. Politeness this man has none, and regulation he has none. The effects he produces are no effects of artists or the arts, but effects of the original eye or arm, or the actual atmosphere of grass or brute or bird. You may feel the unconscious teaching of the presence of some fine animal, but will never feel the teaching of the fine writer or speaker.

Other poets celebrate great events, personages, romances, wars, loves, passions, the victories and power of their country, or some real or imagined incident—and polish their work, and come to conclusions, and satisfy the reader. This poet celebrates himself: and that is the way he celebrates all. He comes to no conclusions, and does not satisfy the reader. He certainly leaves him what the serpent left the woman and the man, the taste of the tree of the knowledge of good and evil, never to be erased again.

What good is it to argue about egotism? There can be no two thoughts on Walt Whitman's egotism. That is what he steps out of the crowd and turns and faces them for. Mark, critics! for otherwise is not used for you the key that leads to the use of the other keys to this well enveloped yet terribly in earnest man. His whole work, his life, manners, friendships, writing, all have among their leading purposes, an evident purpose, as strong and avowed as any of the rest, to stamp a new type of character, namely his own, and indelibly fix it and publish it, not for a model but an illustration, for the present and future of American letters and American young men, for the south the same as the north, and for the Pacific and Mississippi country, and Wisconsin and Texas and Canada and Havana, just as much as New York and Boston. Whatever is needed toward this achievement he puts his hand to, and lets imputations take their time to die.[2]

First be yourself what you would show in your poem—such seems to be this man's example and inferred rebuke to the schools of poets. He makes no allusions to books or writers; their spirits do not seem to have touched him; he has not a word to say for or against them, or their theories or ways. He never offers others; what he continually offers is the man whom our Brooklynites know so well. Of pure American breed, of reckless health, his body perfect, free from taint top to toe, free forever from headache and dyspepsia, full-blooded, six feet high, a good feeder, never once using medicine, drinking water only—a swimmer in the river or bay or by the seashore—of straight attitude and slow movement of foot—an indescribable style evincing indifference and disdain—ample limbed, weight one hundred and eighty-five pounds, age thirty-six years [1855]—never dressed in black, always dressed freely and clean in strong clothes, neck open, shirt-collar flat and broad, countenance of swarthy, transparent red, beard short and well mottled with white hair like hay after it has been mowed in the field and lies tossed and streaked—face not refined or intellectual, but calm and wholesome—a face of an unaffected animal—a face that absorbs the sunshine and meets savage or gentleman on equal terms—a face of one who eats and drinks and is a brawny lover and embracer—a face of undying friendship and indulgence toward men and women, and of one who finds the same returned many fold—a face with two gray eyes where passion and hauteur sleep, and melancholy stands behind them—a spirit that mixes cheerfully with the world—a person singularly beloved and welcomed, especially by young men and mechanics—one who has firm attachments there, and associates there—one who does not associate with literary and elegant people—one of the two men sauntering along the street with their arms over each other's shoulders, his companions some boatman or ship joiner, or from the hunting-tent or lumber-raft—one who has that quality of attracting the best out of people that they present to him, none of their meaner and stingier traits, but always their sweetest and most generous traits—a man never called upon to make speeches at public dinners, never on platforms amid the crowds of clergymen or professors or aldermen or congressmen—rather down in the bay with pilots in their pilot boats—or off on a cruise with fishers in a fishing smack—or with a band of laughers and roughs in the streets of the city or the open grounds of the country—fond of New York and Brooklyn—fond of the life of the wharves and the great ferries, or along Broadway, observing the endless wonders of that thoroughfare of the world—one whom, if you would meet, you need not expect to meet an extraordinary person—one in whom you will see the singularity which consists in no singularity—whose contact is no dazzling fascination, nor requires any deference, but has the easy fascination of what is homely and accustomed—of something you knew before, and was waiting for—of natural pleasures, and well-known places, and welcome familiar faces—perhaps of a remembrance of your brother or mother, or friend away or dead—there you have Walt Whitman, the begetter of a new offspring out of literature, taking with easy nonchalance the chances of its present reception, and, through all misunderstandings and distrusts, the chances of its future reception.[3]

NOTES

1. Transcribed from a photocopy of original in the papers of Herbert Bergman, East Lansing, Michigan. This review can also be found at the Walt Whitman Archive, whitmanarchive.org. This review was written by Whitman himself.

2. Compare to the preface of *Leaves of Grass* (1855): "Of all mankind the great poet is the equable man. Not in him but off from him things are grotesque or eccentric or fail of their sanity. Nothing out of its place is good and nothing in its place is bad. He bestows on every object or quality its fit proportions neither more nor less. He is the arbiter of the diverse and he is the key. He is the equalizer of his age and land . . . . he supplies what wants supplying and checks what wants checking." *Leaves of Grass* (1855), whitmanarchive.org.

3. Compare to Whitman's celebrations of singing groups like the Cheneys and the Hutchinsons. For example, "We beg these young Yankees to keep their manners plain always. The sight of them, as they are, puts one in mind of health and fresh air in the country, at sunrise—the dewy, earthy fragrance that comes up then in the moisture, and touches the nostrils more gratefully than all the perfumes of the most ingen:ious [ingenious] chemist." "Art-Singing and Heart-Singing," *Broadway Journal*, November 29, 1845 (above).

IV

Come Closer to Me

I pass so poorly with paper and types.

—*LEAVES OF GRASS* (1855)

Greenwood Cemetery[1]

Universalist Union

NOVEMBER 16, 1839

Much has been said of late by the different editors in this city concerning the "Greenwood Cemetery;"[2] and being of rather an inquisitive turn of mind, I felt disposed to test the accuracy of the various representations which have been made. Having received a very polite invitation from the Committee of the "American Institute Fair"[3] to accompany them to this future repository of the dead, I gladly availed myself of the favorable opportunity, and was constrained to exclaim with the Queen of Sheba, "the half was not told me."[4]

It is located about two miles from this city, on Long Island, and is almost surrounded by ocean. It comprises an area of two hundred acres of land, which cost the enterprising company one hundred and thirty thousand dollars. It is at present in a high state of forwardness, and it is expected that it will be ready for interments in the course of a few months. Its highest point, which is near the centre of the grounds, is called "Mount Washington"; it is one hundred and sixty feet high, and commands one of the finest prospects in the vicinity of New York. From this elevation may be distinctly seen Brooklyn, the bay and harbor of New York, Staten Island, and the Quarantine. It is, indeed, a second "Mount Auburn,"[5] and is destined at no very distant period to become its rival.

Being a resident of New York, it may perhaps be thought by some of my eastern friends, that I am influenced by sectional prejudices; but I can assure them that such is not the fact, for if I have any partialities, they are in favor of the east. I love Massachusetts. I love its people for their open-hearted frankness and generous hospitality. I love them for their general intelligence and high literary character; and above all, I love them for their religious freedom and christian charity.

While standing on this consecrated ground, I was led into a train of reflections at once pleasing, yet melancholy. How solemn are the thoughts that arise in the mind! What a profound calm pervades the whole scene! Here the silence and solitude of the sepulchre reign triumphant; broken only by the rustling of the sear leaf as it falls from the withered stem, fit emblem of the autumn of human existence, and of the faded hopes and blighted expectations of mortals!

Ah! how many thought I, in yon crowded city, who are now promising themselves years of uninterrupted felicity, shall be arrested in the full tide of health and prosperity by the hand of the "fell destroyer,"[6] and compelled to take up their abode in these "silent halls of death."[7]

Here shall the aged and care-worn pilgrim, who for more than threescore years and ten, has been compelled to "bide the peltings of the pitiless storm"[8] of adversity, "shuffle off this mortal coil,"[9] and lay down his burthen "where the wicked cease from troubling, and where the weary are at rest."[10]

Here shall the children of men resort to learn the vanity of human applause; the shortness of human life; the insignificance of earthly greatness, and the fickleness and instability of all beneath the sun.

Here the man of business, whose mind has been distracted by a multitude of perplexing cares, and whose health has been impaired by a series of adverse circumstances, may find in this secluded spot a solace for all his misfortunes.

Here, too, perchance, the giddy votary of pleasure may direct his course, for the purpose of passing an idle hour; and while the monumental inscription of some newly opened grave shall arrest his attention, he may perhaps be led to pause in his career of folly, and seriously reflect on the more sober realities of life.

Here may be seen the lonely widow, bending in pensive sadness over the tomb of him, in whom, while living, all her earthly happiness was centered, and who now refuses to be comforted, because she shall see his face no more in the flesh.

Here may be seen the orphan, deploring in all the eloquence of grief, the loss of a kind father and mother, feeling the utter helplessness and loneliness of its condition, and realizing the affecting truth, that henceforth it must travel the rugged and uneven journey of life, fatherless and alone.

Here may the fallen statesman come and learn the truth of the poet's description:

"The boast of heraldry, the pomp of power,
　　And all that beauty, and that wealth e'er gave,
Await alike the inevitable hour;
　　The paths of glory lead but to the grave."[11]

Here, too, may be seen the minister of the everlasting gospel, reflecting in the "Depth of nature's silence,"[12] on the transitory nature of all terrestrial objects, and gleaning from the mementoes[13] of mortality by which he is surrounded, lessons of deep and of thrilling interest, which may exert a benign influence on the great mass of thinking matter which lives and moves around him.

Ah! many, very many, shall come, to weep and mourn the loss of near and dear friends, who have been rudely snatched from their embrace and consigned to the silence and solitude of the sepulchre. But how sweet and peaceful will be their slumbers! How calmly will they rest in their silent mansions, till the night, the moonless night of death is passed, and the morning of the resurrection shall usher in a bright, a beautiful, a cloudless day!

> "Thus at the shut of even, the weary bird
> Leaves the wide air and in some lonely brake
> Cowers down, and dozes till the dawn of day,
> Then claps his well-fledged wings and soars away."[14]

W. W.

NOTES

1. This editorial appears in Walt Whitman, *The Journalism, Volume I: 1834–1846,* part of *The Collected Writings of Walt Whitman*, ed. Herbert Bergman, Douglas A. Noverr, and Edward J. Recchia (New York: Peter Lang, 1998), 9–10, from which this transcription is taken.

2. Designed by Henry Evelyn Pierrepont (1808–1888) and David B. Douglass (1790–1849), Greenwood Cemetery was consecrated in 1838 and represented one of the earliest examples of rural cemetery architecture in the United States. Alexandra Kathryn Mosca, *Green-Wood Cemetery* (Charleston, S.C.: Arcadia Publishing, 2008), 11–12.

3. The American Institute Fair was held annually beginning in 1829 by the American Institute of New York City, "For the purpose of encouraging and promoting domestic industry in this state and the United States, in agriculture, commerce, manufactures and the arts ." *Journal of the American Institute* (New York: T. B. Wakeman, 1837), 2:83.

4. "Howbeit I believed not the words, until I came, and mine eyes had seen it: and, behold, the half was not told me: thy wisdom and prosperity exceedeth the fame which I heard." 1 Kings 10:7, KJV.

5. Consecrated in 1831, Mount Auburn Cemetery is located five miles outside of Boston. *Mount Auburn Cemetery Visitor's Reference Book* (Boston: W. H. Safford and Jas. Derby Jr., 1864), 3–4.

6. From William Wordsworth (1770–1850), "The Prelude or, Growth of a Poet's Mind; An Autobiographical Poem" (1850).

7. William Cullen Bryant (1794–1878), "Thanatopsis" (1811, 1821): "So live, that when thy summons comes to join / The innumerable caravan, that moves / To the pale realms of

shade, where each shall take His chamber in the silent halls of death . . . ."

8. From *King Lear*, Act 3, Scene 4: "Poor naked wretches, wheresoe'er you are, / That bide the pelting of this pitiless storm, / How shall your houseless heads and unfed sides, / Your loop'd and window'd raggedness, defend you / From seasons such as these?"

9. *Hamlet*, Act 3, Scene 1: "For in that sleep of death what dreams may come / When we have shuffled off this mortal coil, / Must give us pause. There's the respect / That makes calamity of so long life."

10. Job 3:17, KJV.

11. Thomas Gray (1716–1771), "Elegy Written in a Country Church-Yard" (1751).

12. Edward Young (1683–1765), "The Consolation" (1746): "Lock up thy senses;—let no passion stir;— / Wake all to reason;—let her reign alone; / Then, in thy soul's deep silence, and the depth / Of Nature's silence, midnight, thus inquire, / As I have done; and shall inquire no more."

13. Spelled "momentoes" in original.

14. Robert Blair (1699–1746), *The Grave: A Poem* (1749): "Thus at the Shut of Ev'n, the weary Bird / Leaves the wide Air, and in some lonely Brake / Cow'rs down, and dozes till the Dawn of Day, / Then claps his well-fledg'd Wings, and bears away." Blair's poem represents the popular eighteenth-century genre of cemetery writing.

For the Hempstead Inquirer, Sun-Down Papers.—[No. 1] From the Desk of a Schoolmaster[1]

Hempstead Inquirer

FEBRUARY 29, 1840

I was thinking, the other night, as I sat in mine elbow chair, of the manner in which the past few years of my life had been passed. Sedate minds, it appears to me, take a peculiar pleasure in thus casting a backward glance, and losing themselves among the mazes of old scenes and times. For there is something very delightful in using the beautiful power of memory; and accordingly it has long passed into an axiom, that the old know few occupations of the mind more agreeable than retrospection.

While I was thus engaged in my reveries, the objects present seemed to dissolve and fade away.—Yielding to the gentle influence, I felt myself carried along, as it were, like some expert swimmer, who has tired himself, and to rest his limbs, allows them to float drowsily and unresistingly on the bosom of the sunny river. Real things lost their reality.—A dusky mist spread itself before my eyes.—The Spirit of Ideals came and threw his fantastic spells over me; while Recollection advanced with a slow and ghost-like step, and twined her subtle threads around my heart. I wandered far, far away from my then and there existence.—Quickly and heavily, like waves on the shore, the years seemed to roll back: they gave to my sight scenes long since past, and faces that may never more greet my view—Forms that the coffin shrouds in its white linings; voices that once sounded joyous and light, but which will never again vibrate the air; eyes that laughed and sparkled, and hands that knew full well the grasp of friendship, appeared to my sense. Like a long forgotten dream, a day of childhood was distinct to me.—I saw every particular tree, and hill, and field, my old haunts. Then leaping off again, remembrance carried me a few years farther on the path; and I was surrounded with the intimates of more advanced youth—young companions to whom I long since gave 'good bye.' It is strange how a train of thought will carry a person onward from period to period, and from object to object, until at last the subject of his cogitations bears no affinity to what he first started from. These mental excursions resemble a bold mountaineer, who, in ascending a cliff, springs from rock to rock, and ultimately arrives at the summit, although when he gets there and looks back, it seems impossible that he could have found a path thither.—And I have sometimes amused myself with tracing the chain retrospectively, and examining each idea, as to the one before it, which it took its rise from: so I have gone on backwards to the originator of them all. What a wondrous quality is that of thought in the human mind!—It darts like lightning; and its erratic sweep takes a wider scope than the winds!

As the reveries I have been describing passed off; and as I realized the actual life around me, a saddening influence fell upon my soul. I considered with pain that the golden hours of youth were swiftly gliding; and that my cherished hopes of pleasure had never yet been attained. And shall it, said I to myself, ever continue to be thus?—Shall I become old without tasting the sweet draught of which the young may partake?—Silently and surely are the months stealing along.—A few more revolutions of old earth will find me treading the paths of advanced manhood. —This is what I dread: for I have not enjoyed my young time. I have been cheated of the bloom and nectar of life.—Lonesome and unthought of as I am, I have no one to care for, or to care for me.

In short, my dear reader, I began to feel a regular and most sentimental fit of the *hyp.*—I saw that Low Spirits, a detestable personage who very seldom invades the privacy of my domicilium, was endeavoring to scrape acquaintance with me.—I determined not to admit his familiarities; and cast my thoughts about me for a weapon to repel the attack. All at once, it struck me that it was Sunday evening, the time which has immemorially been held sacred to visits from forlorn bachelors to expecting damsels.—No sooner had this idea popped into my brain, than it was followed by another—that in our neighborhood lived pretty little Kitty Denton.—I seized my hat, and sallied forth to—to—to look at the weather. When I returned, somewhat past the witching hour of night, I was altogether rid of my melancholly.[2]

NOTES

1. This editorial also appears in Walt Whitman, *The Journalism, Volume I: 1834–1846*, part of *The Collected Writings of Walt Whitman*, ed. Herbert Bergman, Douglas A. Noverr, and Edward J. Recchia (New York: Peter Lang, 1998), 13–14, from which this transcrip-

tion is taken. Walt Whitman taught in various Long Island schools from 1836 to 1841. See Jerome Loving, *Walt Whitman: The Song of Himself* (Berkeley: University of California Press, 1999), 36–37; David Reynolds, *Walt Whitman's America: A Cultural Biography* (New York: Alfred A. Knopf, 1995), 53–80.

2. Spelling in original.

Sun-Down Papers.—[No. 7] From the Desk of a Schoolmaster[1]

Long-Island Democrat

SEPTEMBER 29, 1840

I think that if I should make pretensions to be a philosopher, and should determine to edify the world with what would add to the number of those sage and ingenious theories which do already so much abound, I would compose a wonderful and ponderous book. Therein should be treated on, the nature and peculiarities of men, the diversity of their characters, the means of improving their state, and the proper mode of governing nations; with divers other points whereon I could no doubt throw quite as much light as do many of those worthy gentlemen, who, to the delight and instruction of our citizens, occasionally treat upon these subjects in printed periodicals, in books, and in publick[2] discourses. At the same time that I would do all this, I would carefully avoid saying any thing of woman; because it behooves a modest personage like myself not to speak upon a class of beings, of whose nature, habits, notions, and ways, he has not been able to gather any knowledge, either by experience or observation.

Nobody, I hope, will accuse me of conceit in these opinions of mine own capability for doing great things. In good truth, I think the world suffers from this much-bepraised modesty. Who should be a better judge of a man's talents than the man himself? I see no reason why we should let our lights shine under bushels.[3] Yes: I *would* write a book! And who shall say that it might not be a very pretty book? Who knows but that I might do something very respectable?[4]

And one principal claim to a place among men of profound sagacity, by means of the work I allude to, would be on account of a wondrous and important discovery, a treatise upon which would fill up the principal part of my compilation. I have found out that it is a very dangerous thing to be rich. For a considerable time past this idea has been pressing upon me; and

I am now fully and unalterably convinced of its truth.[5] Some years ago, when my judgement[6] was in the bud, I thought riches were very desirable things. But I have altered my mind. Light has flowed in upon me. I am not quite so green as I was. The mists and clouds have cleared away, and I can now behold things as they really are. Do you want to know some of the causes of this change of opinion? Look yonder. See the sweat pouring down that man's face. See the wrinkles on his narrow forehead. He is a poor, miserable, rich man. He has been up since an hour before sunrise, fussing, and mussing, and toiling and wearying, as if there were no safety for his life, except in uninterrupted motion. He is worried from day to day to preserve and take care of his possessions. He keeps horses; and one of them is by him. Look at the miserable brute, (the horse, I mean.) See how his sides pant. I warrant me, the animal has no rest for the soles of his feet.

I don't know when I have been more pleased than I was the other day by an illustration which a friend of mine gave of the trouble of great wealth. Life, said he, is a long journey by steamboat, stagecoach, and railroad. We hardly get fairly and comfortably adjusted in the vehicle that carries us for the time being, when we are obliged to stop and get into another conveyance, and go a different road. We are continually on the move. We may sometimes flatter ourselves in the idea of making a comfortable stop, with time enough to eat our dinner and lounge about a little; but the bell rings, the steam puffs, the horn blows, the waiters run about half mad, every thing is hurry-scurry for a moment, and whizz! we are off again. What wise man thinks of cumbering up this journey with an immense mass of luggage? Who, that makes pretensions to common sense, will carry with him a dozen trunks, and bandboxes, hatboxes, valises, chests, umbrellas, and canes innumerable, besides two dirty shirts in the crown of his hat, and a heavy brass watch that won't keep time, in his waistcoat pocket?

This is, in all sincerity, a true picture of the case. People groan, and grieve, and work, to no other purpose than merely their own inconvenience. And when at last they arrive at the grand stopping place for their travels here, and start on that mysterious train we all go with sooner or later, they find that the Grand Engineer admits no luggage therein. There is no freight car to the Hidden Land. Money and property must be left behind. The noiseless and strange attendants gather from every passenger his ticket, and heed not whether he be dark or fair, clad in homespun or fine apparel. Happy he whose wisdom has purchased beforehand a token of his having settled satisfactorily for the journey!

1. This editorial also appears in Walt Whitman, *The Journalism, Volume I: 1834–1846*, part of *The Collected Writings of Walt Whitman*, ed. Herbert Bergman, Douglas A. Noverr, and Edward J. Recchia (New York: Peter Lang, 1998), 21–23, from which this transcription is taken.

2. Spelling in original.

3. "Neither do men light a candle, and put it under a bushel, but on a candlestick; and it giveth light unto all that are in the house." Matthew 5:15, KJV.

4. Critics have noted the significance of this plan for a "ponderous book." Gay Wilson Allen calls it "extremely ambiguous," but only "half facetious" with "more truth than [Whitman] realizes." See Gay Wilson Allen, *The Solitary Singer* (New York: New York University Press, 1955), 38; Jerome Loving, *Walt Whitman: The Song of Himself* (Berkeley: University of California Press, 1999), 48.

5. For an analysis that connects this recurring theme in Whitman's journalism to the first edition of *Leaves of Grass*, see Jason Stacy, *Walt Whitman's Multitudes: Labor Reform and Persona in Whitman's Journalism and the First* Leaves of Grass, *1840–1855* (New York: Peter Lang, 2008), 114–120.

6. Spelling in original.

Sun-Down Papers.—[No. 8] From the Desk of a Schoolmaster[1]

Long-Island Democrat
OCTOBER 20, 1840

On a pleasant, still, summer evening, I once took a walk down a lane that borders our village. The moon was shining with a luscious brightness; I gazed on the glorious evidences of divinity hanging above me, and as I gazed strange and fitful thoughts occupied my brain. I reflected on the folly and vanity of those objects with which most men occupy their lives; and the awe and dread with which they approach its close. I remembered the strife for temporary and puerile distinctions—the seeking after useless and cumbersome wealth—the yielding up the diseased mind to be a prey to constant melancholy and discontent; all which may be daily seen by those who have intercourse with the sons of men. But most of all, I thought on the troubles caused under the name of Truth and Religion—the dissensions that have arisen between those of opposing creeds—and the quarrels and bickerings that even now prevail among men upon the slightest and most trivial points of opinion in these things. While such imaginings possessed my mind, I unconsciously seated myself on a grassy bank; weariness, induced by the fatigues of the day, overpowered me; I sank into a tranquil sleep, and the spirit of dreams threw his misty veil about my soul.[2]

* * I was wandering over the earth in search of TRUTH. Cities were explored by my enterprise; and the mouldy volumes which for years had lain undisturbed, were eagerly scanned to discover the object of my labours. Among the pale and attenuated votaries of science, I mixed as with kindred spirits; and the proudest of the learned were my familiars. My piercing gaze penetrated far down into the mines of knowledge, endeavouring to reach that jewel fairer, and brighter, and more precious than earthly jewels; but in vain, for it eluded my sight. Through the crowded ranks of men who swarm in thickly peopled places, I took my way, silent and unobserved, but ever on the alert for a clue to guide me towards the attainment of that which was the hope of my soul. I entered the gorgeous temples

where pride, dressed in rich robes, preaches the doctrine of the holy and just Nazarine:[3] I waited at the courts of powerful princes, where pomp, and grandeur, and adoration combined to make a frail mortal think himself mighty: I stood in the presence of the youthful and the gay—beauty, flashing in its bloom—strength, rearing itself in pride—revellers, and dancers, and feasters. But my heart turned comfortless from them all, for it had not attained its desire, and disappointment was heavy upon it. I then travelled to distant and uncivilized regions. Far in the north, among mountains of snow and rivers of ice, I sought what alone could gratify me. I lived, too, with the rude Tartar in his tent, and installed myself in all the mysteries which are known to the Lamas of Thibet.[4] I wandered to a more southern clime, and disputed with the Brahmins, who profess to believe in a religion that has existed for more centuries than any other one has years.[5] The swarthy worshipper of fire made known to me his belief; and the devotee of the camel-driver of Mecca strived for my conversion to his faith.[6] But useless was all my toil, and valueless were all the immense stores of learning I had acquired. I was baffled in all my attempts, and only began new projects to find them meet with as little success as the former.[7]

Sick and disheartened, I retired far from the inhabited portions of earth, and lived in solitude amid a wild and mountainous country. I there spent my time in reflection, and the pursuit of various branches of learning, and lived upon the frugal produce of the neighbouring fields. I had one day travelled to some distance from my usual retreat, and kept insensibly wandering onward and onward, till I found myself suddenly brought to a stand by an immense ledge of rocks which rose almost perpendicularly in front of me, and reaching far away on each side, effectually closed up my advance. The top of this stupendous pile was hidden in the clouds; and so steep was it that it seemed impossible to ascend. I stood perplexed and wondering, incited by curiosity to explore its heights, and warned by prudence to return to my cell, when I heard a low but clear and silvery voice pronounce these words, as if from the cloud over my head:

"Mortal, thou hast now an opportunity of seeing what has been the search of thy life. From the top of the mountain which rises before thee, thou mayest behold on the opposite side the holy altar of Truth. Ascend, and refresh thine eyes with the picture of its loveliness."

Amazed and transported with this assurance, I immediately began to climb the precipice. The ascent was rugged and difficult, but perseverance and incessant vigour enabled me to surmount every bar. I succeeded in reaching the top, and threw myself, panting and covered with sweat, on the stony sand. When weariness had at length given way before the power of repose, I walked onwards over the mountain, which was composed of sterile black rocks and sand, with not a spot of verdure to relieve its gloomy appearance, and at length arrived at the brow of the precipice. On this side, the mountain appeared still more steep, and to advance to the edge was evidently attended with great danger. I did so, however, and my dazzled eyes fell on a sight more beautiful than was ever before revealed to mortals. Far below stretched a country exceeding the imagination of the seeker after pleasure, and more lovely than the dreams which benignant spirits sometimes weave around the couch of youth and innocence. The surface of the land was covered with soft grass, and with fragrant trees, and shrubs, and flowers, far fresher and fairer than those of our world. Here and there it was decked with sparkling streams of water, sweet as the tear which falls in behalf of sorrow from the eye of virtue, and fair as snow-drops in the tresses of beauty. These brooks broke occasionally into little cascades, which gushed forth joyously, and seemed to murmur their happiness in sounds of thankful gratitude to heaven.

But it was not the flowers, or the rich verdure, or the babbling waters that attracted my attention. The scene was delightfully variegated with rolls and slight elevations of land: on the highest of these I beheld a white marble base, on which were raised several columns, and over the whole was thrown a roof of the same material, presenting an edifice of singular appearance, but of the most exquisite finish. I could not at once make out its proportions, for there appeared around it something like a mist, which was the more singular, as in every other place the light was of a radiant clearness. In fact, when I first viewed the spot, though I was on the alert, this temple, if it may be so called, did not strike my eye at all; but now, by dint of the most intent gazing, I could perceive its various parts with tolerable accuracy. While I was communing with myself in what manner I should endeavour to reach the ground below, and explore the very recesses of the marble temple, the silence around me was suddenly broken, and I heard the voice which had once before addressed me at the foot of the mountain, speaking in tones which sounded like the notes of a flute breathed through groves of spicy flowers:

"Seek not, O, child of clay," it said, "to discover that which is hidden by an all seeing God, from the knowledge of mortals! Were thou to attain thy desire, thou wouldst still be impotent, for thine eyes, covered as they are with the dark web of mortality, would be unable to comprehend the awful mysteries which Nature veils from thy mind. But turn thy gaze to the left, below the hill on which the temple stands, and learn a lesson of instruction which will repay all thy fatigue."

The voice ceased, and struck with awe, I looked in the direction it had pointed out to me. I beheld a country different entirely from the one I have just described, and in almost every respect like that earth on which we live. It was not far from the temple of Truth, which could be perceived from it, but the two were divided by an impassable vacuum. Upon the small spot of ground which resembled our native planet, I beheld many people, of all classes, and nations, and tongues and dresses, constantly passing, with their attention directed toward the temple. Each one seemed to view it with the utmost care, and wish to penetrate the surrounding veil of mist that dimmed its clearness. There was one thing, however, which astonished and at first somewhat bewildered me. I observed that each one of these inquirers after Truth held in his hand an optical glass, and never gazed at the temple but through its medium. Upon observing closely, I saw that these glasses were of the most incongruous shapes and forms, and exercised singular and amazing power over the appearance of whatever was beheld through them. With some they were narrow and contracted, making the temple appear insignificant and mean. Some had them of one colour, and others of a different. Many of the glasses were of so gross a texture, that the temple was completely hid from view. Some of them distorted it into the most grotesque shapes and forms: others again would make it appear an ordinary edifice; and few were so true as to give a view of the temple nigh to its correct representation. But of whatever correctness were these glasses, each individual persisted in looking at the object of his attention through their aid. No one, or at least very few, was seen to examine the temple with the clear and undistorted organs which nature had given him: and that few, I found, were scoffed at and persecuted by all the others, who, though they differed to the utmost in their manner of viewing Truth among themselves, yet they united to a man in condemning those who endeavoured to see what little could be perceived of the temple without the false assistance of some glass or other.

I stood gazing on these things, perplexed, and hardly knowing what to think of them, when I once more heard the voice which had twice addressed me. It had lost none of its sweetness, but there was now in it an admonishing tone which sank into my soul as the rich stores of learning penetrate the open ears of attention.

"Behold!" thus it spoke, "and learn wisdom from the spectacles which have been this day unfolded to thine eyes. Thou hast gazed upon the altar of Nature; but hast seen how impossible it is to penetrate the knowledge which is stored within it. Let pride therefore depart from thy soul, and let a sense of the littleness of all earthly acquirements bow down thy head in awe before the mighty Creator of a million worlds. Thou hast seen, that whatever of the great light of Truth it has been deemed expedient to show to mortals—can be most truly and usefully contemplated by the plain eye of simplicity, unaccompanied by the clogs and notions which dim the gaze of most men—and hast with wonder seen how all will still continue to view the noblest object of desire through the distorted medium of their own prejudices and bigotry.[8] The altar of Truth is immutable, unchangeable and firm; ever the same bright emanation from God, and ever consistent with its founder. Though worlds shoot out of existence—though stars grow dim, and whole systems are blotted out of being by the hand of the mighty conqueror, Change—yet will Nature and Truth, for they two in one, stand up in everlasting youth and bloom, and power. Thou seest then, how miserable are all the creeds and doctrines prevailing among men, which profess to bring down these awful mysteries, things which they can fathom and search out. Kneel, then, oh! insect of an hour, whose very formation is subject enough for an eternity of wonder—and whose fate is wrapt in the black shroud of uncertainty—kneel on that earth which thou makest the scene of thy wretched strife after corruptible honors—of thy own little schemes for happiness—and of thy crimes and guilt—kneel, bend thy face to the sand, spread out the puny arms with which thy pride would win so much glory—and adore with a voiceless awe, that Unknown Power, the very minutest idea of whose abode and strength, and formation, and intentions, it would be more difficult for thee to comprehend, than for a stroke of thy hand to push out of their orbits the suns and systems which make the slightest evidence of his strength."

Speechless and trembling, I listened to the sounds of this awful voice. I had sunk to the earth in fear, for a strange and pervading terror had filled my frame, while the unseen spirit had given utterance to his words. But at length I arose, and endeavoured to return the gratitude of my soul for the priceless treasures which had been showered upon my mind.

* * * * * *

The agitation of my thoughts, however, broke my slumbers. I awoke and found that the moon had long raised her radiant face, and was throwing down floods of light to illuminate the earth. The cold mists of night had stiffened my limbs, and were falling heavy around on the wet grass. I slowly wended my way homeward, my soul improved in knowledge, and determined to treasure during life, the instruction I had gained from the vision of that night.

1. Transcribed from Walt Whitman, *The Journalism, Volume I: 1834–1846*, part of *The Collected Writings of Walt Whitman*, ed. Herbert Bergman, Douglas A. Noverr, and Edward J. Recchia (New York: Peter Lang, 1998), 24–27.

2. This scene presages Whitman's famous "loafe" with his soul in the poem that became "Song of Myself":

> I loafe and invite my soul,
> I lean and loafe at my ease . . . . observing a spear of summer grass.
> [. . .]
> I believe in you my soul . . . . the other I am must not abase itself to you,
> And you must not be abased to the other.
>
> Loafe with me on the grass . . . . loose the stop from your throat,
> Not words, not music or rhyme I want . . . . not custom or lecture, not even the best,
> Only the lull I like, the hum of your valved voice.

3. Spelling in original.

4. Tibet.

5. Hinduism.

6. Islam.

7. For a similar rhetorical effect of soaring through global locations, see "Salut au Monde," in Walt Whitman, *Leaves of Grass, 1860: The 150th Anniversary Facsimile Edition*, ed. Jason Stacy (Iowa City: University of Iowa Press, 2009), 243–258.

8. "Bigotry" here means an undue regard for one religion over all others.

Sun-Down Papers.—[No. 9] From the Desk of a Schoolmaster[1]

Long-Island Democrat
NOVEMBER 24, 1840

How I do love a loafer! Of all human beings, none equals your genuine, inbred, unvarying loafer. Now when I say loafer, I *mean* loafer; not a fellow who is lazy by fits and starts—who to-day will work his twelve or fourteen hours, and to-morrow doze and idle. I stand up for no such half-way business. Give me your calm, steady, philosophick[2] son of indolence; one that doesn't[3] swerve from the beaten track; a man who goes the undivided beast. To such an one will I doff my beaver.[4] No matter whether he be a street loafer or a dock loafer—whether his hat be rimless, and his boots slouched, and his coat out at the elbows: he belongs to that ancient and honourable fraternity, whom I venerate above all your upstarts, your dandies, and your political oracles.

All the old philosophers were loafers. Take Diogenes[5] for instance. He lived in a tub, and demeaned himself like a true child of the great loafer family. Or go back farther, if you like, even to the very beginning. What was Adam, I should like to know, but a loafer? Did he do any thing but loaf? Who is foolish enough to say that Adam was a working man? Who dare aver that he dealt in stocks, or was busy in the sugar line?

I hope you will not so far expose yourself as to ask, who was the founder of loafers. Know you not, ignorance, that there never was such a thing as the *origin* of loaferism? We don't acknowledge any founder. There have always been loafers, as they were in the beginning, are now, and ever shall be—having no material difference. Without any doubt, when Chaos had his acquaintance cut, and the morning stars sang together, and the little rivers danced a cotillion for pure fun—there were loafers somewhere about, enjoying the scene in all their accustomed philosophick quietude.

When I have been in a dreamy, musing mood, I have sometimes amused myself with picturing out a nation of loafers. Only think of it! an entire loafer kingdom!

How sweet it sounds! Repose—quietude,—roast duck,—loafer. Smooth and soft are the terms to our jarred tympanums.[6]

Imagine some distant isle inhabited altogether by loafers. Of course there is a good deal of sunshine, for sunshine is the loafer's natural element. All breathes peace and harmony. No hurry, or bustle, or banging, or clanging. Your ears ache no more with the din of carts; the noisy politician offends you not; no wrangling, no quarrelling, no loco focos,[7] no British whigs.[8]

Talk about your commercial countries, and your national industry, indeed! Give us the facilities of loafing, and you are welcome to all the benefits of your tariff system, your manufacturing privileges, and your cotton trade.[9] For my part, I have had serious thoughts of getting up a regular ticket for President and Congress and Governor and so on, for the loafer community in general. I think we loafers should organize. We want somebody to carry out 'our principles.' It is my impression, too, that we should poll a pretty strong vote. We number largely in the land. At all events our strength would enable us to hold the balance of power, and we should be courted and coaxed by all the rival factions. And there is no telling but what we might elect our men. Stranger things than that have come to pass.

These last hints I throw out darkly, as it were. I by no means assert that we positively *will* get up and vote for, a regular ticket to support the 'great measures of our party.'[10] I am only telling what *may* be done, in case we are provoked. Mysterious intimations have been thrown out—dark sayings uttered, by those high in society, that the grand institution of loaferism was to be abolished. People have talked of us sneeringly and frowningly. Cold eyes have been turned upon us. Overbearing men have spoken in derogatory terms about our rights and our dignity. You had better be careful, gentlemen. You had better look out how you irritate us. It would make you look sneaking enough, if we were to come out at the next election, and carry away the palm before both your political parties.[11]

NOTES

1. This editorial also appears in Walt Whitman, *The Journalism, Volume I: 1834–1846*, part of *The Collected Writings of Walt Whitman*, ed. Herbert Bergman, Douglas A. Noverr, and Edward J. Recchia (New York: Peter Lang, 1998), 27–29, from which this transcription is taken.

2. Spelling in original.

3. Original reads "does n't"

4. Or tip his hat. In an image from the 1840s or early 1850s, Whitman wears a wide-brimmed, medium-crowned hat that resembles the famous woodcut in the frontispiece of the 1855 edition of *Leaves of Grass*. See "Pictures and Sound," whitmanarchive.org.

5. Diogenes of Sinope (412–323 BCE) is credited with being the founder of the Cynic school of philosophy.

6. Eardrum.

7. Loco Focos (or Locofocos) were a faction of the Democratic Party aligned against Tammany Hall Democrats, who dominated city hall into the late nineteenth century. First led by William Leggett (1801–1839), Locofocos sought an end of monopolies in the name of free trade and artisan economic rights. Locofocoism was largely incorporated into the mainstream Democratic Party by the early 1840s, though the working-class, anti-Tammany strain continued to reverberate politically in Democratic politics throughout the 1840s and 1850s in New York with the rise of nativist (anti-immigrant) and free-soil (anti-expansion of slavery) factions within the party. Whitman sympathized with Locofoco ideology throughout his life, especially its egalitarian ethos and advocacy of free trade, and he was identified by the *Long-Island Farmer* in 1839 as a "leading Loco Foco." *Long-Island Farmer*, June 19, 1839, fultonhistory.com. A "locofoco" was an early form of match.

8. While Whitman calls these Whigs "British," who were advocates for the constitutional constraints on the power of the Crown, he could also be referring to the American Whig Party, which rivaled Jacksonian Democrats for power throughout the 1840s and 1850s and had the reputation of representing wealth.

9. Here Whitman refers to the overriding political arguments of the day—the tariff, the advent of the manufacturing sector in the North, and the expansion of the cotton system throughout the South.

10. Whitman's disdain for politicking here is a bit misleading, since he played an active role in promoting Democrats in the local elections of 1840 only a few weeks earlier, and had openly campaigned for Martin Van Buren for president. In fact, it appears from a "card" published on October 6, 1840, in the *Long-Island Democrat* that Whitman engaged in a heated public debate with a local Whig and was threatened with "severe and deserved chastisement" by local residents for his rhetorical vehemence. See Walt Whitman, *The Journalism, Volume I: 1834–1846*, part of *The Collected Writings of Walt Whitman*, ed. Herbert Bergman, Douglas A. Noverr, and Edward J. Recchia (New York: Peter Lang, 1998), 23.

11. It is difficult to know here to which two parties Whitman is referring. At the beginning of the editorial, he contrasts the Locofocos (toward whom he was sympathetic) with the "British" Whigs. However, at the end of the article he warns both parties. One side was probably made up of those who supported the American Whig Party in the recent election. The other side could be mainstream Democrats who supported Van Buren. Whatever the case, as a native of New York City and Brooklyn, Whitman would have been something of an interloper in the political affairs of the rural Long Islanders among whom he lived in the summer and fall of 1840.

For the Long Island Farmer, Sun-Down Papers.— [No. 10] From the Desk of a Schoolmaster[1]

Long-Island Farmer and Queens County Advertiser

JULY 20, 1841

We had all made up our minds to take a jaunt in the south bay; and accordingly at the appointed morning, about sunrise might have been seen wending their way toward the place of rendezvous, the various members of our party. There were Bromero, with his clam-rake, and narrow-brimmed straw hat; Senor Cabinet, with sedate face, and an enormous basket, containing a towel, fishing tackle, and incalculable quantities of provisions; Captain Sears with his usual pleasant look; one of the Smith family with a never failing fund of good humor; Kirbus, with his gun, breathing destruction to snipe, and sea-fowl generally; and other personages whose number will prevent their being immortalized in this veracious history.[2]

Having first stowed our persons away in the wagons provided for that purpose, we started for the shore, fifteen precious souls in all; not forgetting to place in safe situations, various baskets, kettles, jugs, bottles, and nondescript vessels, of whose contents we knew not as yet. We hoisted the American flag on a clam-rake handle, and elevated it in the air, very much to our own pleasure, and the edification no doubt of all patriotic beholders. Thus riding along it was discovered by an inquisitive member of our party, that one of us, a married man, had come from home without his breakfast; whereupon an inquiry was instituted that resulted in bringing out the astounding fact that every married man in the company was in the like predicament. An evil-disposed character among us was ungallant enough to say, that the fact was a fair commentary on matrimonial comfort.

When we arrived at the point of embarkation, we found a tight clean boat, all ready for us, with Sailor Bright to superintend the navigation of the same.—Having snugly ensconced ourselves therein, by no means forgetting the baskets, jugs, &c., afore-mentioned, we boldly put forth into the stream, and committed our lives to the mercy of the wind and waves. We reached the mouth of the creek, with no adventure of any importance, except that Kirbus came very near getting a wild duck who was seen foraging on the waves not far from us; it would have been very easy to have got him, if Kirbus had shot him. I had like to have forgot mentioning that Senor Cabinet got the tail of his black coat quite wet by dragging it in the salt water, as he was seated on the gunwale of the boat.

We had brought a musical instrument with us, and accordingly in due time we proceeded to give some very scientific specimens of the concord of sweet sounds. The popular melodies of 'Auld Lang Syne,' and 'Home, sweet Home,' were sung with great taste and effect.—Thus the time passed away very pleasantly until we arrived at the beach; when some of us dashing boldly through the water to dry land—and the more effeminate being carried thither on the back of Sailor Bright, we started forth to visit the other side, whereon the surf comes tumbling, like lots of little white pigs playing upon clean straw. Before we went thither, however, I must not forget to record that we were entertained with some highly exquisite specimens of Shakespearian eloquence by one of our company, formerly a member of the "Spouting Club"; and, therefore, entitled to be called a *whaler.*

Having arrived at the surf, a portion of our party indulged themselves in the luxury of a bathe therein.[3] The rest returned to the boat, and forthwith each arming himself with a clam-rake, did valourously set to work a-scratching up the sand at no small rate. After a while, the individual, before spoken of, as belonging to the Smith family, not feeling contented with his luck where he was, did, in company with another discontented personage, betake himself off in the little skiff, which had accompanied our larger vessel. He rowed most manfully, for half a mile, to a place where he thought he could better himself. By dint of pulling and hauling there nearly an hour, he managed to catch one clam, and then was contented to return from whence he came. Thus was exemplified in the fortunes of this Smith individual, the truth of the old maxim: "Let well enough alone."[4]

But my limits will not allow me to expatiate upon the events of this interesting voyage. I shall therefore not say a word about the astonishing appetite of Senor Cabinet; or the fun we had in Bromero's laughable stories; or how a hat belonging to one of our chaps, blew off into the wide waters, and was recovered again by the Smith individual, but with the loss of a short necked pipe, which had for many days before been safely kept therein. Nor shall I tell how we cut up divers clams into small bits, and thrust the said bits upon fish-hooks, and let down the said hooks by long lines into the water, and then sat patiently holding the lines, in the vain hope of nabbing some stray members of the finny tribe.

Passing over all these, and other like important matters, I shall wind up this most accurate account by saying, that we returned home perfectly safe in body, sound in limb, much refreshed in soul, and in perfect good humour and satisfaction one with another.

P. S.—I came very near forgetting to say, that some of us had our faces highly improved in colour, and that Kirbus, and others of the married men, after we came ashore, bought several shillings' worth of eels and clams, probably in order to ward off the danger that would inevitably have followed their return empty-handed.

NOTES

1. Transcribed from scanned original at fultonhistory.com. This editorial also appears in Walt Whitman, *The Journalism, Volume I: 1834–1846*, part of *The Collected Writings of Walt Whitman*, ed. Herbert Bergman, Douglas A. Noverr, and Edward J. Recchia (New York: Peter Lang, 1998), 31–32. Following Bergman's lead, the roman numeral "X" in this editorial has been changed to the Arabic "10" to match the other editorials in this series. Also, the original version of this editorial hyphenates "School-master," whereas, according to Bergman, the other Sun-Down Papers do not. For the sake of uniformity and following Bergman, "Schoolmaster" has not been hyphenated in this transcription.

2. While many of these names appear to have had some significance, probably for humorous effect, the editors have been unable to locate their origins or meaning.

3. From *Leaves of Grass* (1855): "Twenty-eight young men bathe by the shore, / Twenty-eight young men, and all so friendly, [. . .] The beards of the young men glistened with wet, it ran from their long hair, / Little streams passed all over their bodies."

4. This could be a subtle political reference in support of free trade and low tariffs, since "Let well enough alone" appears to have been something of a slogan of the Locofocos, the faction of the New York Democratic Party that supported free trade and an egalitarian ethos. An editorial in the *Long-Island Farmer* against Locofocoism called "Let well enough alone" a "detestable sentiment." *Long-Island Farmer*, June 19, 1839, fultonhistory.com.

Life in New York[1]

New York Aurora

MARCH 14, 1842

Whoever does not know that "our city" is the great place of the western continent, the heart, the brain, the focus, the main spring, the pinnacle, the extremity, the no more beyond, of the New World—whoever does not know this, we say, must have been brought up in a place where they "didn't take the papers," and where the Aurora, in particular, had never scattered its effulgent light.

The two great channels of communication through the city, are Broadway, and Chatham street, of which the Bowery is nothing more than a continuation. At a little before sunrise, if you are an early riser, you may behold a slight human stream, beginning to set down Broadway. The milkmen's carts, and occasionally a carriage from one of the landings where steamboats arrive early in the morning, dash hastily along the street. The pedestrians are nearly all workmen, going to their daily toil, and most of them carrying little tin kettles containing their dinner; newsmen, also, with bundles of damp morning papers strapped to their sides; people now and then, of a more fashionable appearance, who have wisely roused themselves from torpid slumber, and come forth to snuff the morning air. Frequently, too, you may meet a sleepy looking boy, neatly dressed, and swinging a large brass key as he goes along. He is an under clerk in some store, and on his way to open the establishment, sweep it out, and, if need may be, kindle the fire. Be careful, as you pass, lest you get a sousing from some of those Irish servant women, scrubbing the marble stoops, and dashing pails of water upon the flagging of the side walks.

As the sun mounts the horizon, the scene assumes another and a far different aspect. Gradually the working-day appearance of Broadway is changed, and the patricians of our great metropolis take possession in force. On the sunny side as the noon draws on, beautiful women and good looking men, occasionally interspersed with an overdressed dandy, meet the eye. It may well be said, indeed, that in America there is only *the* Broadway.

If you have travelled over the world, you will hardly remember a livelier or more brilliant and dashy scene, than the pave presents in Broadway from two till four o'clock in the afternoon of a pleasant day.

At sunset, the direction of the current is contrary to what it was in the morning—setting upward, that is, from the Bowling Green to Union Park. The same people who went down in the[2] morning now return, carrying with them the same little tin kettles. But the crowd is at this time so much greater that the infusion of the homeward bound working men is but as a drop in the bucket.

NOTES

1. Transcribed from scanned original at the Walt Whitman Archive, whitmanarchive.org. This editorial also appears in Walt Whitman, *The Journalism, Volume I: 1834–1846*, part of *The Collected Writings of Walt Whitman*, ed. Herbert Bergman, Douglas A. Noverr, and Edward J. Recchia (New York: Peter Lang, 1998), 53–54.

2. Original reads "th*" with the letter "e" inverted.

Life in a New York Market[1]

New York Aurora
MARCH 16, 1842

One Saturday night, not long since, a fantasy popped into our brain that we would like to take a stroll of observation through a *market*. Accordingly, sallying forth, we proceeded to put our wishes into execution. A short distance brought us to that large, dirty looking structure situated in Grand street, where much store of meats, vegetables, et cetera, is daily dispensed to the sojourners of that section of our city.

We entered. What an array of rich, red sirloins, luscious steaks, delicate and tender joints, muttons, livers, and all the long list of various flesh stuffs, burst upon our eyes! There they hung, tempting, seductive—capable of begetting ecstacies[2] in the mouth of an epicure—or curses in the throat of a Grahamite.[3] By the powers of cookery! the condition of the republic is not so grievous after all; we cannot be on the verge of despair, when such spectacles as these may be witnessed in the land![4]

How the crowd rolls along! There comes a journeyman mason (we know him by his *limy*[5] dress) and his wife—she bearing a little white basket on her arm. With what an independent air the mason looks around upon the fleshly wares; the secret of the matter is, that he has his past week's wages in his pocket, and therefore puts he on the devil-may-care countenance. So marvellous[6] an influence hath money in making a man feel valiant and as good as his neighbor.

Notice that prim, red cheeked damsel, for whom is being weighed a small pork steak. She is maid of all work to an elderly couple, who have sent her to purvey for their morrow's dinner. How the young fellow who serves her, at the same time casts saucy, loveable glances at her pretty face; and she is nothing loth, but pleased enough at the chance of a little coquetry. Cunning minx! she but carries out the foible of her sex, and apes her superiors.

With slow and languid steps moves along a white faced, thin bodied, sickly looking, middle aged man. He is dressed in a shabby suit, and no doubt will look long and watchfully before he spends the two ten cent pieces to which his outlay is limited. Poor fellow! he is evidently a member of one of those trades which require a man to stay cooped up in the house in some constrained bodily position. The healthy air, and the pleasant sunshine, and the delicious influences of the outer world, have not been showered upon him; and here he is, fast sinking into the grave. What a mockery of the benefits of civilization!

That fat, jolly featured woman, is the keeper of a boarding house for mechanics, and every one else who chooses to take up with good solid accommodations, for a moderate price. She is foraging for her Sunday dinner. What is it to be? She has piece after piece taken down from its hook, but none seem to suit her. She passes on.

A heterogeneous mass, indeed, are they who compose the bustling crowd that fills up the passage way. Widows with sons, boys of twelve or fourteen, to walk with them for company; wives, whose husbands are left at home to "take care of the children;"[7] servant women; cooks; old maids (these are the especial horror of every salesman in the market;) careful housewives of grades high and low; men with the look of a foreign clime; all sorts and sizes, kinds, ages, and descriptions, all wending, and pricing, and examining, and purchasing.

But those butchers! what jovial dogs they are! Notice with what easy impudence they accost every passer by, and how they swear by all that's sacred, that on *their* stall may be found exactly what the said passer by desires to purchase. With sleeves rolled up, and one corner of their white apron tucked under the waist string—to whoever casts an enquiring glance at their stand, they gesticulate with the grace, the affected bendings and twistings of a French dancing master. Neither does rebuff discourage them. With amusing perseverance they play off on every new passenger the same lures and the same artifice that have been tried and failed in so many previous cases. And then when they have nothing else to do, they amuse themselves with a jig, or a break down.[8] The capacities of the "market roarers" in all the mystery of a double shuffle, it needs not our word to endorse. And the whistling—the butcher boy's whistling!—whose ear has not drank in the full, rich melody thereof?

Perhaps, search the whole land through, you will not find a handsomer, more manly looking set of men than our butchers. They may be known by their clear complexions, healthy look, bright eyes—and by their saucy good nature, their bull dog courage, their impudent wit, their hankering for a frequent "muss," and their disposition to rows and fights generally.

Walking along to another section of the place—we are in the region of vegetable stands, huckster women, and poultry sellers. Near by, is a coffee and cake stall.

Every now and then a hungry boy, or a man whose pressure of business has caused him to go without his supper, or some one else, tempted by the savory fumes of the coffee and the rich "kraulers,"[9] seats himself or herself, and commences murderous attacks upon the good things of the fair maid officiating behind the counter. Within three yards, notice those two urchins eyeing the "kraulers" with envious eyes; let us open the flood gates of our charity, and give the youngsters a half dime, that they may revel in the tit bits that have evidently so taken their fancy. There! the fashionable may laugh our notions to scorn—but we feel more satisfaction from having bestowed on those awkward boys a ten minutes' joy, than if we had received sunny greetings from the proudest belle in Broadway, or heard that "our party" had gained the gubernatorial contest.

Such are some of the scenes of "life in a New York market."[10] It would be no loss for a man who loves to see the workings of human nature—the uncouth, natural outpourings of the feelings of the heart—to take a stroll, now and then, in the mazes of these miniature worlds. Lessons may be learnt there, and pictures of life seen there, which the gilded halls of rank, and the refined circles of the ton, with all their boasted privileges, cannot confer.

NOTES

1. Transcribed from scanned original at the Walt Whitman Archive, whitmanarchive.org. This editorial also appears in Walt Whitman, *The Journalism, Volume I: 1834–1846*, part of *The Collected Writings of Walt Whitman*, ed. Herbert Bergman, Douglas A. Noverr, and Edward J. Recchia (New York: Peter Lang, 1998), 55–57.

2. Spelling in original.

3. A reference to Sylvester Graham (1794–1851), who promoted health and morality through vegetarianism and sexual self-control.

4. Whitman could be referring to the lingering effects of the Panic of 1837 here, which most historians claim ended only in the mid-1840s. See Alasdair Roberts, *America's First Great Depression: Economic Crisis and Political Disorder After the Panic of 1837* (Ithaca, N.Y.: Cornell University Press, 2012).

5. As a mason, he would be covered in the residue of limestone.

6. Spelling in original.

7. The quotes in this statement could imply that the husband is out of work. A contemporary source relates the story of an unemployed artisan whose wife goes into the factory to work for inferior wages and "[t]he husband is left to take care of the children and of the domestic concerns. He chafes at the wrong done to himself and to his wife—feels himself degraded by her being subjected to a masculine and himself to a feminine employment—

with the idle husbands around him he becomes a frequenter of the public house." E. W. Chester, "The Wrongs of Woman," *Christian Parlor Magazine*, May 1844, 11.

8. "The butcher-boy puts off his killing-clothes, or sharpens his knife at the stall in the market, / I loiter enjoying his repartee and his shuffle and breakdown." *Leaves of Grass* (1855), 20, Walt Whitman Archive, whitmanarchive.org.

9. Or crueller, a glazed, textured doughnut.

10. Original does not close quotation marks.

An Hour in a Balcony[1]

New York Aurora

MARCH 23, 1842

Though during yesterday and the preceding night our city had a short touch of the quality of winter—every man, woman, and child in New York must recollect that for several days previous the weather was of the mildest, most summerlike description. On an afternoon of one of these pleasant days, as we sauntered out of the west gate of the Park, feeling in an observative mood, we recollected an old custom of ours, long since disused—we went up the stairs of the American Museum,[2] entered the first room, took a chair, placed it in a roomy niche made by the setting in of one of the front windows—and in that chair ensconced we ourself. Out before us was the busiest spectacle this busy city can present. One mighty rush of men, business, carts, carriages, and clang.[3]

How true it is, what travellers say about our population always being in a hurry. With what restless and feverish steps they move along! It seems as though each knew his appointed time, and was determined to make the most of it. Let us pass a few remarks upon the scenes and the people that may be beheld from that balcony window.

The noisiest things which attract attention in that part of Broadway, are the omnibusses.[4] Rumbling and bouncing along, they come, now and then stopping as some person on the sidewalk holds up his finger—a signal that he wants to take passage.[5] The omnibus drivers are a unique race. Winter and summer, rain or shine, there they are, perched up on the tops of their vehicles, and driving ahead just the same. What a life! over the same track, and along the same street, hour after hour, and day after day. Moving and changing as is the scene, can it be otherwise than monotonous to them?[6]

A group of fashionable ladies next attracts our eyes. What splendid creatures they are—even amid the tinsel and distortion of milliners and dress makers. After all, say what poets and rural lovers may—there is something about a polished, splendidly dressed, graceful and dashy city lady, that eclipses all else of the sex![7] There; we have come to a conclusion on that point.

Notice those carriages, with liveried servants. Such sights are particularly pleasing to plain republican eyes. In this imitative style, the gentleman rolls along Broadway, pompous as a militia colonel on review day—no matter if his hands be a little soiled by the measuring of broadcloth, or his clothing still retain the scent of the sugar box, the tobacco keg, the rappee pot,[8] rum cask, or even, what is worse than all, the scent of Wall street verdigris—no matter, we say; for the glory of the style aristocratic so mystifies the senses of the democratic plodders on the way side, that they can only wonder and adore.

But what objection can there be to this kind of "showing off?" Not the slightest. It indicates a great mind, a laudable ambition, an ambition to make a show in the world—and though it is merely a puppet show, it is the sort most pleasing to children and fools; and such people are the only ones whom men of sense should attempt to interest or improve. Sir Isaac Newton had not half the judgment that the countryman had who continually rang a hand bell as he passed in the streets, saying that he was determined to make some noise in the world. These worthies possess just as much sense as the countryman, only they do not show it in quite so harmless a way.[9]

And we further contend that our Broadway aristocrats do good in the community. Laughing is an agreeable and healthy exercise.

But it is no joke, after all. These gentry discover their consummate folly in this sort of aping of the customs of Europe. We have no aristocracy in this country; but these poor, deluded people think that by wrapping themselves in the cloak of the true aristocrat they will be able to pass for genuine. They should remember the ass in the lion's skin.[10] Where are their manors, their long lines of "illustrious predecessors," their identity with the government itself, their rights, titles and treasures which the wind of popular caprice cannot waft to the hand of another?

But our republican aristocrats! Who are they? They are those whose brains would be more likely to breed grasshoppers than ideas—whose pedigrees should be sought for in the tinker's shop. But it may be asked, do they not do good, by scattering thus broadcast, the money which, in early life, they wrought hard and lived frugally to amass? No. A good many worthy arguers have split upon this rock. The lavish expenditure of money is not doing good unless it be spent for proper objects.

As our cogitations have already extended to a "pretty considerable" length, we shall give the remainder of them at some future time.

NOTES

1. Transcribed from scanned original at the Walt Whitman Archive, whitmanarchive.org. This editorial also appears in Walt Whitman, *The Journalism, Volume I: 1834–1846*, part of *The Collected Writings of Walt Whitman*, ed. Herbert Bergman, Douglas A. Noverr, and Edward J. Recchia (New York: Peter Lang, 1998), 66–67.

2. P. T. Barnum's American Museum, on Broadway and Ann Streets, existed between 1841 and 1865. See Edwin Burrows and Mike Wallace, *Gotham: A History of New York City to 1898* (Oxford: Oxford University Press, 1999), 644.

3. "The blab of the pave . . . the tires of carts and sluff of bootsoles and talk of the promenaders." *Leaves of Grass* (1855), 18, Walt Whitman Archive, whitmanarchive.org.

4. Spelling in original.

5. "The heavy omnibus, the driver with his interrogating thumb." *Leaves of Grass* (1855), 18, Walt Whitman Archive, whitmanarchive.org.

6. From *Specimen Days* (1892): "Yes, I knew all the drivers then, Broadway Jack, Dressmaker, Balky Bill, George Storms, Old Elephant, his brother Young Elephant (who came afterward,) Tippy, Pop Rice, Big Frank, Yellow Joe, Pete Callahan, Patsy Dee, and dozens more; for there were hundreds. They had immense qualities, largely animal—eating, drinking, women—great personal pride, in their way—perhaps a few slouches here and there, but I should have trusted the general run of them, in their simple good-will and honor, under all circumstances."

7. "I saw the rich ladies in full dress at the soiree, / I heard what the run of poets were saying so long." *Leaves of Grass* (1855), 85, Walt Whitman Archive, whitmanarchive.org.

8. Tobacco snuff.

9. Whitman expressed similar anticonsumerist sentiments in "Sun-Down Papers.—[No. 7] From the Desk of a Schoolmaster," *Long-Island Democrat*, September 29, 1840 (above).

10. From Aesop's fables.

A Peep at the Israelites[1]

New York Aurora
MARCH 28, 1842

For the first time in our life, we went on Saturday morning last, to spend an hour in a Jewish synagogue. Accompanied by a friend, and starting at 10 o'clock, we wended our way through Centre street, and thence into Crosby, in which, a block or two above Grand, we found the place of our destination.[2] The front to the street was bordered by a high fence, with banister work on the top. Passing through a gate, and down two or three rods[3] by the side of the building, we went up the steps of a porch in the rear, where we found the entrance.

Fearful lest we should go somewhere or do something that might be totally malapropos, we waited a few moments, until, seeing a gentleman enter, we followed him through a side door into the main body of the house. There, we were politely ushered to a convenient seat, from whence we had a fair view of all the performances.

The whole scene was entirely new; never had we beheld any thing of a similar description before. The congregation (we don't know what other word to use) were all standing, each one with his hat on. A white silken mantle, somewhat like a scarf, was worn by every person; it encircled the neck, falling down the back, and the ends in front reaching to the floor. In the middle of the room was a raised platform about four yards square, with a heavy balustrade of bronze work and mahogany around it. Upon the centre of this platform was a figure which, by the voice coming from it, we knew to be a man. None of the lineaments of the human form, however, were visible; for one of the large silk mantles alluded to was thrown over his head, and completely shrouded him. He was speaking; but as his language was Hebrew, we could not understand a word he uttered.

At the further end of the room stood an erection very much resembling the front that pictures give the ancient Parthenon. Under it was a semi circular partitioned enclosure, of panelled wood, which from the ornaments and expensive tracery lavished upon the whole affair, seemed intended to contain something either very valuable, or very sacred. Upon the platform which made part of this structure, there was another figure standing, half shrouded in a white mantle, like the personage before described. He was also speaking.

And there we were amid the Jews worshipping in their temple. The people of Solomon and Saul, of Ruth and Mary Magdalene, of the traitor Judas, and John, the beloved of the Son of God—the people of the very Christ himself—these were they who stood around. And they were speaking in the same tones as those which at night bade the shepherds to follow the guidance of the star in the east—the same tones which Jonathan and Saul used in their beautiful friendship—which sounded out from the plaintive Hagar in the wilderness—through which Absalom, "that too beauteous boy,"[4] made rebellion against his father—with which the widow's son, who was dead, and brought to life again, gladdened his desolate mother's heart;—the tones and the native language of the holy Psalmist, the lovely Rebecca of Scott, and the Malignant Shylock of Shakespeare.[5]

And here was a remnant of the mighty nation, who routed the warlike dwellers in Canaan, and who received the Law from the great I Am upon the mountain of clouds;—their ancient pride swept to the winds—their name a jeering and mark for contempt—their might humbled, their old homes taken by the hand of the spoiler, and clouds and dark frowns for ages spread around them;—yet here, scoffed, scouted, and scorned, they came, to worship their God after the manner of their ancestors.

The heart within us felt awed as in the presence of memorials from an age that had passed away centuries and centuries ago. The strange and discordant tongue—the mystery, and all the associations that crowded themselves in troops upon our mind—made a thrilling sensation to creep through every nerve. It was indeed a sight well calculated to impress the mind with an unwonted tone.

As our account has already stretched to the limits beyond which it is not judicious to go in a paper like ours, we shall give the remainder of what we saw during our stay at the synagogue, in the Aurora of tomorrow.

NOTES

1. Transcribed from scanned original at the Walt Whitman Archive, whitmanarchive.org. This editorial also appears in Walt Whitman, *The Journalism, Volume I: 1834–1846*, part of *The Collected Writings of Walt Whitman*, ed. Herbert Bergman, Douglas A. Noverr, and Edward J. Recchia (New York: Peter Lang, 1998), 76–77.

2. Probably the temple of Shearith Israel, built in 1833. Founded in 1654, Shearith Israel was the first Jewish congregation in North America. Its founders were Sephardi Jews originally from Spain and Portugal who emigrated from Brazil when the Portuguese conquered the Dutch settlement at Recife and instituted the policies of the Inquisition. Today, Congregation Shearith Israel is located at 8 W. 70th Street in New York City. shearithisrael.org.

3. About 50 feet (1 rod = 16.5 feet).

4. Ben Johnson, *Cynthia's Revels, or The Fountain of Self-Love* (1600), in *The Works of Ben Johnson: With Notes Critical and Explanatory and a Biographical Memoir* (London: Bickers and Son, 1875), 2:221

5. "Shakspeare" in original.

Untitled[1]

New York Aurora

APRIL 6, 1842

Reader, we fear you have, by way of novelty, a *poor* Aurora this morning. We felt dull and inactive all yesterday, "pottered" as Fanny Kemble[2] would express it, during the earlier hours of the day; and after dinner, (we dine at 2) and chatting fifteen minutes, (for the benefit of digestion) we came round to our accustomed editorial nook, and took up the pen, intending to dash into Bishop Hughes,[3] Webster,[4] or Justice Matsell,[5] and knock those worthies into a disarranged chapeau.[6] But it was no go! We had the pleasant influences of a good dinner moving our breast to love everything, and be indulgent toward every body, (O! Mrs. C. you little know what power you and the cook down below have upon the popular pulse, as said pulse is acted on through Aurora!)[7] and so we repented us, and politely desisted from our pugnacious intentions.

Then, finding it impossible to do any thing either in the way of "heavy business," or humor, we took our cane, (a heavy, dark, beautifully polished, hook ended one) and our hat (a plain, neat, fashionable one, from Banta's, 130 Chatham street, which we got gratis, on the strength of giving him this puff,) and sauntered forth to have a stroll down Broadway to the Battery. Strangely enough, nobody stared at us with admiration—nobody said "there goes *the* Whitman, of Aurora!"—nobody ran after us to take a better, and a second better look—no ladies turned their beautiful necks and smiled at us—no apple women became pale with awe—no news boys stopped, and trembled, and took off their hats, and cried "behold the man what uses up the great Bamboozle!"[8]—no person wheeled out of our path deferentially—but on we went, swinging our stick, (the before mentioned dark and polished one,) in our right hand—and with our left hand tastily thrust in its appropriate pocket, in our frock coat, (a grey one.)

Well, (are you interested, dear reader?) in due time we arrived at the ponderous iron gates which give ingress to the Battery. We entered. We strolled along—casting a side glance now and then at the beautiful green that was just "being put on" by the grass—and arrived, after a while, at the south extreme of Gotham's glorious promenade. Then we turned. We walked slowly and lazily back, enjoying the fresh air, and the delicious sunshine, and the intoxicating sweetness of the beauty of nature that appeared all around.

A number of children were at play—some kind of a game which required that they should take each others' hands and spread themselves so as to make a large ring. When we came up, they were just in the crisis of their game, and occupying clear across the walk.

"Ah!" said one, with a peevish air, to a companion, "we shall have to break the line. There comes a gentleman."

The boy spoken to was a fine, handsome fellow, of twelve or thirteen years. He turned and looked at us for a moment; then the expression changed, and his face greeted ours with an arch confiding smile, as much as to say "I know, my dear sir, you are too good natured to disturb us, merely to save the trouble of turning out a step!" It is needless to add, we *did* turn out. What wonderful powers children have of discriminating who is possessed of a courteous, kindly, manful and creditable disposition!

Then we came up, and out, and along Broadway, to whence we started. And for the next two or three hours, we possess no recollection of having done any thing in particular. And at half past 8, P. M. (fifteen minutes before this present writing) the chilling consciousness came over us that we hadn't written any thing for a leader.[9] And so, we concocted the foregoing (what were you about, at half past 8, last night, dear reader?)

And all we have to add is, that if you read it over a second time you will find more meaning in it, by far, than you might at first imagine.

NOTES

1. Transcribed from scanned original at the Walt Whitman Archive, whitmanarchive.org. This editorial also appears in Walt Whitman, *The Journalism, Volume I: 1834–1846*, part of *The Collected Writings of Walt Whitman*, ed. Herbert Bergman, Douglas A. Noverr, and Edward J. Recchia (New York: Peter Lang, 1998), 99–100.

2. Frances Anne Kemble (1809–1893) was a British actress who temporarily left the stage in 1834 upon marrying Pierce Butler, a South Carolinian cotton and rice planter. Throughout her *Journal of a Residence in America* (1836), Kemble used the term "pottered" to mean undertaking small and unorganized activities: "They talked politics, abused republicanism, lauded aristocracy, drank tea, took snuff, ate cakes, and pottered a great deal."

"After dinner, [I] pottered about, and dressed at once." "When I came down, found—in the drawing-room with my father: paid him my bill, and pottered an immensity." Fanny Kemble, *Journal of a Residence in America* (Paris: A. and W. Galinani, 1835), 126, 159, 206. This term for a time was infamously Kemble's. A reviewer of her *Journal* wrote, "How revolting must be that language which even Miss Kemble calls inelegant and unrefined. Among beauties of her style we find, 'I dawdled about most dreadfully.' 'I pottered an immensity.'" *Religious Magazine* 2, no. 9 (June 1835), 417. "Or all the modern writers of German opera who have plodded and 'pottered an immensity' (to quote Mrs. Fanny Kemble's quaint phrase), among the Lindpaintners and the Lachners, and the contrivers and the combiners, Weber stands out as *the one* man." *All Year Rounder*, no. 3326 (July 22, 1865), 610.

3. Bishop John Hughes (1797–1864) represented Irish Catholics in New York in the pursuit of public funding for parochial schools through the Maclay Bill. See "Americanism" and "Organs of the Democracy," *New York Aurora*, March 23 and 29, 1842 (above).

4. Daniel Webster (1782–1852) was a prominent Whig politician whose politics were opposed to those of the Democratic *Aurora*.

5. George Washington Matsell (1811–1877), who organized night patrols in New York City to bolster the outdated system of night watchmen. These patrols became the inspiration for the activities of the New York police force, created by the Municipal Police Act (1844). Matsell later served as chief of police.

6. French for "hat." A "disarranged chapeau" means to knock someone off balance or to knock them flat.

7. Probably a reference to the "Mrs. C—" in Whitman's *Aurora* editorial "New York Boarding Houses" of March 18, 1842, where he refers to her as the "proprietor" whose name was "displayed on the door" of the house, signifying one of the "better houses." In *Walt Whitman: The Song of Himself*, Loving notes that this was "Mrs. Chipman at the corner of Chambers and Center, in the northwest shadow of City Hall" (61).

8. Whitman exposed a plagiarized text in the *New World* on March 28, a scandal that he referred to as "The Great Bamboozle." See Whitman, *The Journalism, Vol. I*, 77.

9. In the *Aurora* the "leader" appeared in the first column on page 2.

Life and Love[1]

New York Aurora

APRIL 20, 1842

Damps and chills continued—would have been a very good motto for yesterday. Five minutes to one P. M. we stood at the window, drumming idly on the pane with our fingers, and gazing at the magnificent prospect outside. Drizzle, drizzle, drizzle—drop, drop, drop—hour after hour, and no cessation. The omnibusses[2] roll along, dragged by their melancholy horses; shivering pedestrians pass with a kind of dog trot on the side walks; and the old apple woman who generally occupies the corner over the way, is no where to be seen.

What a variety of umbrellas!

After gazing at the scene, and making divers philosophic speculations upon matters and things in general, we determined to perpetrate a few paragraphs of sentiment. Reader, get a fresh handkerchief.

Life and love! The words are certainly short, and make no great show in print; yet has each, in its four little letters, a mighty volume of mystery, and beauty. Were we disposed to be fanciful, we might divide the body's life from the mind's life, and compare them together. The first, men share equally with irrational animals.

But the soul's life! The soul—so grand and noble in its capacities, so thirsty for knowledge, so filled with the germs of illimitable progress—the soul, that has such awful powers, is endued with such quickness, such judgment, such ability of thinking strange and unearthly thoughts, such a desire of assimilating itself to perfection and godlike purity, such insatiable anxiousness to discover hidden things, such unfathomable good will for its fellows, such undying faith in the efficacy of truth, and such towering ambition, that it may well be lost in wonder at itself. O, what venturesome mariner shall launch forth, and explore it, and take a plummet in his hand and sound its depths?

And part of the life of the soul is *love;* for the chambers of the heart are pleasant as well as costly. Things of surpassing fairness are there—thoughts that glow and dazzle—benevolence—innocent and holy friendship. Among their windings, restless and sparkling like rays of sunshine, lurk a hundred promptings and capabilities for delight. They are planted by God—and he who would stifle them is a bigot and a fool.

Ever faithful, too, there is the monitor Conscience, sitting on her throne, with a sleepless eye, and a never tiring finger. And down, deep down, from the innermost recesses, wells up the pure fountain of affection, the sweetest and most cheering of the heart's treasures.

What a superb verse that is of Coleridge's:

"All thoughts, all passions, all delights—
 Whatever stirs this mortal frame,
Are but the ministers of *love,*
 And feed his sacred flame."[3]

So let us be more just to our own nature, and to the gifts the Almighty has made ineradicable within us. Casting our eyes over this beautiful earth, where so much of joy and sunshine exist—looking on the human race with the gentle orbs of kindness and philosophy—sending our glance through the cool and verdant lanes, by the sides of the blue rivers, over the crowded city, and among those who dwell on the prairies, or along the green savannahs of the south—and we shall see that every where are the seeds of *happiness* and *love*. Yet unless they are fostered, they will lie entombed forever in the darkness—and their possessors may die and be buried, and never think of them but as baubles and worth no care.

NOTES

1. Transcribed from scanned original at the Walt Whitman Archive, whitmanarchive.org. This editorial also appears in Walt Whitman, *The Journalism, Volume I: 1834–1846*, part of *The Collected Writings of Walt Whitman*, ed. Herbert Bergman, Douglas A. Noverr, and Edward J. Recchia (New York: Peter Lang, 1998), 132–133.

2. Spelling in original.

3. Samuel Taylor Coleridge (1772–1834), "Love." The poem was written in 1799 for William Wordsworth's future sister-in-law, Sara Hutchinson.

The Ocean[1]

New York Aurora
APRIL 21, 1842

It is not easy for a person who has resided only upon the seaboard, to conceive of the feelings which fill the bosom of one, when for the first time he comes in sight of the ocean. How many thousands pass their lives without one glimpse of that glorious "creature," which, next to the canopy above, is the most magnificent object of material creation.

Here is one who has spent the years of childhood, youth, and early manhood in the far off inland districts. The green hills, briar studded crags, and mossy battlements of rock, have echoed with the bellowing of the thunder and the mountain blast, but with the deep rolling murmur of the ocean, never. He has seen the flowers of the glen nod, and the treetops of the forest wave in the wind, and when the fury of the tempest came, the air filled with mangled branches and stripped off verdure; but never has he seen the ocean "wrought up to madness by the storm,"[2] the angry billows leaping up, and in battle array invading the province of the very clouds, or dashing in spent fury upon the trembling rocks. Calmly has he seen the moon throw down her light upon the rural bound, and all things revelling[3] in quiet beauty; but never the moonlight rocked upon the rolling deep, nor the reflected stars rising and falling there, gems upon a mighty bosom swelling with darkness and mystery. Over wide spread fields of green, dotted with copse and mansion, has his eye wandered; but never over a boundless field of brightest blue, variegated only by the sunny sail and sable hull. What, then, can we imagine to be his feelings, as he stands now for the first time upon some lofty sea shore crag, with the boundless expanse before him? His soul must be stirred by its magnificence, and his thoughts take a new and loftier[4] flight into regions of beauty and grandeur.

A few days ago we were quietly treading our way among the bales, boxes and crates upon one of the East river quays, when our progress was arrested by a very aged man, who wished to have pointed out to him the different kinds of vessels.

He said he had never before seen vessels of any kind, this being the first time he had ever been near the ocean. He had read of the various classes, but had no definite conception on the subject. At first we thought him quizzing, but after being satisfied of his perfect sincerity, endeavored to point out the peculiarities. He soon had no difficulty in recognising[5] the various denominations—ships, barks, brigs, schooners, sloops, &c.; and as well as our limited nautical attainments would admit of, we endeavored to show the peculiar advantages of the different modes of rigging. The old man seemed much gratified, and doubtless will with pleasure, should it ever be our lot to peregrinate in the region of his home, point out to us the peculiarities, virtues, beauties and uses of the various productions of his soil. And that practical knowledge of his is of far greater value than all the fanciful smattering that is usually caught up in the city rounds. A man cannot acquire all knowledge, and therefore it becomes him to direct his attention to the acquisition of that which is of the greatest worth. Teaching a bean to wind up its pole, is a more useful, though perhaps not so *manly* or elegant an employment, as teaching a lap dog to jump.

But we were speaking of the ocean—that eternal fountain of the sublime and mysterious. We love to listen to the deep and ceaseless tones of its music, when the repose of midnight has fallen upon it. There is a sublimity in its angry tossing, when wrought to madness by the assaults and goadings of the storm king. We love to think of the riches, and the lost, that lie beneath its wave, and to carry the thoughts forward to that eventful hour when it must give up its treasures and its dead—when the sands which now form its bound will melt away with "the fervent heat,"[6] and its waves be lost in the ocean of eternity.

NOTES

1. Transcribed from scanned original at the Walt Whitman Archive, whitmanarchive.org. This editorial also appears in Walt Whitman, *The Journalism, Volume I: 1834–1846*, part of *The Collected Writings of Walt Whitman*, ed. Herbert Bergman, Douglas A. Noverr, and Edward J. Recchia (New York: Peter Lang, 1998), 133–134.

2. Perhaps a loose quotation of "They [the Apostles] had hitherto breasted the storm in silence and without shrinking, but now their feelings were wrought up even to madness, and they began to look abroad upon the darkness of the scene, and seek with anxious eyes the gladsome light of home." H. K. Honjosef, "Peace—Be Still," *American Magazine, and Repository of Useful Literature* 2, no. 1 (January 1842), 10.

3. Spelling in original.

4. Spelled "lofter" in original.

5. Spelling in original.

6. "But the day of the Lord will come as a thief in the night; in which the heavens shall pass away with a great noise, and the elements shall melt with fervent heat, the earth also and the works that are therein shall be burned up." 2 Peter 3:10, KJV.

Dreams[1]

New York Aurora

APRIL 23, 1842

Dreams, to the pure of heart, are always messengers of love and beauty; be he the son of wealth or of poverty, they are to him a gilding which serves to adorn and beautify the roughest deformities of life. There are dreams of the day and dreams of the night, but around all fancy twines a magic wreath.

Here is a mother watching her tender babe. What dreams must fill her anxious heart. By night, while on her breast that sweet one calmly breathes, and timid sleep has gently closed her eyes, she dreams of nought but beauty, love, and tenderness. By day she dreams of the proud moments when those pure lips will lisp the name of "mother;" then, when by her side it ambles to the fields, to revel with the flowers, and join its laugh with the gay robin's song; then to the school she follows it; and then to the distant and more sombre path beset by manhood's cares and duties, where she sees him, by his acts of honor and of virtue, shedding lustre on the name she gave; and then, in "melancholy pleasure," she dreamily reverts to the hour when old age will throw down his frosts upon her head, and find him by her side, a watchful one, who will support her tottering step, and smooth the pillow for her dying head. Sweet are the mother's dreams.

And here is the toiling aspirant for wealth. We let him pass. His dreams are sordid, unsatisfying, and unworthy of the form he bears. By day, his thoughts are running among boxes, bales, and tierces; notes, and bills, and bullion; ships, and lands, and houses;—and by night, the order only is reversed—they are running in his thoughts. Anxious and unsatisfying are the worldling's dreams.

And here is the blooming maiden. Her day dreams rest on fair and bright, though evanescent joys. The present is a sparkling holiday—the future, a sealed book, which she seldom urges fancy to step forward and unfold. And when her day of little cares has passed, and her quelled spirit seeks repose upon her virgin couch, visions of purity and peace hover around her head. Fair are the dreams of joyous maidenhood.

And here is the poor poet, with ashy cheek, but eye whose power discovers beauty in the smallest thing of earth. Night's shadows fall, and his limbs, wearied with wandering, are stretched upon his coarse pallet; the gnawing pangs of appetite are eased by dreams of present love and future glory. Now he revels in the fields of brightness spread around, and anon tosses in nervous anticipation of that triumphant hour, when, on the glittering wings of genius he will soar to regions of such surpassing lustre as will dazzle all beholders, and far overpay his own physical toil and suffering. And from the waking dream he gently passes into that more glowing, less alloyed, one of sleep. Far brighter scenes than even he had viewed in waking hours, now crowd around his path; and even while they change and flit his newly opened vision, deems them enduring. But fleeting is that hour of immaterial radiance, and he wakes again to find himself upon the couch of poverty.

But yet his spirit sinks not. Poor though he be in worldly wealth he has a soul which in Nature's volume reads a lesson which imparts content, nay, highest happiness. That is a holy volume, filled with the most true and glorious illustrations which the universe affords, and is opened wide to all—as well to the meanest beggar as the mightiest lord—and he to whom God gave the soul to comprehend it, and to love its varied pages, is the happiest of his race, though poorest in the eye of undiscerning fools. And he who never drew life from that pure fountain, is poorest of the earth worm race, though bathing in a fount of gold. And this poor poet rises from his dreaming couch, to walk a dreaming path; and if but a crust of bread and a cup of water are his to stay the stern demands of hunger, he casts his eye upon morn's mantling blushes, the retreating mists, and opening flowers, and is well satisfied. Finally, as life progresses, he finds that one by one his earlier dreams—that all his earthborn dreams—are fading into nothingness; and as his mind has long been drawn from earth's corroding cares and gold increasing toils, he wakes—aye, *wakes* to revel in the glories of that world beyond the veil.

And there are children's dreams—fair, but transient. They come, like the zephyr, to impart warmth and cheer to the tender spirit. By night, like little stars, they twinkle through the mists of undeveloped intellect, and by day throw a veil of undefined beauty over the play ground and the fair scenes of home.[2]

NOTES

1. Transcribed from scanned original at the Walt Whitman Archive, whitmanarchive.org. This editorial also appears in Walt Whitman, *The Journalism, Volume I: 1834–1846*, part of *The*

Collected Writings of Walt Whitman, ed. Herbert Bergman, Douglas A. Noverr, and Edward J. Recchia (New York: Peter Lang, 1998), 136–137.

2. From *Leaves of Grass* (1855), compare this editorial to:

How solemn they look there, stretched and still;
How quiet they breathe, the little children in their cradles.

The wretched features of ennuyees, the white features of corpses, the livid faces of drunkards, the sick-gray faces of onanists,
The gashed bodies on battlefields, the insane in their strong-doored rooms, the sacred idiots,
The newborn emerging from gates and the dying emerging from gates,
The night pervades them and enfolds them.

The married couple sleep calmly in their bed, he with his palm on the hip of the wife, and she with her palm on the hip of the husband,
The sisters sleep lovingly side by side in their bed,
The men sleep lovingly side by side in theirs,
And the mother sleeps with her little child carefully wrapped.

The blind sleep, and the deaf and dumb sleep,
The prisoner sleeps well in the prison . . . . the runaway son sleeps,
The murderer that is to be hung next day . . . . how does he sleep?
And the murdered person . . . . how does he sleep?

The female that loves unrequited sleeps,
And the male that loves unrequited sleeps;
The head of the moneymaker that plotted all day sleeps,
And the enraged and treacherous dispositions sleep.

I stand with drooping eyes by the worst suffering and restless,
I pass my hands soothingly to and fro a few inches from them;
The restless sink in their beds . . . . they fitfully sleep.

Retrieved from the Walt Whitman Archive, whitmanarchive.org.

An Hour at a Bath[1]

Evening Tattler
AUGUST 11, 1842

Toward the latter part of the afternoon, when our labors for the day are nearly over, we delight to go down to that beautiful promenade, the Battery; take a few turns there—then make the *entree* to Rabineau's bath,[2] order a sherry cobbler,[3] (which by the way is concocted in a style to tempt the gods from their nectar,) and take a comfortable seat up on the outer promenade, in full view of our beautiful bay.

How noble and lovely a prospect! Far away stretches the bosom of the dark green waters—and clouds of all fantastic shapes play over the top of the land in the distance.

A splendid ship is coming up the harbor, with every sail set. How steadily and gracefully she moves along—with what swiftness she cuts her passage through the tide, though favored neither by that or the wind. She bears, likely, a number of curious eyes and throbbing hearts from the Old World—travellers to this home of the injured and refuge for the children of weariness. Let them come! and sore be the tongue that would insult them for their peculiarities, novel to us—or for their having been born in a land three thousand miles away!

Off some couple of furlongs, lies the French steamer Gomer, with the tricolor at her mast head. She is a ponderous looking craft; it would seem to require no small impetus to move her. There comes a boat from the Frenchman. It is painted black all over; and the men are dressed in broadcloth, notwithstanding the warmth of the day. We have hardly ever seen a more robust set of fellows than those French sailors, with their brown cheeks, their thick shoulders, and vivacious eyes. The officers of the Gomer are magnificent in their personal appearance.

It is one continued and beautiful moving panorama—the view from here. Sloops, schooners and brigs—vessels of all sizes, from the little skiff to the stupendous line-of-battle ship, are in sight, anchored or sailing with the breeze.

We might say a good deal more—but our cobbler is out, and the sun has sunk behind the Jersey shore. We will wind up our essay.

NOTES

1. Transcribed from Walt Whitman, *The Journalism, Volume I: 1834–1846*, part of *The Collected Writings of Walt Whitman*, ed. Herbert Bergman, Douglas A. Noverr, and Edward J. Recchia (New York: Peter Lang, 1998), 150–151.

2. "Rabineau's baths, in the Astor House, entrance on Vesey-street, is a very neat and popular establishment, and is entitled to patronage. Medicinal baths are prepared here, under the care of the proprietor, who is a physician. There are several other establishments about town of an inferior class, but very much frequented by the public, and open at low prices." Edwards Ruggles, *A Picture of New-York in 1846* (New York: Homans and Ellis, 1846), 116.

3. "*Sherry Cobbler* is made as Mint Julep, *sans* lemon-peel or mint, sherry being substituted for brandy; and when served, nutmeg is grated over the top." John Timbs, *Hints for the Table: or, The Economy of Good Living* (London: Kent, 1859), 141.

A Visit to Greenwood Cemetery[1]

Sunday Times & Noah's Weekly Messenger

MAY 5, 1844

On Tuesday, we mounted a gallant steed in Brooklyn and rode out to Greenwood. We were induced to make this visit by learning from the director's report, that Greenwood "was in a very flourishing situation, there having been a large number of interments there during the past year." You laugh, reader, but why should not the proprietors of a grave-yard, like the proprietors of fancy stores, calculate their success by the number of their customers?

Greenwood is a beautiful spot. There is no denying this. It is romantically broken up into hill and dale; here a secluded little nook, where a disappointed and broken hearted man would like to lie down and be at rest, there a little sunlit knoll, fit for the happiest and purest being that ever breathed, to rest within. A beautiful lake, the surface of which is as quiet as the graves around, its depths as passionless as the forms, that having dismissed their spirits, now crumble away to dust, adds to the poetic beauties of the place. By the side of this sheet of water, is poor Macdonald Clarke's grave.[2] We read the simple yet touching inscription, and gazed on the medallion likeness, so faithful, lacking nothing but life. A more fitting spot for the repose of this strange child of genius, this impulsive creature, whose own terrible imaginings made life to him so dark and dreary, could not have been chosen. Its stillness and beauty are in striking contrast, with the storm and cloudiness of his existence. And now, the sympathy which he in vain yearned for while living, is freely given to him dead. There are few who pass his grave, who do not pause to read his name, and bestow a tender thought on his memory.[3] This is the way of the world. It never finds out a man's virtues until he is dead, and quite indifferent to its opinion, good or bad.

A few steps from Clarke's grave is the tomb of the Indian Princess.[4] It is unpretendingly beautiful. A block of marble, on which is inscribed the name and rank of the maiden, who far away from her home, died amongst strangers. Some benevolent ladies of this city, assisted by Mr. Barnum of the Museum, procured her burial in this sweet dell, and erected to her memory this stone. It was a kindly act, and is appreciated by all visitors to Greenwood.

A most pretending mausoleum of free stone, owned by George W. Browne, Esq, demands by its uncouthness the attention of visitors. It is built in the style of an old fashioned Dutch farm house, and is certainly the clumsiest contrivance for the living or the dead, that our eyes ever rested upon. In perfect keeping, are a couple of stone dogs on either side of the entrance. What an odd idea of poetry must the designer[5] of the whole structure have had. We presume he intended the dogs to be emblematic of faithful remembrance, but as they are crouching down, with their eyes distended, they look as though they were set there to watch. And now we think of it twice, that was the idea intended to be conveyed. Wouldn't a regular New York watchman, with his club and cap answer better?

On the hill side not far from the lake, are two very beautiful monuments. The artist was engaged in completing on one of them a medallion likeness of a most lovely woman. She was young, only twenty two, at the time of her death. We forget her name, but remember that she was from Ohio—a wife, and the affection of her husband had raised the pile, and placed upon it in imperishable stone, the features of her angelic countenance. There is true poetry of the heart here.

In driving quietly through the grounds, we surprised a young couple, who appeared to be making love. We laughed outright, notwithstanding the sacredness of the place. We have heard of love among the roses, but never before of love among the graves. And yet it was all right enough, nay appropriate. True, it would dampen the ardor of youthful hearts, the solemn truth forcing itself upon their remembrance in such a place, that the brightest, the purest, the holiest sentiment of earth is not immortal. Here is the altar, there the grave; to-day the wild throbbings of ecstacy; to-morrow the pall, the bier, the tomb. No, a grave yard is not the place for dreams of love and happiness. It is the place for sorrow to come and learn endurance, for disappointment to acquire patience, for the weary of earth to gather up their remaining disappointment to acquire patience, for the weary of earth to gather up their remaining strength and plod on—on to rest and forgetfulness. Bless us, how sentimental we are getting.

There is a beautiful hill in Greenwood, the summit of which overlooks the bay and a portion of the city of New York. A very animating prospect, bespeaking life, and bustle, and activity, and contrasting strangely enough, with the quiet of the cemetery. On the side of the hill several tombs are already built, and others are now constructing. A hundred lots, we should think by the names attached to them, are sold but as yet unbuilt upon. When they are improved,

Greenwood will rival in its melancholy beauty, the far famed Mount Auburn, in the vicinity of Boston. Its natural advantages are quite as great, and it only needs a thick undergrowth of wood and shrubbery, and the erection of monuments, to make it one of the most interesting places of sepulture in the world. Our citizens should generally visit it.

NOTES

1. Transcribed from Walt Whitman, *The Journalism, Volume I: 1834–1846*, part of *The Collected Writings of Walt Whitman*, ed. Herbert Bergman, Douglas A. Noverr, and Edward J. Recchia (New York: Peter Lang, 1998), 190–191. One of Whitman's first editorials was written about Greenwood Cemetery. *Universalist Union*, November 16, 1839.

2. McDonald Clarke (1798–1842) was known as the "mad poet of Broadway"; see Part III of this volume. Whitman wrote eulogies for Clarke in the *Aurora* (March 8 and March 12, 1842), the first of which is published in this volume as "Untitled" in Part III. Spiritualists during the 1850s gathered at Clarke's grave at Greenwood Cemetery, as reported by the *New York Times*, but "Several of the party . . . gave up all hope of 'getting manifestations'; and well they might have for as poor Clarke was not careful of his appointments while in the land of the living, he could hardly be expected to be more punctual after having resided so long in the city of the dead." *New York Times*, September 21, 1855, nytimes.com.

3. Whitman had a large tomb built for himself. The *New York Times* described it as "a substantial structure, built of massive rough granite blocks, some of them weighing over seven tons. The door is of granite, six inches thick. The tomb contains receptacles for eight caskets or coffins, arranged in two tiers. They are constructed of marble. The top of the tomb bears the name 'Walt Whitman.' The tomb was erected 'on the side of the hill, near a grove' where, according to the poet he could 'go in to the woods.'" *New York Times*, March 27, 1892, nytimes.com.

4. Do-Hum-Me (1824–1843) became a celebrity between March and September 1843 when she visited New York as a member of a delegation of Native Americans representing the Sac Indians and met and married Cow-Hick Kee of the Iowas. The couple remained in New York as an attraction of P. T. Barnum's American Museum, until Do-Hum-Me took ill and died unexpectedly. Her monument at Greenwood was described as follows: "The whole being six feet in height. The inscriptions are simple and appropriate. On one side is inserted a tablet of Italian marble, on which is sculptured in relief, the figure of an Indian sitting upon the broken trunk of a tree, in a bending posture, his face buried in his hands, which rest upon one knee, and his bow and quiver lay neglected at his feet." *Universalist Union* 8, no. 3 (September 23, 1843), 724.

5. Richard Upjohn (1802–1878).

Ourselves and the 'Eagle.'[1]

Brooklyn Daily Eagle
JUNE 1, 1846

We have arrayed ourselves in new apparel, and present us to the public with a 'clean face,' to-day—as per the current paragraph, and all after it! We might say a great deal, herewith, about what we are going to do, etc.; but we think it about as well to 'let our acts speak for us.' We shall do as well as we can; and our journal will be 'devoted' to—what is put into it.

The democratic party of Brooklyn should (*and do*) handsomely support a handsome daily paper.—For our part, too, we mean no mere lip-thanks when we say that we are truly conscious of the warm kindness with which they have always treated this establishment. To those in Brooklyn who, not taking a daily local print, feel inclined to subscribe to one, we respectfully suggest that they 'try us,' now. If, at the end of a fortnight, or month, they don't think they get the worth of their money, we will cheerfully mark them off again. We really feel a desire to talk on many subjects, to *all* the people of Brooklyn; and it *ain't* their ninepences we want so much either. There is a curious kind of sympathy (haven't you ever thought of it before?) that arises in the mind of a newspaper conductor with the public he serves. He gets to *love* them. Daily communion creates a sort of brotherhood and sisterhood between the two parties. As for us, we like this. We like it better than the more 'dignified' part of editorial labors—the grave political disquisition, the contests of faction, and so on.[2] And we want as many readers of the *Brooklyn Eagle*—even unto the half of Long Island—as possible, that we may increase the number of such friends. For are not those who daily listen to us, friends?

—Perhaps no office requires a greater union of rare qualities than that of a *true editor*. No wonder, then, so few come under that flattering title! No wonder that we are all derelict, in some particular! In general information, an editor should be complete, particularly with that relating to his own country. He should have a fluent style: elaborate finish we do not think requisite in daily writing. His articles had far better be earnest and terse than polished; they should ever smack of being uttered on the spur of the moment, like political oratory.—In temper, Job himself is the lowest example he should take. And even that famed ancient, we trow, cannot be said to have achieved the climax of human endurance—since types and printing presses were not in vogue at his era. An editor needs, withal, a sharp eye, to discriminate the good from the immense mass of unreal stuff floating on all sides of him—and always bearing the counterfeit presentment of the real. This talent is so rare that many newspapers have built up quite a reputation on the merit of their selections alone. Here, in this country, most editors have far far *too much to do*, to make good work of what they do.[3] Abroad, it is different. In London or Paris, the payment for a single 'leader' is frequently more than the month's salary of the best remunerated American editor. Crowding upon one individual the duties of five or six, is, indeed, the greatest reason of all why we have in America so very few daily prints that are artistically equal to the European ones. Is it not astonishing, then,—not that the press of the United States don't do better, but that it don't do worse?

With all and any drawbacks, however, much good can always be done, with such potent influence as a well circulated newspaper. To wield that influence, is a great responsibility. There are numerous noble reforms that have yet to be pressed upon the world. People are to be schooled, in opposition perhaps to their long established ways of thought.—In politics, too, the field of improvement is wide enough yet; the harvest is large, and waiting to be reaped—and each paper, however humble, may do good in the ranks. Nor is it a mere monotonous writer after old fashions that can achieve the good we speak of...... We shall have more to say on this theme, at a very early period.

NOTES

1. Transcribed from scanned original at the Walt Whitman Archive, whitmanarchive.org. This editorial also appears in Walt Whitman, *The Journalism, Volume I: 1834–1846*, part of *The Collected Writings of Walt Whitman*, ed. Herbert Bergman, Douglas A. Noverr, and Edward J. Recchia (New York: Peter Lang, 1998), 391–392.

2. Ironically, it was probably Whitman's support in print for the "Barnburners," a faction of the Democratic Party that advocated for new western territories to be closed to slavery, that cost him his position at the *Daily Eagle*. See "Letter from Gen. Cass.," *Brooklyn Daily Eagle*, January 3, 1848 (above).

3. On September 11, 1849, over one year after Whitman left the paper, the editors of the *Eagle* claimed that "Mr. Whitman . . . lacks . . . the industry and tact so necessary to the conduct of a political paper; and is more gifted in alienating friends than in making them."

Gayety of Americans[1]

Brooklyn Daily Eagle
SEPTEMBER 23, 1846

The passed morning, (23d) has been very beautiful. The sun rose clear and cloudless—the air is fresh and just warm enough to be without chilliness. And though the streets in Brooklyn are tolerably, and in the great Babel over the river superlatively, covered with dirt, there is somehow or other no dust to annoy eyes or mouth, this mornings . . . . We had occasion to pass through Broadway, in N.Y.; and never have we seen that famed thoroughfare present a brighter aspect. Walking there, if we had been asked to mention the particular characteristic which would in all probability first impress a stranger visiting New York, we should reply that it was a *gay activity*. This is surely the most striking feature of the population. We have often wondered, of a bright morning, how every body could dress so well, and where on earth they could find business enough to employ them, and make it necessary for them to hurry along at the helter-skelter pace.

We are not sure but it is unjust to this country after all, to attribute the want of 'fun' to it, which most European travellers attribute. Go through the streets, and see for yourself, almost any where, in pleasant weather, particularly at the beginning of 'business hours.' For the early time of the day, there is, too, an aspect of *youth* impressed upon N. York. Two thirds of the persons you meet in the street are young men or boys nearly grown—clerks, apprentices, office-boys,[2] and so on. These with their bright faces, and their exact attire, form by no means the least agreeable part of the scene. Dull and torpid must that man be who can walk any distance in the streets of the metropolis, of a morning, and not become imbued with the cheerfulness so evident everywhere around.[3] The capital of France is a gay city—but the gayety we speak of is quite different from the flippant gayety of the Parisian population. Theirs is a spirit which seems to partake of the thoughtlessness of the savage—a disposition to enjoy to-day, and take no care for to-morrow. Ours, we think, is more the disposition to make business a pleasure—to work, but to work with smiles and a bright heart. Theirs is a repast, all flowers and fine dishes, but with little for the appetite; ours forgets not the ornamental part of the feast, but retains the solid, too.

It is somewhat singular that few or none of the travellers in America have noticed these truths—or rather that none have noticed *all* the truth—for they have generally given us quite credit enough, and too much, for application to business, and little, or none at all, for enjoyment. The mistake is, probably, that they find few idle pleasures popular in America. There is undoubtedly here a great—a very much too great—eagerness for wealth, and a forgetfulness, in feverish speculation, of the humble philosophy of living while we live; but at the same time there is a powerful current of smiles and liveliness running through the national character, and developing itself, so far, in the way we have mentioned . . . . . . What can afford a livelier spectacle for instance, than the lower part of Fulton street, or of Atlantic st., Brooklyn—than Broadway, the Bowery, Grand street, Canal street, and nearly all of the large N.Y. thoroughfares, on a fine morning or afternoon? Of course, many of the persons who look so gay there have their own special troubles and cares, no doubt, as it is the lot of all mortality to have. But, for the hour, they have forgotten them. Sunshine of the mind beams over their faces, and they find relief in the excitement of so much bustle and noise—the spectacle of so much fashion and beauty. And, indeed, all through the day, in almost all parts of New York, this activity never flags. Surely there can be no town on earth that has less of a sleepy look than that. It is always "wide awake," and the throbbings of its pulse beat forever . . . . . . We commend this spirit, for we commend whatever is opposed to idleness and melancholy. Life is short enough to make the most active hands, joined with the quickest brain, slow to do what ought to be done—and dark enough to render all that throws sunshine around us welcome indeed. We might, perhaps, if we tried, offer some suggestions of improvement; but to tell the truth, we are not among those who prefer to dwell on the deficiencies[4] of a community, than on its merits; and we are quite satisfied with Brooklyn and New York character as it is—confident that though it might be better, there are hardly[5] two cities elsewhere, take them all in all, in which it is as well.

NOTES

1. Transcribed from scanned original at the Walt Whitman Archive, whitmanarchive.org. This editorial also appears in Walt Whitman, *The Journalism, Volume II: 1846–1848*, part of *The Collected Writings of Walt Whitman*, ed. Herbert Bergman, Douglas A. Noverr, and Edward J. Recchia (New York: Peter Lang, 2003), 63–64.

2. Hyphen in original.

3. Perhaps an allusion to Wordsworth's "Composed Upon Westminster Bridge":

"Earth has not anything to show more fair:
Dull would he be of soul who could pass by
A sight so touching in its majesty:
This City now doth, like a garment, wear
The beauty of the morning; silent, bare,"

4. Original reads "deficiences."

5. Original reads "hard y."

PHILOSOPHY OF FERRIES.[1]

Brooklyn Daily Eagle
AUGUST 13, 1847

Our Brooklyn ferries teach some sage lessons in philosophy, gentle reader, (we like that time-honored phrase!) whether you ever knew it or not. There is the Fulton, now, which takes precedence by age, and by a sort of aristocratic seniority of wealth and business, too. It moves on like iron-willed destiny. Passionless and fixed, at the six-stroke the boats come in; and[2] at the three-stroke, succeeded by a single tap, they depart again, with the steadiness of nature herself. Perhaps a man, prompted by the hell-like delirium tremens, has jumped over-board and been drowned: still the trips go on as before. Perhaps some one has been crushed between the landing and the prow—(ah! that most horrible thing of all!) still, no matter, for the great business of the mass must be helped forward as before. A moment's pause—the quick gathering of a curious crowd, (how strange that they can look so unshudderingly on the scene!)—the paleness of the more chicken hearted—and all subsides, and the current sweeps as it did the moment previously. How it deadens one's sympathies, this living in a city![3]

But the most 'moral' part of the ferry sights, is to see the conduct of the people, old and young, fat and lean, gentle and simple, when the bell sounds three taps. Then follows a spectacle, indeed—particularly on the Brooklyn side, at from seven o'clock to nine in the morning. At the very first moment of the sound, perhaps some sixty or eighty gentlemen are plodding along the side walks, adjacent to the ferry boat—likewise some score or so of lads—with that brisk pace which bespeaks the 'business individual.' Now see them as the said three-tap is heard! Apparently moved by an electric impulse, two thirds of the whole number start off on the wings of the wind! Coat tails fly high and wide! You get a swift view of the phantom-like semblance of humanity, as it is sometimes seen in dreams—but nothing more—unless it may be you are on the walk yourself, when the chances are in favor of a breath-destroying punch in the stomach. In their insane fury, the rushing crowd spare neither age nor sex. Then the single stroke of the bell is heard; and straightway what was rage before comes to be a sort of extatic[4] fury![5] Aware of his danger, the man that takes the toll has ensconced himself behind a stout oaken partition, which seems only to be entered through a little window-looking place: but we think he must have more than ordinary courage, to stand even there. We seriously recommend the ferry superintendant[6] to have this place as strong as iron bars can make it.

This rushing and raging is not inconsistent, however, with other items of the American character. Perhaps it is a developement[7] of the 'indomitable energy' and 'chainless enterprise' which we get so much praise for. But it is a very ludicrous thing, nevertheless. If the trait is remembered down to posterity, and put in the annals, it will be bad for us. Posterity surely cannot attach any thing of the dignified or august to a people who run after steamboats, with hats flying off, and skirts streaming behind! Think of any of the Roman senators, or the worthies of Greece, in such a predicament.—(The esteem which we had for a certain acquaintance went up at least a hundred per cent, one day, when we found that, though a daily passenger over the ferry, he never accelerated his pace in the slightest manner, even when by so doing, he could 'save a boat.')

A similar indecorum and folly are exhibited, when the boat approaches the wharf. As if some avenging fate were behind them, and the devil indeed was going to "take the hindermost," the passengers crowd to the very verge of the forward parts, and wait with frightful eagerness till they are brought within three or four yards of the landing—when the front row prepare themselves for desperate springs. Among many there is a rivalry as to who shall leap on shore over the widest stretch of water! The boat gets some four or five feet from the wharf, and then the springing begins—hop! hop! hop!—those who are in the greatest hurry generally stopping for several minutes when they get on the dock to look at their companions behind on the boat, and how *they* come ashore! Well: there is a great deal of inconsistency in this world.[8]

The Catharine ferry at the foot of Main street has plenty of business too, though not near as much as the one whose peculiarities we have just been narrating. It has lately had some new boats—or new fixings and paint, we don't know which—and presents, (we noticed the other day, in crossing,) quite a spruce appearance. The Catharine ferry is used by many working people: in the morning they cross there in prodigious numbers. Also, milk wagons, and country vehicles generally. During the day a great many of the Brooklyn dames go over this ferry on shopping excursions to the region of Grand street and Catharine street on the other side. The desperation to get to the boat, which we have mentioned above, does not prevail so deeply here. Long may the contagion 'stay away'! for we must confess that we don't like to see it. This ferry, (like all the others,) is a very profitable investment; and from those profits we are warranted in saying—as we have said once or twice before—that the price for foot passengers should be put down to one cent, and horses and wagons in proportion.

The South ferry has more dainty and 'genteel' character than either of the other places. The broad avenue which leads to it, and the neighborhood of the aristocratic heights, from whom it receives many of its passengers, keep it so. Business is not so large there as at either of the other ferries we have mentioned; but the accommodations are of the first quality. The boats are large and clean; and the more moderate bustle and clatter make it preferable, during the summer afternoons, for ladies and children—the latter often taken by their nurses and remaining on board the boats for an hour, for the pleasant sail.

Besides these, we have the ferry from the foot of Jackson street on the Brooklyn side, to Walnut st. New York side. This consists of only one boat, and a rather shabby one at that. Many workmen at the navy yard use this means of conveyance; and it is also of course patronized by citizens in that vicinity. We should think much better and[9] more rapid accommodations would be desirable there.—The boat is half the time prevented by her own unwieldiness from getting into her slip under half an hour's detention. She seems to be some old affair that has been cast off for years.

We have also two other ferries, in the limits of Brooklyn, which in time will be as much avenues of business as either of the rest. One of those goes from Whitehall to the foot of Hamilton avenue, and accommodates the region of the Atlantic dock, and of farther South Brooklyn, which is daily assuming more and more importance. The other goes also from Whitehall to the long wharf near Greenwood cemetery. This also is necessary for the accommodation of a rapidly increasing mass of citizens who are attracted by the salubrity[10] of that section of Brooklyn joined with the cheapness of the land, and the nearness of the beautiful grounds of the cemetery.

The ferry at the foot of Montagu street is in progress; and will probably be in operation next spring. The Bridge street ferry is also determined upon, and may be completed by the same time.

NOTES

1. Transcribed from scanned original, Brooklyn Public Library—Brooklyn Collection, eagle.brooklynpubliclibrary.org. This editorial also appears in Walt Whitman, *The*

Journalism, Volume II: 1846–1848, part of *The Collected Writings of Walt Whitman*, ed. Herbert Bergman, Douglas A. Noverr, and Edward J. Recchia (New York: Peter Lang, 2003), 308–310, and in Walt Whitman, *The Uncollected Poetry and Prose of Walt Whitman*, ed. Emory Holloway (Gloucester, Mass.: Peter Smith, 1972), 1:168–171.

2. In the original, the word "and" is repeated here.

3. In the poem "Crossing Brooklyn Ferry," *Leaves of Grass* (1860) (Walt Whitman Archive, whitmanarchive.org), the city inspires the opposite:

> Now I am curious what sight can ever be more stately
> and admirable to me than my mast-hemm'd Manhatta,
> My river and sun-set, and my scallop-edged waves of
> flood-tide,
> The sea-gulls oscillating their bodies, the hay-boat in
> the twilight, and the belated lighter;
> Curious what Gods can exceed these that clasp me
> by the hand, and with voices I love call me
> promptly and loudly by my nighest name as I
> approach,
> Curious what is more subtle than this which ties me
> to the woman or man that looks in my face,
> Which fuses me into you now, and pours my meaning
> into you.

4. Spelling in original.

5. Compare to:

> Crowds of men and women attired in the usual costumes! how curious you are to me!
> On the ferry-boats, the hundreds and hundreds that
> cross, returning home, are more curious to me
> than you suppose,
> And you that shall cross from shore to shore years
> hence, are more to me, and more in my meditations, than you might suppose.

6. "superintendent."

7. Spelling in original.

8. Two weeks later, Whitman made a more explicit warning about jumping from an arriving ferry to the dock. "An Anecdote with a Moral," *Brooklyn Daily Eagle*, August 31, 1847.

9. Original contains repetition of the word "and."

10. Health.

East Long Island Correspondence [Letter III].[1]

Brooklyn Daily Eagle
SEPTEMBER 20, 1847

Southold, Sept. 14th—Seeing, to-day, as I passed one of the country stores, a real *Indian,* (at least as far as there are any of that race, now-a-days; that is, perhaps, an Indian whose blood is only thinned by two or three degrees of mixture,) my thoughts were turned toward the aboriginal inhabitants of this island. A populous and powerful race! for such they once were. Some authorities assert that, at the earliest approach of the whites to this part of the continent, and for a time after, the Indian inhabitants of Long-Island[2] numbered a million and a half. This may be an over-estimate; but the red race here was certainly very numerous, as is evidenced by many tokens. "An ancient Indian," says one tradition, "more than a hundred years ago, declared to one of the earliest inhabitants of Easthampton, that within his recollection the natives were *as many as the spears of grass.* And if, said he, stretching his hands over the ground, you can count these, then, when I was a boy, you could have reckoned their number."[3] . . . . Another token is the immense shell-banks, at intervals, all along the shores of the island—some of them literally "mountain high." Another is the immense tract devoted to the fields of Indian corn.

Unlike the present arrangement, the seat of the greatest aboriginal population and power was on the eastern extremity of Long Island. On the peninsula of Montauk dwelt the royal tribe; —and there lived and ruled the noble Wyandanch;[4] (*will* not the Union ferry company be persuaded to take off that most miserably wrong terminative of "dank," from the boat they pretend to christen after the old chief?) This chief held a position not unlike our American president. On the island were thirteen separate tribes, (our Kings county was occupied by the "Canarsees,")[5] who were united in one general confederacy, at the head of which was Wyandanch. From Montauk, whose white sides resounded forever with the mighty voice of the sea, went forth the supreme commands and decisions. Here, too, was the holiest of the burial places, the sacred spots to all savage nations, and peculiarly so to our North American Indians. On Montauk, even now, may also be seen remains of aboriginal fortifications, one of which at what is now called "Fort Hill," must have been a work of art indeed.[6] It had ramparts and parapets, ditches around, and huge towers at each of four corners—and is estimated to have afforded conveniences for three or four hundred men, and to evince singular knowledge of warfare, even as understood among what we call civilized nations. Wars, indeed, added to pestilence, and most of all the use of the 'fire-water,' thinned off the Indian population from the earlier settlement of the whites until there are hardly any remaining. I believe there are but two clusters of Indian families that can be called settlements, now on the island. One is at Shinnecock,[7] and consists of some hundred and forty or fifty persons: the other is down on Montauk, and does not comprise a baker's dozen.[8] Sad remnants, these, of the sovereign sway and the old majesty there!

NOTES

1. Transcribed from scanned original, Brooklyn Public Library—Brooklyn Collection. This editorial also appears in Walt Whitman, *The Journalism, Volume II: 1846–1848,* part of *The Collected Writings of Walt Whitman*, ed. Herbert Bergman, Douglas A. Noverr, and Edward J. Recchia (New York: Peter Lang, 2003), 329–330, and Walt Whitman, *The Uncollected Poetry and Prose of Walt Whitman*, ed. Emory Holloway (Gloucester, Mass.: Peter Smith, 1972), 1:180–181.

2. Hyphen in original. See Whitman, *The Journalism, Vol. II*, 468.

3. Lost Native American populations in the Northeast provided a rich subject for this kind of historical thinking among well-known writers like James Fenimore Cooper. This is an early example of Whitman's own use of Native Americans to generate anecdotal memories that establish a personal, rather than didactic, relationship with the past. In *Leaves of Grass*, Whitman constructed a similar kind of anecdotal memory of Native Americans along Long Island:

> Now I tell what my mother told me today as we sat at dinner together,
> Of when she was a nearly grown girl living home with her parents on the old homestead.
>
> A red squaw came one breakfasttime to the old homestead,
> On her back she carried a bundle of rushes for rushbottoming chairs;
> Her hair straight shiny coarse black and profuse halfenveloped her face,
> Her step was free and elastic . . . . her voice sounded exquisitely as she spoke.
> My mother looked in delight and amazement at the stranger,
> She looked at the beauty of her tallborne face and full and pliant limbs,

The more she looked upon her she loved her,
Never before had she seen such wonderful beauty and purity;
She made her sit on a bench by the jamb of the fireplace . . . . she cooked food for
her,
She had no work to give her but she gave her remembrance and fondness.

The red squaw staid all the forenoon, and toward the middle of the afternoon she
went away;
O my mother was loth to have her go away,
All the week she thought of her . . . . she watched for her many a month,
She remembered her many a winter and many a summer,
But the red squaw never came nor was heard of there again.

Leaves of Grass (1855), Walt Whitman Archive, whitmanarchive.org.

4. Wyandanch (1620–1660) was a chief of the Algonquin-speaking Montaukett people. By the 1650s he had become the chief intermediary between native peoples on Long Island and European settlers.

5. An Algonquin-speaking people. The name "Canarsie" is derived from the Lenape word for "fenced-in place." Evan T. Pritchard, *Native New Yorkers: The Legacy of the Algonquin People of New York* (San Francisco: Council Oak Books, 2002), 101.

6. Montauk means "fortified place." Ibid., 321.

7. The Shinnecock now reside on Long Island, in Southampton, New York, in a self-governing reservation of 1,292 people. "U.S. Recognizes an Indian Tribe on Long Island, Clearing the Way for a Casino," *New York Times*, June 25, 2010, nytimes.com.

8. According to the 2010 census, of the 3,326 people in Montauk, New York, seven claimed Native American ancestry and nine claimed a mixed ancestry of Native American and European. U. S. Census (2010), factfinder2.census.gov.

Excerpts from a Traveller's Note Book—[No. 3] Western Steamboats—The Ohio[1]

New Orleans Daily Crescent

MARCH 10, 1848

Having crossed the Alleghanies during Saturday night, and spent the ensuing day in weary stages, from Uniontown[2] onward, we arrived at Wheeling[3] a little after 10 o'clock on Sunday night, and went aboard the steamer *St. Cloud,* a freight and packet boat, lying at the wharf there, with the steam all up, and ultimately bound for New Orleans.[4] This was my "first appearance" on a Western steamboat. The long cabin, neatly carpeted, and lit with clusters of handsome lamps, had no uncomfortable look; but the best comfort of the matter lay in (what I myself soon laid in) a good state room, of which I took possession, and forthwith was oblivious to all matters of a waking character. Roused next morning by the clang of the breakfast bell, I found that we had during the night made a good portion of our way toward Cincinnati.

Like as in many other matters, people who travel on the Ohio, (that most beautiful of words!) for the first time, will stand a chance of being somewhat disappointed. In poetry and romance, these rivers are talked of as though they were cleanly streams;[5] but it is astonishing what a difference is made by the simple fact that they are always and altogether excessively muddy—mud, indeed, being the prevailing character both afloat and ashore. This, when one thinks of it, is not only reasonable enough, but unavoidable in the very circumstances of the case. Yet, it destroys at once the principal beauty of the rivers. There is no romance in a mass of yellowish brown liquid. It is marvellous,[6] though, how easily a traveller gets to drinking it and washing in it. What an india-rubber principle, there is, after all, in humanity!

To one who beholds steamboat-life on the Ohio for the first time, there will of course be many fresh features and notable transpirings. One of the first and most unpleasant, is the want of punctuality in departing from places, and consequently the same want in arriving at them. All the steamers carry freight, that being, indeed, their principal business and source of profit, to which the accommodation of passengers, (as far as time is concerned) has to stand secondary. We on the *St. Cloud*, for instance, picked up all sorts of goods from all sorts of places, wherever our clever little captain made a bargain for the same. What he brought down from Pittsburg, the Lord only knows; for we took in afterward what would have been considered a very fair cargo to a New York liner. At one place, for instance, we shipped several hundred barrels of pork; ditto of lard; at another place, an uncounted (by me) lot of flour—enough, though, it seemed, to have fed half the office-holders of the land—and that *is* saying something. Besides these, we had bags of coffee, rolls of leather, groceries, dry goods, hardware, all sorts of agricultural products, innumerable coops filled with live geese, turkeys, and fowls, that kept up a perpetual farmyard concert. Then there were divers living hogs, to say nothing of a horse, and a resident dog. The country through which the Ohio runs is one of the most productive countries—and one of the most buying and selling—in the world; and nearly all the transportation is done on these steamboats. Putting those two facts together, one can get an idea of the infinite variety, as well as amount of our cargo. To my eyes it was enormous; though people much used to such things didn't seem to consider it any wonder at all.

About half past 6 o'clock, on board these boats—I begin at the beginning, you see—the breakfast bell is rung, giving the passengers half an hour to prepare for the table. Of edibles, for breakfast, (as at the other meals, too,) the quantity is enormous, and the quality first rate. The difference is very wide between the table here and any public table at the northeast; the latter, as many starved wight can bear testimony, being, in most cases, arranged on a far more economical plan. The worst of it is, on the Western steamboats, that everybody gulps down the victuals with railroad speed. With that distressing want of a pleasant means to pass away time, which all travellers must have experienced, is it not rather astonishing that the steamboat breakfast or dinner has to be dispatched in five minutes?[7]

During the day, passengers amuse themselves in various ways. Cheap novels are in great demand, and a late newspaper is a gem almost beyond price. From time to time, the boat stops, either for wood or freight; sometimes to pick up a passenger who hails from the shore. At the stopping places on the Kentucky side, appear an immense number of idlers, boys, old farmers, and tall, strapping, comely young men. At the stopping places on the northern shore, there seems to be more thrift and activity. The shore, each way, is much of it barren of interest; though the period must arrive when cultivation will bend it nearly all to man's use. Here and there, already, is a comfortable house; and, at intervals, there are tracts of well-tilled land, particularly on the Ohio line.

In the evening, (the reader must remember that it is not for *one* evening only, but sometimes for ten or twelve,) the passenger spends his time according to fancy. In our boat, the *St. Cloud*, the two large cabin tables were sometimes surrounded by readers; and the stove by smokers and talkers. The ladies appeared to have rather a dull time of it in their place. Most of them would sit listlessly for hours doing nothing—and, so far as I could learn, saying nothing!

Among the principal incidents of the voyage was crossing the falls of the Ohio, just below Louisville. Our boat was very deeply laden; and there is a canal around the ticklish pass; our captain, with Western hardihood, determined to go over the "boiling place." For my own part, I didn't know till afterwards, but that it was an every hour occurrence. The bottom of the boat grated harshly more than once on the stones beneath, and the pilots showed plainly that they did not feel altogether as calm as a summer morning. We passed over, however, in perfect safety. The Ohio here has a fall of many feet in the course of a mile. Does not the perfection to which engineering has been brought afford some means of remedying this ugly part of the river? Besides the canal around on the Kentucky side, the Indiana Legislature has lately granted a charter for one on its shore, too.

From Louisville down, one passes through a long stretch of monotonous country—not varied at all, sometimes for dozens of miles. The Ohio retains its distinctive character of mud, till you get to the very end of it.

Cairo,[8] at the junction of the Mississippi, pointed our passage into the great Father of Waters. Immense sums of money have been spent to make Cairo something like what a place with such a name ought to be. But with the exception of its position, which is unrivalled for business purposes, everything about it seems unfortunate. The point on which it is situated is low, and liable to be overflowed at every high flood. Besides, it is unwholesomely wet, at the best. It is doubtful whether Cairo will ever be any "great shakes," except in the way of the ague.

NOTES

1. This editorial also appears in Walt Whitman, *The Uncollected Poetry and Prose of Walt Whitman*, ed. Emory Holloway (Gloucester, Mass.: Peter Smith, 1972), 1:186–189, from which this transcription is taken.

2. Uniontown, Pennsylvania.

3. Wheeling, West Virginia.

4. Whitman probably arrived in New Orleans on the *St. Cloud* on February 26, 1848. William Kernan Dart, "Walt Whitman in New Orleans," *Publications of the Louisiana Historical Society* 7 (1913–1914): 97–113, 99.

5. "Race of races, and bards to corroborate! / Of them, standing among them, one lifts to the light his west-bred face, . . . Making its rivers, lakes, bays, embouchure in him, / Mississippi with yearly freshets and changing chutes—Missouri, Columbia, Ohio, Niagara, Hudson, spending themselves lovingly in him, . . ." *Leaves of Grass* (1860), Walt Whitman Archive, whitmanarchive.org.

6. Spelling in original.

7. Charles Dickens also wrote critically of a breakfast served aboard a canal boat on his journey west in *American Notes for General Circulation* (1842): "As we have not reached Pittsburg, yet however, in order of our narrative, I may go on to remark that breakfast was perhaps the least desirable meal of the day. . . . Many of the gentlemen passengers were far from particular in respect of their linen, which was in some cases as yellow as the little rivulets that had trickled from the corners of their mouths in chewing, and dried there." Charles Dickens, *American Notes for General Circulation* (London: Chapman and Hall, 1842), 2:61. Whitman was a lifelong fan of Dickens's works and actively defended the British novelist in the *New York Aurora*, among other newspapers, when Dickens's *American Notes* was published to great uproar in the United States. See "Dickens and Democracy," *New York Aurora*, April 2, 1842 (above).

8. Cairo, Illinois.

Letters from a Travelling Bachelor [No. III][1]

New York Sunday Dispatch
OCTOBER 28, 1849

SOME POETICAL COMPARISONS BETWEEN COUNTRY AND CITY.—THE OLD COUPLE ON SHELTER ISLAND.—A BIT OF ARGUMENT—OR AN ATTEMPT ANY HOW

Southold, L.I., 24 Oct.

Quiet, homely and passionless, is the life of these East Long Islanders, compared with existence in a great city like New York. Now that old Dutch Dr. Zimmermann, who wrote so profoundly and acted so foolishly, commends "solitude" as the greatest developer and establisher of virtuous conduct, and intellectual and scientific improvement.[2] Also, it is a common way among writers to speak in the same strain—to make much of "the soothing pleasures of retirement,"[3] and the "calm delights of obscurity."[4] We hear these gentlemen talk about life in the country as surely productive of a fine unsophisticated character in man or woman.

I know from the frequent bent of my own feelings, that yearning for the freshness and quiet of the country—that love of freedom from the ligatures and ceremonies of a life in town. But to be born and "brought up" in an out of the way country place, and so continue there through all the stages of middle life—and eat and drink there only, and "dress up" of a Sunday and go to church there—and at last die and be buried there—is that an enviable lot in life? No, it is not. The burying part may be well enough, but the living is much such living as a tree in the farmer's door-yard.

Undoubtedly as a general thing we United Statesers have enough of the restless in us, never to settle anywhere, longer than a few seasons. But Long Island is an exception. The people are tenacious of the place, and the places, from the brown sand of Napeague Beach, far east, to the white sand of Coney Island Point, far west. Here about the eastern parts, in particular, I find whole villages, or rather scattered hamlets, whose residents were born, and will live and die here, many of them having been only once or twice away from home over night, and very many who never visit the city of New York, during their whole lives! A very large majority never entered a theatre or read a play, or saw a piano or any thing worthy to be called sculpture or painting. Only a fraction of them take newspapers—and the book I frequently find to be nothing later than the "Children of the Abbey," "Rinaldo Rinaldini," "Alonzo and Melissa," or those interesting horrors of Calvinism by Masters Fox and Baxter.[5] I am aware that these people might be very intelligent, and very manly and womanly, without ever having seen a play or a piano—and therefore I only mention that as a specimen of their primitiveness. But the vegetating forever in one little spot of this wide and beautiful world—the absence of books—the getting *set* in the narrow notions of the locality where they live—serve to dwarf and distort much of the goodly elements of their own nature; and increase the same rude effects to the third and fourth generation.

Yes, Messrs. of the city: I have found no precept more strongly taught, by my rambles among this often hospitable and quite invariably honest and sturdy race, then that of, *Let everyone mix for at least some part of his earlier life with the bustling world of the great towns.* Such towns have, for many an age, borne the accusations of moralists, and been warned against by timid fathers and affectionate mothers. Yet were we a coarse and unhewn structure of humanity without them. Living in the country, in an insulated way, never wears off the husk upon one's manners, never sharpens conversational powers, rarely develops the intellect or the morals to the perfection they are capable of—and generally leaves a man in that condition of unbakedness, appropriately called "raw." Advantages there are, truly; but they are preserved on the same principle as the father's who, fearing his son *may* be drowned, lets him never go in the water to learn to swim.

Isolated country life, I perceive, encourages avarice and a singular sort of egotism. Penuriousness is almost universal among the farmers here, and their families; and "living by one's self" is carried to a remarkable extreme.

The other afternoon, tired and sweaty, after a long scramble over the hills and among the woods of Shelter Island, (a fertile "collection of land surrounded by water," in extent of some ten miles by three,) I came down to the shore, opposite Greenport, and found myself just too late for the little ferry boat, which crosses only at long intervals. Nigh the shore ran up a beautiful creek, the water whereof was as clear as plate glass; and the mouth of this creek and the shore helped form a fine knoll whose sides were adorned with thrifty oaks and so forth, altogether a very goodly and wholesome spot. Through a gate, some five or six rods, was a large two-story double house, and the barns and outbuildings gave token to the fatness of the land. The whole air of the spot was so inviting, that I dispatched a ragged little urchin who came down to view me, back again to the house, asking if I could get a bowl of bread and milk. They had no bread, was the answer sent me, but I could have some milk and hominy. I presently found myself at the table of this well-stored dwelling, spooning up some skimmed milk and coarse burnt hominy. An old woman, the mistress of the place, bustled about, and regaled my repast with many words: her husband had gone over to Greenport after "things": she had no servants, and never wanted any: she had had nine children, all of whom were living, but none lived home: they, that is her husband and herself, had settled there thirty-eight years ago. Wasn't she sometimes lonesome? No, she never wanted company—her husband and she found they "got along" best as they were. I noticed large numbers of cows in the neighboring fields: were they hers? Yes: the cheese and butter were sent to market. Those thrifty orchards? Yes, they produced well; the apples were sold. Divers fatting hogs, in the pens; they also were designed for market. Those flocks of poultry, and the daily products of eggs. O, they were not for "poor folks" to consume—they, too, increased the weight of the money bags.

Shortly, the farmer himself came home. He had been across the bay, to "the store," for various purchases. I was amazed to notice that they were just such articles as a workingman's family in New York might get, butter, bread, candles, lard, salt fish, and so on—all by the small quantity! And I discovered, by-and-by, that this man had a good farm of nearly three hundred acres, and money out at interest, and two or three other farms for sale! His farms he put out on shares: all his part of the product was sold over to the stores, and he purchased, by the peck and pound, just enough to live on, from season to season.

Notwithstanding all the old woman's apologies, and protestations, I saw plainly enough that they always lived in this half starving manner. I really could not eat the thin milk and coarse burnt corn; but, as I rose, I put down a shilling on the table. The fierce clutching look of the woman's eyes, as she sidled toward the money, made me sick. It told more than I could write on pages of paper; and it told a degrading story of avarice and wretchedness.[6]

Thirty-eight years agone, that couple, then probably just married and young, had settled down there; and from that time forward they had made money and raised children—the latter, probably, because they found it more economical than hiring people to work on the farm. I cannot describe to you their remarkable queernesses of look and manner. The old woman was fat, but her face, the color of copper, had none of the jolly or motherly expression of most fat old women. Her restless black eyes shifted constantly to and fro, and she seemed to be under the influence of an unsatisfied demon of motion, for she waddled and trotted without a single moment's cessation. Neither a physiognomist nor a phrenologist would have been pleased with her face and head—or the man's either.

The old man had piercing gray eyes, that fixed upon you firmly, and looked you through, with an intense look. His manner and the still-expression (you know what I mean?) of his features didn't trouble one like the woman's; for one don't notice such things so strikingly in a man. But that expression corresponded perfectly with the facts aforesaid—that not one of their nine children lived home—that they had no servants—that they were rich—and that they seized ravenously on my shilling! I almost forgot to say that the wife's mother, a superannuated relic of mortality, aged ninety-two, still lived with them.

I have been somewhat particular in drawing this little "family picture" for you, because, with fewer or greater modifications, it stands good for a sadly large number of Long Island and New England country people, with probably one exception. There are few of the farmers, or farmers' wives about east Long Island who will take shillings for a cup of milk and a slice of bread to the wayfarer. Doubtless the same exception holds good in New England.

You would be amazed, in peregrinating around these quarters, at finding out the number of people who *live alone*. The other day, I turned off the road to call at the hut of a venerable hermitess, that used to remind me of some of the old women in Scott's novels,[7] with her short blanket-cloak, her horn-rimmed spectacles, and her long hickory staff. I made the acquaintance of the dame of a Sunday, some years since, on which occasion she gave me specimen of her vocal powers, evidently then in full vigor. A small gift purchased her good will, and our acquaintance has been preserved by annual installments.[8] Poor, half-deranged, old creature! She lived all alone, in a miserable cottage, some distance from the road—all alone, for many years, though those who were related to her, and who were rich, would have taken her to stay with them, but she would not. Strange and ridiculous, and—but sacred be the poor old crone's weak traits, for she is under the sod. I found the old cottage unoccupied. The paper blinds were up at the windows, and a wild black cat scampered under the house; and a neighbor told me that the old woman had died some six months ago.

To the north of the village, again, in a small two-roomed dwelling, lives a man by himself—an old fellow, who for years has done his own cooking and washing—and made his own shirts, for what I know. He is a fat, stolid looking old man. Benevolence and philoprogenitiveness[9] have made themselves scarce on his skull-cap.

Truly, I might go on, and jot down a long string of these solitary people, who betake themselves aside from their kind, and seem to resist companionship the more they need it by growing old. Sometimes, in the middle of wide "plains," or on the edge of extensive woods, or otherwheres at a great distance from any neighbor, I find families living, who see no one but their own members for days in succession. They hear no news, till it is old—sometimes not the most startling and important occurrences, till months after they are printed in the city papers. And all this within a hundred miles of New York!

From the people themselves I have learned that, generally, at first, it was irksome to them, and they felt solitary enough; but in a very few seasons they liked it better, and by and by it was inexpressibly annoying to be long in a thick town, or surrounded closely by neighbors. They came to *love* their far-removed habitations, and, if their children went away, the old people would stick with double tenacity; and if one of the old people died, the other would still remain in the same place, and would not move away!

Such were the ones, who, when newly married, had bought lands very cheap in those remote spots, and gone to make a living there. But there were others, who from childhood had grown up on similar farms by themselves, surrounded by deserts of plain, or pine, or scruboak;[10] and this class, too—so individuals of them told me—felt happier in their solitude than they could bring themselves to feel where the dwellings were less sparse.

Does some one suggest that from the scattered nature of a country population, vice is scarcer? It appears so, but it is not probably so in reality. *In proportion*, there is as much wickedness in country as in towns. What I mean is this: Suffolk county, L. I., has about 40,000 inhabitants, New York city has eight or ten times that number—does any one suppose that any fair average eighth part of the city generates more vice, or contains more, than Suffolk county? And I believe that the county I mention has as sternly honest a race of inhabitants as any in the Republic.

There is also a great amount of error as to the physical advantages of country life. The *air* is wholesomer, of course; but that advantage is generally counterbalanced by evils in other points. The country child is put to hard work at an early age; he soon loses the elasticity of youth, and becomes round-shouldered and clumsy. He learns to smoke, chew, and drink, about as soon as his town prototype. The diet of country people is generally abominable; pork and grease, doughy bread, and other equally indigestible dishes, form a large portion of their food. They work very much too hard, and put too heavy labors upon the youthful ones. The excessive fatigue of a hurried harvest, in the hottest season of the year, thoroughly breaks the constitution of many a boy and young man.

So much have I informally written, because what I *have* written is by no means the popular view, although the truth. Does any one infer that I would advise country-boys to betake themselves to the city right off? God forgive me, if it should tend that way: no! The city hath its perils, too, and very likely the novice would find them great ones. Yet would I have no child reared up in the barbarous ignorance of so many quite well-off country families. And I say that, no matter what moralists and metaphysicians may teach, *out of cities the human race does not expand and improvise so well morally, intellectually, or physically.* Nor do I yield the point when some one goes farther than our own land, to London, or Paris, or manufacturing Glasgow or Manchester.

PAUMANOK[11]

NOTES

1. Transcribed from Joseph Jay Rubin, *The Historic Whitman* (University Park: Pennsylvania State University Press, 1973), 318–323.

2. Johann Georg Zimmermann (1728–1795) was, in fact, born in Switzerland. His four-volume *On Solitude* was written between 1756 and 1785. Zimmermann suffered from depression and hypochondria, which may have been the cause of the foolish actions that Whitman refers to here. Ellen Judy Wilson et al., *Encyclopedia of the Enlightenment* (New York: Facts on File, 2004), 641.

3. Perhaps from S. C. Walford, *Recollections of a Ramble during the Summer of 1816, in a Letter to a Friend* (London: Smith and Elder, 1817), 70: "At that time, doubtless, when there was no safeguard against individual wrong, then the scholar and the man of letters found no security but in retiring from the scenes of active life, to the soothing pleasures of retirement." Considering the title of this book, Whitman may have sought models for his "Letters from a Travelling Bachelor" when he came across this quote. A more obvious model for Whitman here is James Fenimore Cooper's *Notions of the Americans: Picked up by a Travelling Bachelor* (1828).

4. "I fought the calm delights of obscurity; but I have no will save that of Heav'n; adversity has taught me to bend every secret wish to its all wise decrees." M. Peddle, *The Life of Jacob* (Sherborne, England: R. Goadby, 1785), 76.

5. *Children of the Abbey* (1795) by Regina Maria Roche (1764–1845), *Rinaldo Rinaldini, the Robber Captain* (1797) by Christian August Vulpius (1762–1827), and *Alonzo and Me-*

lissa (1804) by Isaac Mitchell (1759–1812) were Gothic thrillers. Whitman contrasts them here to *Book of the Martyrs* (1563) by John Foxe (1517–1587) and *The Saints' Everlasting Rest* (1650) by Richard Baxter (1615–1691) to portray a rural print culture as both retrograde and zealous.

As a young schoolteacher, Whitman similarly portrayed rural Long Island society in his letters to Abraham Leech: "I believe when the Lord created the world, he used up all the good stuff, and was forced to form Woodbury and its denizens out of the fag ends, the scraps and refuse: for a more unsophisticated race than lives hereabouts you will seldom meet with in your travels." Arthur Golden, "Nine Early Whitman Letters, 1840–1841," *American Literature* 58, no. 3 (1986): 342–360, 347.

6. While Whitman appears shocked here, his letters of 1840–1841 to Abraham Leech express a similar disdain for what he perceived as a particularly rural kind of greed: "The principal feature of the place is the money making spirit, a gold-scraping and wealth hunting fiend, who is the foul incubus to three fourths of this beautiful earth." Ibid., 356.

7. Walter Scott (1771–1832), from *Waverley* (1814): "Once upon a time there lived an old woman, called Janet Gellatley, who was suspected to be a witch, on the infallible grounds that she was very old, very ugly, very poor, and had two sons, one of whom was a poet, and the other a fool, which visitation, all the neighbourhood agreed, had come upon her for the sin of witchcraft."

8. Original reads "instalments."

9. "Philoprogenitiveness" was a phrenological term that referred to the inclination of an individual to feel parental love toward offspring. Phrenology itself was a proto-psychology pioneered by Johann Gaspar Spurzheim (1776–1832) that analyzed personality by mapping the particular ridges and bumps on a person's skull.

10. Scrub oak.

11. "Paumanok" was ostensibly a Native American word for Long Island that Whitman often used as a pen name, first, in "Letters from a Travelling Bachelor," and later, in 1851, in the series "Letters from Paumanok." In the 1860 edition of *Leaves of Grass*, he used the term in the poem "Proto-Leaf," which was later retitled "Starting from Paumanok."

From a Travelling Bachelor [Number IX][1]

New York Sunday Dispatch
DECEMBER 16, 1849

SITUATION OF MONTAUK POINT—LIGHTHOUSE—FERTILITY—AN INVALID FISHERMAN—OPIUM EATING—STRANGE DOINGS AT MONTAUK—SICKENING TURN OF AFFAIRS—A DINNER AT LAST SECURED—THE PROCESSION—THE DINNER—THE START FOR HOME—NIGHT—A DASH OF SENTIMENT—SUNRISE—BREAKFAST—MORE EXCITEMENT—ARRIVAL HOME

[16 Dec. 1849]

Montauk Point![2] how few Americans there are who have not heard of thee—although there are equally few who have seen thee with their bodily eyes, or trodden on thy green-sward. Most people possess an idea, (if they think at all about the matter,) that Montauk Point is a low stretch of land, poking its barren nose out toward the east, and hailing the sea-wearied mariner, as he approacheth our republican shores, with a sort of dry and sterile countenance. Not so is the fact. To its very extremest verge, Montauk is fertile and verdant. The soil is rich, the grass is green and plentiful; and the best patches of Indian corn and garden vegetables I saw last autumn, were within gun shot of the salt waves of the Atlantic, being just five deg. east longitude from Washington, and the very extremest terra firma of the good state of New York.

Nor is the land low in situation. It binds the shore generally in bluffs and elevations. The point where the lighthouse stands—and it is the extreme point—is quite a high hill; it was called by the Indians *Wamponomon*[3]—by modern folks Turtle-hill. The lighthouse here is a very substantial one of an old-fashioned sort, built in 1795; the lights are two hundred feet above the level of the sea.[4] Sheltered in a little vale, near by, is the dwelling of the keeper and his family, the only comfortable residence for many miles. It is a tolerably roomy cottage—a sort of public house; and some inveterate sportsmen and lovers of nature in her wild aspects, come here during the summer and fall, and board awhile, and have fun.

I went out to the very edge of the cliff, and threw myself down on the grass, and tossed aside my slouchy wool hat, and looked to the eastward. The sea was in one of its calmest phases. A hoarse low roar, only, gave some token of its fiercer vitality—a sort of *living* roar, it seemed to me, for it made me think of great storms, and wrecks; and the despairing and dying who had groaned erewhile upon those waters. In a former letter I have described the appearance of the catchers of blue-fish, darting about in their swallow-like boats and trailing their lines. It was upon these men and their maneuvers that I was now gazing.

An invalid-looking man came slowly up the hill while my eyes were out upon the sea there. He seemed to be about nothing in the way of employment, and as he looked curiously and half-bashfully toward me, I called to him. He was a fisherman he told me, by occupation, and had come there to work with the rest.

"But I couldn't stand it," he continued, coughing in a bad hacking way, "went out in the water, and got pretty cold, I had a dead pain all over here," placing his broad hands over the regions of his stomach, lungs, and heart.

We got directly into conversation—which, by-and-by merged into an account of his life, fortunes, and sickness. He further confessed to me that he had for years been in the habit of eating large quantities of opium. He had also lost his appetite.

"Have you had no medical advice?" I asked.

"No"; he felt no faith in doctors; besides it was expensive and troublesome. Notwithstanding his ailments, however, he still continued his opium eating.

That man, at my request, showed me one of the globules which he was in the habit of taking daily. It was frightfully large! He was also becoming troubled frequently with a pain and swelling in one of his legs, which would ache and then remain torpid awhile, so that he could not walk, and then swell up to double its natural proportion. He was a large robust-sized man, of good original development, but very much emaciated in the face, and with bad stuff in his eye balls. He told me that he worked whenever he could, and liked well to come a-fishing, from which sport he was only deterred by the imperious suddenness of the before-mentioned pain in all the important vital organs, that followed his getting wet and chilled. He was better dressed than the ordinary fisherman and—probably gratified at the interest of a city stranger, and liking to talk over his troubles and be condoled—he told me that he had parents who lived toward the middle of the island, who were well off, and wished him to come home to them. He had married, years ago, and moved near Sag Harbor; though his wife was dead, and he had no family.

From the man's statement, it needed not much physiological knowledge, to tell that there was a general abstraction of the vital stimulus of the great organs,—the "dead pain" as he well-expressed it,—a lethargic slowness of the functions of the heart, stomach, and liver. Besides he must have had some pulmonary affection; the cough signified a sorry state of things that way. Opium was a poison to him—and had undoubtedly brought him to the pass I saw, and was vitiating his blood, as instanced in the swelled and painful leg.

I advised him by all means to stop his fishing employments—for he expressed a design to stay until the party he was with went home, and meanwhile to go out with them whenever he felt well enough. I was at a loss to enjoin the cessation of the opium or not; but, laying before the poor frightened fellow the plain condition and probabilities, I told him by all means to get himself home to his old mother's nursing care, to lay by for a while, and to get the advice of a trusty physician, after stating all the symptoms and habits he had just related. And his accidental talk with me was the first rational colloquy the man had had with any living being on the subject.

We talk a great deal about "the intelligence of the age," and so on; but truly there is ignorance enough yet among the masses to grow up in mountains of sickness, destitution and vice.

By the by, this opium eating, may be more prevalent in county districts than one would think.[5] At Southold not many days before, I had come across a man, who, from the same practice, achieved himself into a helpless state, and a painful swelling of the limbs. For many years, he had supported himself and family, by fishing, gunning, and light jobs; but out of his narrow income he must invariably get the little monthly box of opium! The day I saw him at Southold, he was going to the alms house, and there the poor helpless fellow is at this moment.

As every man was master of his time between our arrival, and the period of dinner, I took a good long ramble for several miles to and fro. To a mineralogist, I fancy Montauk Point must be a perpetual feast. Even to my unscientific eyes there were innumerable wonders and beauties all along the shore, and the edges of the cliffs. There were earths of all colors, and stones of every conceivable shape, hue, and density, with shells, large boulders of pure white substance, and layers of those smooth round pebbles called "milk-stones" by the country children. There were some of them tinged with pale green, blue, or yellow—some streaked with various colors—and so on.

We rambled up the hills to the top of the highest—we ran races down—we scampered along the shore, jumping from rock to rock—we declaimed all the violent appeals and defiances we could remember, commencing with "Celestial states, immortal powers, give ear!"[6] away on the ending which announced that

Richard had almost lost his wind by dint of calling Richmond to arms.[7] I doubt whether those astonished echoes[8] ever before vibrated with such terrible ado. Then we pranced forth again, like mad kine—we threw our hats in the air—aimed stones at the shrieking sea-gulls, mocked the wind, and imitated the cries of various animals in a style that beat nature all out! We challenged each other to the most deadly combats—we tore various passions into tatters—made love to the girls, in the divine words of Shakespeare and other poets, whereat the said girls had the rudeness to laugh till the tears ran down their cheeks in great torrents. We indulged in some impromptu quadrilles, of which the "chasez" took each participant couple so far away from the other that they were like never to get back. We hopped like crows; we pivoted like Indian dervishes; we went through the trial dance of *La Bayadère*[9] with wonderful vigor; and some one of our party came nigh dislocating his neck through volunteering to turn somersets like a circus fellow. Every body caught the contagion, and there was not a sensible behaved creature among us, to rebuke our mad antics by comparison.

Most appalling news met us on returning from this nice exercise! *Our master of the revels had utterly failed to negotiate a dinner for us at the cottage!* Three several parties had been in advance of ours, that day, and had eaten up the last crumb in the house! Wasn't this enough to make Rome howl?

But it was no time to howl any more—we had already sharpened our appetites quite enough by that sort of sport. Something must be done, and quickly. A very fat, tender, plump-looking young woman, was already trying to hide herself from the ravenous looks of two or three of the most alimentively[10] developed of our party—when we luckily spied a flock of well grown chickens feeding near the cottage door. We still had lots of bread and butter aboard the sloop. Moreover, were there not the freshest and finest fish to be bought within stone-throw? And couldn't we get potatoes from that garden, and onions likewise? And what was better than *chowder*?

Our almost collapsed hearts were now bounded up again like young colts. We proceeded in solid phalanx to the landlady,—the Mrs. Lighthouse-Keeper—and with an air which showed we were not going to stand on trifles, gave voice to our ultimatum. The landlady attempted to demur, but the major domo loudly proposed that if all else failed, we should eat the landlady herself; and this motion being passed by acclamation, the good woman gave in.

Six fat pullets had their heads off in as many minutes—and shortly afterwards we made a solemn procession down to the water, each man carrying a part of the provender, in its raw state. For we determined to cook our meal on board the sloop, and owe no thanks to those inhospitable shores. Our faithful major at the head, carried a large sea-bass; next followed the young sailor with six headless chickens, whose necks (like Pompey's statue,) all the while ran blood;[11] next the fat girl with a splendid head of cabbage—behind whom marched the continuation of us, each furnished with something to make up the feast. Toward the rear came I, possessed of a stew-pan, purchased at a great price, and borne by me, I hope, with appropriate dignity.

All worked to a charm. Amid laughter, glee, and much good sport, (though I and the fat girl cried bitterly, peeling onions,) we cooked that dinner. And O ye Heavens, and O thou sun, that looked'st upon that dinner with a glow just as thou wast dipping thy red face below the western horizon—didn't we enjoy it? The very waters were as quiet as a stone floor, and we made a table by placing three boards on some barrels, and seats by other boards, on half barrels. But the strongest part of all is that when we got through there were fragments enough to rival the miraculous remains of the feast of the five loaves and two fishes. I shall remember that dinner to my dying day.

We pulled up stakes, and put for home. But we had overstaid our time, and the tide too—Night came on. It was calm, clear and beautiful. The stars sparkled, and the delicate figure of the new moon moved down the west like a timid bride. I spread a huge bear-skin on the deck, and lay flat on it, and spoke not a word, but looked at the sky and listened to the talk around me. They told love stories, and ghost stories, and sang country ditties; but the night and the scene mellowed all, and it came to my ears through a sort of moral distillation; for I fear, under any circumstances, 'twould have appeared stale and flippant to me. But it did not then; indeed quite the contrary.

I made my bed in the furled sail, watching the stars as they twinkled, and falling asleep so. A stately and solemn night, that, to me—for I was awake much and saw the countless armies of heaven marching stilly in the space up there—marching stilly and slowly on, and others coming up out of the east to take their places. Not a sound, not an insect, interrupted the exquisite silence,—nothing but the ripple of the water against the sides of the vessel. An indescribable serenity pervaded my mind—a delicious abnegation of the ties of the body. I fancied myself leaping forward into the extent of the space, springing as it were from star to star. Thoughts of the boundless Creation must have expanded my mind, for it certainly played the most unconscionable pranks from its tabernacle lying there in those fields of hempen duck.

Sunrise found us alive and stirring. We he-creatures departed for an island near by, on whose sedgy creeks there was the look of wild birds. Over the sand, here, we issued a second edition of the proceedings on the hills and shores of Montauk. But, owing to the absence of the terraqueous girls, we didn't have as good a time. After all, what a place this wretched earth would be without the petticoats!

A plentiful breakfast was ready when we returned: the Lord only knows whence came all the viands, for they appeared to rise, like Venus, from the froth of the sea. However, I asked no questions, but ate thankfully.

Up sails, then, and away!—a clear sky still overhead, and a dry, mild wind to carry us before it. I was astonished at the amount of vitality that resides in man, and woman too. One would have thought the exertions and outpourings we had performed within the last twenty hours, should have left us cooled down a little. Angels bless you, sir! 'twas no such thing. Fast and loud rose the voices again, the clear upper notes of the girls, and laughter and singing. We knew we should soon be home—down amid the clouds and commonplaces—and we determined to make the most of it. And we *did*.

Ah, my dear friend, I despair of putting upon paper any true description of that condensed Babel. Our shouts transpierced the wounded air. Even the dullest of us seemed filled with mental quicksilver which rose higher and higher, until there seemed some chance of not enough being left in our heels to anchor us fast upon earth. Truly those were wonderful hours!

We hove in sight of the steeples and white-paint of home, and soon after, the spirits we had served deserted us. (There was no brandy aboard, mind, and hadn't been.) We landed at the dock, and went up to the village, and felt the tameness of respectable society setting around us again. Doubtless it was all right; but as for me, I fancied I felt the mercury dwindling down, down, down into the very calves of my legs.

PAUMANOK

NOTES

1. Transcribed from Joseph Jay Rubin, *The Historic Whitman* (University Park: Pennsylvania State University Press, 1973), 341–347. According to Rubin, the shortened title of this article is in the original.

2. This is the second of two of Whitman's excursions to Montauk Point reprinted in this volume. The first is "East Long Island Correspondence [Letter III]," *Brooklyn Daily Eagle,*

September 20, 1847 (above).

3. Perhaps derived from "wampum," a shell used by Algonquin peoples as a form of currency.

4. Montauk Point Light, designed by the architect John McComb (1763–1853), was funded by the U.S. government and completed in 1797. The light stands 160 feet above sea level. Francis Ross Holland, *America's Light Houses: An Illustrated History* (Mineola, N.Y.: Dover, 1972), 83.

5. According to J. Hector St John de Crevecoeur (1735–1813), Nantucket residents ingested a dose of opium each morning. J. Hector St John de Crevecoeur, *Letters from an American Farmer* (New York: Fox, Duffield, 1904, originally published in 1782), 211; see also Rubin, 387. The image of the opium addict was popularized in the nineteenth century by *Confessions of an Opium Eater* (1822) by Thomas De Quincey (1785–1859). For a discussion of American involvement in the opium trade, see Thomas N. Layton, *The Voyage of the "Frolic": New England Merchants and the Opium Trade* (Stanford, Calif.: Stanford University Press, 1997). As the opium trade with China increased, the drug increasingly entered popular consciousness. For example, a search for the word "opium" in publications between 1820 and 1840 shows a rise in the frequency of the term in English language publications during this period (1820: 0.00058837 percent, 1840: 0.0011375012 percent). "Google Books, Ngram Viewer," books.google.com/ngrams.

6. Jove (Zeus) from Pope's translation of *Iliad*: "Celestial states, immortal gods! Give ear, / Hear our decree, and reverence what ye hear; / The fix'd decree which not all heaven can move; / Thou, Fate! fulfil it: and, ye powers! approve!" Book III.

7. In Shakespeare's *Richard III*, Act 4, Scene 2, Richard is unsettled by a remembered prophecy where Richmond (Henry Tudor) becomes king: "Richmond! When last I was at Exeter, / The mayor in courtesy show'd me the castle, / And call'd it Rougemont: at which name I started, / Because a bard of Ireland told me once /I should not live long after I saw Richmond."

8. Original reads "echos."

9. A ballet by Daniel Auber (1782–1871). Thanks to Gertrud Due Elisberg for finding this reference.

10. A phrenological term for the "feeding instinct." Whitman used phrenological terms throughout his earliest editions of *Leaves of Grass*.

11. In Shakespeare's *Julius Caesar,* Pompey's statue is covered with Caesar's blood (Act 3, Scene 2).

From a Travelling Bachelor [Number X][1]

New York Sunday Dispatch
DECEMBER 23, 1849

AN INTERESTING JOURNEY DOWN FULTON STREET AND ACROSS FULTON FERRY—OBJECTION TO STRAIGHT STREETS—ARCHITECTURE OF THE LANDING—HOLT'S HOTEL, AND THE BUILDER—THE CLERKS—THE BOAT—VIEW FROM THE RIVER—CROSSING IN THE DEPTH OF WINTER, AND IN A DENSE FOG—SCENES—ACCIDENTS—THE BRIDGE PROPOSITION

[23 Dec. 1849]

Many books have been written, to describe journeys between the Old and New World, and what was done or seen therein, and afterward. But we know of no work—at least we feel sure none has yet been issued by the Harpers, Appletons, or any of our great publishers—describing a voyage accross[2] the Fulton Ferry. This is the more remarkable, as that is a jaunt taken every day by myriads of people. Besides, we have ourself seen authors, editors, reporters and all departments of the "press-gang" go aboard the boats of the Fulton Ferry Company, (after depositing two cents with the gentleman at the gate,) and cross over—sometimes even coming back again on the same boat. (This latter, doubtless, to get the pure air, at the economical price of a penny a trip.)

Fulton street—we are going down the one on the New York side—is not what may be called the prettiest one in town. Neither is it after the straightest sect of streets. On the contrary, it is rather ugly, and very much crooked. It is an old street. It probably came in with the Knickerbockers.[3] We are free to assume that it once had some Dutch name, before it was christened after the great applier of steam to boat moving. We suggest an inquiry that way to some antiquarian, and solemnly believe that if he were to burrow out the facts which bear on this interesting subject, he would get something more than his labor for his pains.[4]

While upon the subject, let us in confidence reader, just whisper to you that we are no friend to thoroughfares that are rigid and right-angular. The checker-board[5] principle applied to laying out a town is our abomination. What romance is there about it? Such exactness reduces one to despair! What is left for you to see, after you have traversed *one* of such avenues? Nothing. When you "go" one, you have gone the whole. Much more do we prefer the winding and curvicular arrangement. We like to come upon new shows—to turn a bend, and behold something fresh. Uniformity! Why it's the taste of the vulgar. Nature hath nought of it. The skies, the earth, the waters, and the woods laugh in your face, at such rectangular tediousness. But we are digressing.

Architecturally there is nothing great in Fulton street—unless it be the United States Hotel,[6] down near the Ferry. When it was built, that was the greatest specimen of a Hotel in New York. Mr. Holt, the putter-up, had made a hundred thousand dollars out of cheap eating houses under the Fulton market. He commenced with less than ten dollars; he and his wife did the work, and waited on the customers. The ambition of the man's heart was to build *a great Hotel*. Accordingly, in "dear times," he put out contracts for the tall-storied concern we have mentioned. He spent his hundred thousand dollars, and went on giving notes and mortgages for some twice as much more. He finished it. Proudly and contentedly he entered it as lord and master. But alas, alas! how transitory is human pride! The "days of the speculation" passed like a dream, after having lighted many fools the way to dusky death. Mr. Holt was unable to satisfy his mortgages, which, somehow, *had* to be satisfied. Consequently the great Hotel was sold, for just short of the amount of the aforesaid mortgages, and poor Mr. Holt was left without a dollar of his hundred thousand!

But here we are at the Ferry entrance, after having passed, without personal outrage, the stream of carts, omnibusses, and all sorts of wheeled horrors, that surround, (like things Milton describes,[7]) the entrance to the great space beyond. The piece of architecture before us is of wood, well painted. It is of the simplest order of the genus roof. Under its shadow are many small edifices—besides a large plank floor.

It has been a wonder to us that the Ferry Company do not put up, there, substantial and useful buildings, of stone and iron, with fine large entrances. They are rich enough to do it, and the investment would be better than any stocks in Wall street. Put this hint in your memory, gentlemen.

Pause a moment under this pine canopy, and you will find food for observation, and thought too. There is the special room where "No gentlemen are admitted unless accompanying ladies." There are two other rooms for the masculine gender. Outside there is always a crowd waiting, stamping its feet with impatience for the boats—as if Time didn't fly fast enough without wanting to hurry it. The most impatient gentlemen here are the young clerks. It is perfect agony for them to be just half a second too late for the boat. On such occasions you may see what a struggle it costs them to restrain their legs from leaping into the river. The time until the arrival of the next boat, (which extends from a second to three quarters of a minute,) these excited youths pass in a state of mind which must be felt before it can be realized. Then to see them wait at the very edge of the wharf, and spring on the incoming boat, to the manifest danger of fat personages standing placidly in front! Afterward, the rush for the farther end—the sharp glance around, to see whether there are any fashionable coats aboard—the intense earnestness with which our youthful friends watch for the premonitory symptoms of the boat's starting! Ah, these city clerks are a peculiar race; on all occasions, you can tell them with as much certainty as you can tell a New England voice.

Then we put off—for the bell has tapped twice. Perhaps we have come on the "Manhattan," the newest of these steamers. Behold the roomy and high-ceiling'd ladies' cabin, its clear, open, airy sweep, and the colored glass windows, giving a glow to the light. The seats are cushioned most comfortably, and all around run pipes containing "hot stuff" to warm the air these cold winter times. The ladies, too, *they* form not the least part of the pleasantness. When the cabin is full, and they are seated in close rows all along from one end of the cabin to the other, it takes a fellow of some nerve to run the gauntlet through that cabin. For our part, we always feel our heart beat quicker when we attempt it—and are fain to pop down in a seat before we get half way. But then every body knows we have an unusual amount of modesty.

Who has crossed the East River and not looked with admiration on the beautiful view afforded from the middle of the stream? The forests of the New York shipping, lining the shores as far as one can see them—the tall spire of Trinity looming far up over all the other objects—various other spires—the tops of the trees on the Battery and in the Parks—these we have left behind us. In front stands Brooklyn—Brooklyn the beautiful! The Heights stretch along in front, lined now with dwellings for nearly the whole extent; but with space still left for a Public Promenade, if it be applied to that purpose *soon.* To the left of the Heights, the open mouth of Fulton street, the great entrance to the city—up whose vista you can see many of the principal Brooklyn buildings, particularly the square squatty tower of St. Ann's Church. Away to the left lies the Navy Yard, and the great Dry Dock, now nearly finished. Then Williamsburgh, another place of beauty. She too, has her high banks, and they show admirably from the river.

On the other side our eyes behold a still more varied scene. Governor's Island, in shape like a well proportioned wart, looks green even at this season of the year; and those straight, regularly planted poplars are in perfect accordance with the military character of the place. Far to the distance is Staten Island, and the Jersey shore. The Battery Point is hidden by the masts of the shipping.

A moving panorama is upon all parts of the waters. Sail craft and steamboats are in every direction. Observe, too, the dexterity with which our pilot plies between the crowd that cross his way. He can shave by, to the verge of a hair. He makes all allowances for the strength of the tide, and "brings her in" at the appointed time, as a fine rider manages a well-trained horse.

Nor should we omit to mention a good point connected with the management of these boats. Each one has a respectable person, elderly and staid, who keeps things strait, and acts, when there may be need, as chevalier to the ladies. My old friends, Mr. Doxsey[8] and Mr. Van Duyne[9] are in this department.

Soon, now, will come the time for big cakes of ice in the river. We have a fondness for crossing then,—particularly when we have to go "all the way round Robin Hood's barn."[10] Why, bless your soul! in our day, we have taken a forced trip, and a merry one, round Governor's Island, between starting from Brooklyn and arriving at New York; filling up time enough, in clear sailing, to go from New York to Poughkeepsie. It is now several winters since the ice has been so "fixed," as to permit crossing the East River on foot. We remember such things, however, and have, on our own legs, done that feat of courage. We came marvellously near taking a trip down the day, however, for the ice got dislodged again and was moving maliciously off—leaving us just time, by hard "scrouging," to hop on the end of a certain pier, with the determination never again to trust our flesh on a mass of congealed water.

There is another favorite time we have for crossing at the Fulton Ferry. It is when a heavy fog spreads itself. We like to start out, and listen to the muffled tolling of the bell in the distance, and go prowling slowly along, with divers men on the look-out for breakers. We are not sure but we enjoy a bit—just a *little bit*, of danger—nothing, of course, that would give us the chance of taking to the cold water, but just a spice of excitement. After some time, we come out, perhaps, near the Catharine Ferry. Then the nervousness of those who are in a great hurry—merchants wanting to get to their business, clerks, and people who have engagements that they fear will have to be broken.

There is "a great deal of human nature," to be seen in crossing the Fulton Ferry. All imaginable sorts and styles of rational and irrational life, besides a variety of manufactured matter, transmits itself there, from one shore to the other. We like too, to cross at night, when there is a clear sky; always feeling sorry that the jaunt isn't ten times as long. Yes, yes; for some of the nicest of the "happy ten minutes" that glitter in one's experience, have we been indebted to the Fulton Ferry.

Fortunately for our nerves, we have never yet seen a serious accident on this great passage line. It is sickening, though, what things do sometimes happen here! A fellow in his haste, jumps *at* the landing, from the incoming boat—misses his footing!—slips!—O, horrible!—falls between the steam-moved mass, and the solid timbers of the wharf![11] Stout faces, then, grow ashy, and the bravest are appalled! But the hands attached to the boat, spring to the rescue. What they do, depends upon the circumstances of the case; but they always act promptly, effectively, and for the best.

We notice there is much talk, just at present, of *a Bridge* to Brooklyn. Nonsense. There is no need of a bridge, while there are incessantly plying such boats as the Manhattan, the Wyandance, and the Montauk.[12] If there be any spare energy, let it be applied to improving the indifferent accommodations at Catherine ferry, and the wretchedness of that at Jackson street. Also, to completing the proposed lines from the bottoms of Montague street and Bridge street.

PAUMANOK

NOTES

1. Transcribed from Joseph Jay Rubin, *The Historic Whitman* (University Park: Pennsylvania State University Press, 1973), 347–352. Jerome Loving, in *Walt Whitman: The Song of Himself* (Berkeley: University of California Press, 1999), speculates that with this editorial, Whitman may have already begun thinking of his later poem, "Crossing Brooklyn Ferry" (148). Whitman's crossing for the poem also took place in December: "I too many and many a time crossed the river the sun half an hour high, / I watched the December sea-gulls, I saw them high in the air floating with motionless wings oscillating their bodies . . . "

2. Spelling in Rubin, from which this transcription is made.

3. Originally a Dutch surname, "Knickerbocker" came to be a popular term for New York's established upper class. Its most well known use was in Washington Irving's *A History of New-York from the Beginning of the World to the End of the Dutch Dynasty, by Diedrich*

Knickerbocker (1809).

4. Fulton Street was named for Robert Fulton (1765–1815) and was laid out in 1704 as part of the King's Highway. Leonard Benardo and Jennifer Weiss, *Brooklyn By Name: How the Neighborhoods, Streets, Parks, Bridges, and More Got Their Names* (New York: New York University Press, 2006), 45.

5. Hyphen in original.

6. The United States Hotel was opened in 1833 and demolished in 1902. It was originally called "Holt's Hotel," after its first proprietor. The *New York Times* described the building having an "almost square edifice, having about 100 feet frontage on Pearl, Fulton, and Water Streets. A grant promenade was the feature of the roof, and surmounting this was a cupola, over 125 feet from the street, from which one of the best views of the city and the harbor was to be had in its palmy days." "Stephen Holt and His Folly," *New York Times,* March 12, 1902, nytimes.com.

7. John Milton (1608–1674) is best known for his epic *Paradise Lost.*

8. In 1844, Samuel Doxsey was named in the *Brooklyn Daily Eagle* as "Superintendent of the Poor." See, *Brooklyn Daily Eagle,* October 31, 1844, http://bklyn.newspapers.com/newspage/50254181/.

9. Probably John Van Duyne, Inspector of Customs, *New York General & Business Directory for 1840–41* (Brooklyn, N.Y.: T. & J. W. Leslie & W. F. Chichester, 1840), bklyn-genealogy-info.com/Directory/1840.html.

10. Since Robin Hood was an outlaw who lived in Sherwood Forest, all of the fields of the region were his "barn." So, to go around "Robin Hood's barn" is to travel far and wide. This colloquial phrase was commonly used in popular print culture in the nineteenth century. The editors found examples in periodicals such as *Lady's Companion* (1839), *New York Teacher and American Educational Monthly* (1869), *Atlantic Monthly* (1872), and *Journal of the Maine Ornithological Society* (1899).

11. Whitman had worried about this sort of thing earlier. See, for example, "Philosophy of Ferries," *Brooklyn Daily Eagle,* August 13, 1847, and "An Anecdote with a Moral," *Brooklyn Daily Eagle,* August 31, 1847.

12. The Brooklyn Bridge was completed in 1883.

Letters from Paumanok [No. 2][1]

New York Evening Post
JUNE 28, 1851

Greenport, L.I., June 28th.

A VILLAGE WITH A NEW NAME

The turnpike on the peninsula of which Orient, (formerly Oysterponds,) is the eastern point, is a pleasant and thrifty looking road. It is laid quite thickly with farm cottages, none of them very grand in their appearance; but then there are hardly any that seem remarkably mean, either.

One new and costly house, on the north side of the turnpike, is the residence of Dr. Lord, formerly member of Congress, and the owner of large tracts of land here.

Strolling on through the neighborhood, I came to a thicker collection of houses, formerly known as Rocky Point, but now christened with the more romantic appellation of "Marion."

Very great confusion arises on Long Island, from the numerosity of names, belonging to one and the same place. Hardly one fourth of the neighborhoods retain the same names for twenty years in succession! Letters, packages, and even travellers are constantly getting lost, through this unfortunate propensity.

I MAKE THE ACQUAINTANCE OF AN OLD FELLOW

As I was passing the "store" at Marion, I was accosted by an old fellow, with a pipe in his mouth, and a clam-basket and hoe in his hands. He had evidently put a dram or two into his stomach, more than it could cleverly stand; but it probably made him better company than he would have been without the liquor.

I must give you a description of him, for I responded to his salute and we walked on a way together.

His trousers were originally bright blue homespun, but they had long since seen their good times, and were now variegated with patches of many colors—particularly about the "seat," which was of the style that tailors call "baggy." His vest was of a spotted dirt color, and of a cut like those you see worn by Turkish slaves, or by "supes"[2] in a melo-drama, at the Bowery Theatre. Its points hung down in front. The figure of the old man was short, squat and round-shouldered, but of Herculean bone and muscle. His hair was not very gray, and he showed palpable signs of strength.

But his hat! It was a hat which I am sorry now I did not buy up and present to one of the Broadway "merchants" in that line, or to the eating house near the Fulton ferry, whose window has such amusing curiosities. It was a truly wonderful hat! It was not a large hat; neither could it have been called a small hat. It was unquestionably a very old hat, however. It had probably stood the storms of many winters, and the sun of many summers. Yet it held itself tolerably erect, with various undulations and depressions in its surface; but an unfortunate paucity of brim. True, there was an apology for a brim, but it was a very narrow apology. It was laughable to see that hat!

While the old man was telling us that he owned a certain windmill, which we were then and there passing, and that he was now on his way to get a basket of soft clams, for bait to catch fish, a wagon came along, in which he was furnished with a ride, and so left us.

THE ROAD—THE BRIDGE—THE FISH

The various windows of Rocky Point doubtless exhibit a flitting array of heads on all occasions of strangers passing. It was, therefore, the case, that our walk, for a while, was quite a public passage. Indeed, had there been a little hurrahing, we might, (my companion and I,) have fancied ourselves some distinguished people, taking the honors.

A bend in the road brought us to an old mill, on the broad railing of whose bridge I sat down to rest. Underneath, as I leaned over, I saw in the stream myriads of little fish endeavoring to get up, but balked by an obstruction, and apparently in council, as if at a loss what to do. The water was as clear as glass.

Directly two or three large eels crawled lazily along, wriggling their tails, and sucking up whatever they found on the bottom. Then came a couple of little black fish; after which a real big one, twenty inches long, opening his great white mouth, and behaving in a very hoggish manner. Also, there were crabs, and divers small fry.

Had I possessed a hook and line, there is no telling what feats might have been performed.

A couple of rods from the shore, and near at hand, was the old gentleman, with the remarkable hat; he had arrived before us, and was busily engaged with his hoe, digging a basket of soft clams, "for bait," as he said. He procured quite a mess in fifteen minutes, and then brought them up, and sat down on the bridge by me, to rest himself.

A COLLOQUY—"AUNT REBBY"

Lighting his pipe very deliberately, he proceeded to catechise me as to my name, birth-place, and lineage—where I was from last, where I was staying, what my occupation was, and so on. Having satisfied himself on these important points, I thought it no more than fair to return the compliment in kind, and so pitched into him.

He was born on the spot where he now lived; that very same Rocky Point. He was sixty-seven years old. For twenty years he had kept a butcher's stall in Fly Market, in New York, and left that business to move back on the "old homestead."

He volunteered the information that he was a Universalist in his religious belief, and asked my opinion upon the merits of the preachers of that faith, Mr. Chapin,[3] Mr. Thayer,[4] Mr. Balch,[5] and others. He also commenced what he probably intended for a religious argument; and there was no other way than for me to stop him off, by direct inquiries into the state of his family and his real estate.

He was "well off" in both respects, possessing a farm of over a hundred acres, running from the turnpike to the Sound, and being the father of numerous sons and daughters. He expatiated on the merits of his land at great length; and was just going into those of his bodily offspring, when our confab was fated to receive a sudden interruption. For at this moment came along an old woman with a little tin kettle in her hand.

"Aunt Rebby," at once exclaimed the old gentleman, "don't you know me ?"

But Aunt Rebby seemed oblivious.

"Is it possible you don't know me? Why we've bussed one another many a time in our young days!"

A new light broke upon the dim eyes of the old dame.

"Why Uncle Dan'l!" cried she, "can this be you?"

Uncle Dan'l averred that it wasn't any body else. And then ensued a long gossip, of which I was the edified and much-amused hearer. They had not met each other, it seems, for years, and there needed to be a long interchange of news.

"What a fine mess of clams you've got," said the old lady.

"Yes," responded Uncle Dan'l.

"But I," rejoined the old lady, in a mournful voice—"I have no body to dig clams for me now."

"No, I s'pose not," said the other composedly; "your boys are all gone now."

Supposing that the "boys" had emigrated to California, or married and moved off, I ventured an inquiry as to where they had gone.

Three young men, all the sons of the old woman, had died of consumption. The last was buried only a short time before.

Old times were talked of. Aunt Rebby expressed it as her positive opinion that the young folks of the present day don't enjoy half as much fun as the young folks of fifty years ago, and a little longer, did. She was seventy years old, and remembered the days of General Washington. Those were jovial times, but now "it was all pride, fashion and ceremony."

At the mention of pride, Uncle Dan'l interrupted her with an invitation to look at him and his apparel, and say whether he furnished any exhibition of that vice.

WE RETURN HOMEWARD

The afternoon being now pretty far advanced, Aunt Rebby wended on her way towards the east; and the old man, with I and my companion, turned our courses westward. The old fellow shouldered his heavy basket, which dripped down his back.

I made him tell me the personal history of the affairs of each family, as we passed the houses on our way. But, although I was much amused and interested with the narration, perhaps your readers wouldn't be, and so I pass it by.

About twenty-eight months ago, the old man's two eldest sons, the one of 33, the other 24 years of age, had sailed off in the new and fine sloop "Long Island," bound for some port nearly down to Florida. He had never heard from them since. They were lost in a terrible storm that came up while they were out at sea. They owned half the sloop, which was worth $5000.

When we arrived at the old fellow's house, he invited us in and treated us to good berries. And so, at sundown, we had a nice cool walk of three miles, back to our quarters.

NOTES

1. Transcribed from Walt Whitman, *The Uncollected Poetry and Prose of Walt Whitman*, ed. Emory Holloway (Gloucester, Mass.: Peter Smith, 1972), 1:250–253.

2. "Estimable individuals who lay down carpets and carry off chairs and tables." "Theatrical Supes," *New York Times*, June 9, 1872, nytimes.com.

3. Perhaps Augusta Jane Chapin (1836–1905), Universalist minister.

4. Thomas Baldwin Thayer (1812–1886), Universalist minister.

5. William Stevens Balch (1806–1887), Universalist minister.

Long Island is a Great Place![1]

Brooklyn Daily Times
JULY 30, 1857

For thirty years past, there has been a suggestion made by spasms, sometimes in joke, sometimes in earnest, that Long Island should become a State by itself! The comparison is made between its extent of surface, the number of its population—and then in the comparison, Rhode Island and Delaware are brought in.

Long Island is about a hundred and twenty miles long—two thirds of it being occupied by Suffolk County—"Old Suffolk," with forked snout thrust forth into the Atlantic, and "Turtle Hill," (the eastern extremity on which is built the light house,)[2] like a verdant wart on one of the projections.

Going east, by the Long Island Railroad, after you leave Hicksville, you travel ten or twelve miles through the Plains to Deer Park; and then the succeeding forty or fifty miles is mostly a barren and uninviting route, the soil flat, whitish, coarse, sometimes hard, more often friable, and sandy, not good to retain manure, with parts of the surface covered with tough grass, lichens, and patches of "kill calf."

But the more prevailing feature of the route through which the Long Island Railroad runs, beyond Deer Park, is the spread of medium-sized pines—not the grand trees of the southern states, or of the far north, but a different thing altogether. The tracts of Long Island pines are never left to attain their growth; the farmers use them, without stint, for firewood—and devastating fires rage every year through some portions of them.

Another more modern reason is that Charcoal-burning has, within the past ten years, become quite a great business, through that half of the Island. As you pass along you see the conical stacks, covered with earth and turf, smoking through crevices in the sides, and at the top. Occasionally too the huts of the charcoal-burners are visible—rude, undeveloped, original houses, formed of branches of trees, earth, and perhaps a few cheap boards.

Whiskey, cider, cheap rum, or some other stimulant, is an indispensable part of the stores in these huts. Pork, sea-biscuit, and coffee, are mostly likely there; but liquor may be counted upon as certainly there. The Charcoal burners themselves are a class of men worth studying a little, and writing about—all of which we leave for another opportunity.

Slowly, but quite surely, these vast tracts of pine are being cleared from the heart and breast of Long Island. In twenty-five or thirty years from now, perhaps the clearance will be quite general. The land will then warrant the outlay required before it can be made useful for human sustenance, through agriculture.

But the strange passenger through this Island must not receive what he sees along these barrens, plains, and pineries, as a sample of the whole; for they form indeed but a fraction of the Island. Both on the south side, and on the north side, the main part of the soil is good. Take them all through, the lands of Long Island are certainly better, in their native condition, than those of any one of the New England States.

All the peninsula of Montauk is good soil. It is now unsettled—fifteen or twenty miles without as many houses or farms. It is largely used for commons and pasture; rights for grazing are also hired out by the towns. The towns have the ownership of Montauk, in usufruct. They use it, or sell the use of it, but cannot sell the land with complete title. We believe the Indians have yet a legal foothold here. Some way will have to be found to "extinguish" their title.[3]

Shelter Island is another unknown, untraveled, but interesting part of Long Island. It is about the size of Staten Island, and is equally picturesque. It lies in the waters of the Peconic, and is enclosed, as in the opened and half-embracing claws of a huge lobster, sheltering it all around; hence its name.

The south side—the Great South Bay—the fishing and fowling—the fishermen, the natives, the curious and original characters, so quaint, so smacking of salt and sea-weed—the sand-islands out in the bays—Fire Island—the wrecks and wreckers—all these richly repay the journeyer and explorer, from Rockaway to the Hamptons.

The North side is more hilly, and has many promontories, coves, &c. It is exceedingly beautiful in parts, as any one must acknowledge who goes on a day's sail through the Sound. The North side is very favorable to fruit—apples, pears, cherries, grapes, and the wild berries.

Thus dashing off at random a very few of the points of interest and note, belonging to Long Island, we think we are safe in making the assertion at the head of this article.

We have to add, in conclusion, that our readers may soon expect in our columns a running series of letters, depicting the places, scenes, shores, improvements, and the salient traits of the people also, through Long Island, penned *con amore* from the same hand as the foregoing.

NOTES

1. From a transcription in the papers of Herbert Bergman, East Lansing, Michigan. The editors also consulted a badly damaged version of this editorial in scanned format from the Brooklyn Public Library—Brooklyn Collection. This editorial is listed as Whitman's in *I Sit and Look Out* as "Long Island is a Great Place" (190), and in White's bibliography of Whitman's journalism (35). Whitman, in this editorial, echoes themes in both "Letters from a Travelling Bachelor" and "Brooklyniana."

2. See "From a Travelling Bachelor [Number IX]," *New York Sunday Dispatch*, December 16, 1849 (above).

3. See "East Long Island Correspondence [Letter III]," *Brooklyn Daily Eagle*, September 20, 1847 (above).

A Gossipy August Article.[1]

Brooklyn Daily Times
AUGUST 12, 1858

Well, here we are, pretty well toward the end of the summer months—looking out, as we write this article upon the clear August sunshine, and penning down whatever happens to flow from the point of our pen. Take notice, therefore, that we may perhaps gossip from theme to theme—and that we do not promise whether we shall write any thing very profound or not. Perhaps the better for you reader. For, after all, a little lazy and indolent reading is not to be despised. Have you not observed that those fellows, companions or authors, who are forever so sensible and solid, we sometimes feel it a huge relief to escape from?

Yes, the summer will now soon draw to a close. The indications are unmistakeable.[2] The days are an hour and a half shorter than they were, when at the longest. People begin more generally to say, Have you *been* in the country? While the future tense, in their interrogatories on the subject, has become disused for the season.

At the same time, let us remark, as our private opinion, that there is no preferable period for jaunting off into the rural regions, than these forthcoming and cooler weeks of later summer, and all the time of autumn. Surely it is far ahead of the burning June and July. You don't go into the country to be baked, do you? Then give us the latter days, when we can count on fresh air by rising early, and when the cool evenings begin to smell of ripening apples, and the corn is full-grown in the fields, and water-melons are ripe in the patch, (with alas! often irresistible invitations to be purloined and stealthily eaten, in the shade of some hedge-bushes or covert wood.) Give us, we say again, the latter days, in preference to the former days; for what is there in your June and July in the country? Now we can have new ripe potatoes, and all the varieties of "garden sass." Now Nature, in her beauty and bounty, bestows herself upon us, not like a captious and undeveloped girl, (always a torment, though sometimes extremely fascinating)—but like a woman of ripe growth, reliable, full-sized, and "worth something."

But is it indispensable that one should go into the country in order to see the beauties of nature, or have a good time? By no means. There are plenty of spots around Brooklyn and New York, within walking distance, that afford a healthful and inspiriting recreation to all who wish. Few, we think, realize how magnificently Brooklyn is situated, with all the diversity of hills, fine walks and roads, and a superb shore and water prospect.

The shores of Greenpoint, the walks through Bushwick, the hills in the neighborhood of Ridgewood Reservoir, the green streets of Bedford, the Clove Road, Prospect Hill, South Brooklyn, the Heights—how many persons there are that probably often give their thoughts to some distant and far inferior spots, and read exaggerated descriptions of them, while of these Brooklyn localities we have just named, though abounding in points of interest, they never visit them, and perhaps even know nothing about them.

How few, for example, know by their own experience that we have here in Brooklyn one of the finest public grounds in the world; we allude to Washington Park.—Of a fine morning or evening, it affords a promenade which, from features peculiar to the spot, can no where else be surpassed. From its elevated position, you stretch your eye over a vast expanse of land and water; you see the city of New York, the distant grey buildings of Blackwell's Island, the heights of Weehawken, Greenwood Cemetery, the ships sailing down the Narrows to the South, and the boats on the East River to the North;—while Brooklyn itself lies spread out like a huge map in all directions about you.

Nor do we believe there are anywhere in the Old World or New, any grounds comparable, in romantic beauty, variety, and with finer natural advantages than our celebrated cemeteries, Greenwood, Evergreens and Cypress Hills. While travelers are expatiating in their letters over some famed places abroad, it is forgotten that we have, in our own borders, these noble public grounds we have mentioned. Such as they, if one is disposed for a day's enjoyment in solitude and out of the din of the streets, possess advantages which we would like to see our citizens make a commoner habit of availing themselves of.

NOTES

1. Transcribed from a photocopy of original in the papers of Herbert Bergman, East Lansing, Michigan. This editorial is listed as Whitman's in *I Sit and Look Out* (194), and in

White's bibliography of Whitman's journalism (50). Topics like the celebration of loafing and a self-referential description of editorial writing lead us to believe that it is Whitman's. See, for example, "Sun-Down Papers.—[No. 9] From the Desk of a Schoolmaster," *Long-Island Democrat*, November 24, 1840; "Untitled," *New York Aurora*, April 6, 1842 (above).

2. Spelling in original.

Letter From Washington[1]

Our National City, After all, Has Some Big Points of Its Own—Its Suggestiveness To-day—The Figure of Liberty Over the Capitol—Scenes, Both Fixed and Panoramic—A Thought on Our Future Capital.[2]

New York Times

OCTOBER 4, 1863

Washington, Thursday, Oct. 1, 1863.

It is doubtful whether justice has been done to Washington, D.C.; or rather, I should say, it is certain there are layers of originality, attraction, and even local grandeur and beauty here, quite unwritten, and even to the inhabitants unsuspected and unknown. Some are in the spot, soil, air and the magnificent amplitude of[3] the laying out of the City. I continually enjoy these streets, planned on such a generous scale, stretching far, without stop or turn, giving the eye vistas. I feel freer, larger in them. Not the squeezed limits of Boston, New-York, or even Philadelphia; but royal plenty and nature's own bounty—American, prairie-like. It is worth writing a book about, this point alone. I often find it silently, curiously making up to me the absence of the ocean tumult of humanity I always enjoyed in New-York. Here, too, is largeness, in another more impalpable form; and I never walk Washington, day or night, without feeling its satisfaction.

Like all our cities, so far, this also, in its inner and outer channels, gives obedient reflex of European customs, standards, costumes, &c. There is the immortal black broadcloth coat, and there is the waiter standing behind the chair. But inside the costume, America can be traced in glimpses. Item, here,[4] an indolent largeness of spirit, quite native. No man minds his exact change. The vices here, the extravagancies, (and worse), are not without something redeeming; there is such a flowing hem, such a margin.

We all know the chorus: Washington, dusty, muddy, tiresome Washington is the most awful place, political and other; it is the rendezvous of the national universal axe-grinding, caucusing, and of our never-ending ballot-chosen shysters, and perennial smouchers, and windy bawlers from every quarter far and near. We learn, also, that there is no society, no art, in Washington; nothing of the elaborated high-life attractions of the charming capitals (for rich and morbid idlers) over sea. Truly this particular sort of charm is not in full blossom here; *n'importe.* Let those miss it who miss it, (we have a sad set among our rich young men,) and, if they will, go voyage over sea to find it. But there are man's studies, objects here, never more exhilarating ones. What themes, what fields this national city affords, this hour, for eyes of live heads, and for souls fit to feed upon them!

This city, this hour, in its material sights, and what they and it stand for, the point of the physical and moral America, the visible fact of this war, (how at last, after sleeping long as it may, one finds war ever-dearest fact to man, though most terrible, and only arbiter, after all said about the pen being mightier, &c.) This city, concentre to-day of the inauguration of the new adjustment of the civilized world's political power and geography, with vastest consequences of Presidential and Congressional action; things done here, these days, bearing on the status of man, long centuries; the spot and the hour here making history's basic materials and widest ramifications; the city of the armies of the good old cause, full of significant signs, surrounded with weapons and armaments on every hill as I look forth, and THE FLAG flying over all. The city that launches the direct laws, the imperial laws of American Union and Democracy, to be henceforth compelled, when needed, at the point of the bayonet and the muzzle of cannon—launched over continental areas, three millions of square miles, an empire large as Europe. The city of wounded and sick, city of hospitals, full of the sweetest, bravest children of time or lands; tens of thousands, wounded, bloody, amputated, burning with fever, blue with diarrhœa. The city of the wide Potomac, the queenly river, lined with softest, greenest hills and uplands. The city of Congress, with debates, agitations, (petty, if you please, but full of future fruit,) of chaotic formings; of Congress knowing not itself, as it sits there in its rooms of gold, knowing not the depths of consequence belonging to it, that lie below the scum and eructations of its surface.

But where am I running to? I meant to make a few observations of Washington on the surface.

THE DOME AND THE GENIUS.[5]

We are soon to see a thing accomplished here which I have often exercised my mind about, namely, the putting of the Genius of America away up there on the top of the dome of the Capitol. A few days ago, poking about there, eastern side, I found the Genius, all dismembered, scattered on the ground, by the basement front—I suppose preparatory to being hoisted. This, however, cannot be done forthwith, as I know that an immense pedestal surmounting the dome, has yet to be finished—about eighty feet high—on which the Genius is to stand, (with her back to the city).

But I must say something about the dome. All the great effects of the Capitol reside in it. The effects of the Capitol are worth study, frequent and varied;[6] I find they grow upon one. I shall always identify Washington with that huge and delicate towering bulge of pure white, where it emerges calm and lofty from the hill, out of a dense mass of trees. There is no place in the city, or for miles and miles off, or down or up the river, but what you see this tiara-like dome quietly rising out of the foliage; (one of the effects of first-class architecture is its serenity, its *aplomb*.)[7]

A vast eggshell, built of iron and glass, this dome—a beauteous bubble, caught and put in permanent form. I say a beauty and genuine success. I have to say the same, upon the whole, (after some qualms, may be,)[8] with respect to the entire edifice. I mean the entire Capitol is a sufficient success, if we accept what is called architecture the orthodox styles,[9] (a little mixed here,) and indulge them for our purposes until further notice.

The dome I praise, with the aforesaid Genius, (when she gets up, which she probably will by the time next Congress meets,) will then aspire about three hundred feet above the surface. And then, remember that our National House is set upon a hill. I have stood over on the Virginia hills, west of the Potomac, or on the Maryland hills, east, and viewed the structure from all positions and distances; but I find myself, after all, very fond of getting somewhere near, somewhere within fifty or a hundred rods, and gazing long and long at the dome rising out of the mass of green umbrage, as aforementioned.

The dome is tiara or triple. The lower division is surrounded with a ring of columns, pretty close together. There is much ornament everywhere, but it is kept down by the uniform white; then lots of slender oval-topt windows. Ever as I look, especially when near, (I repeat it,) the dome is a beauty, large and bold. From the east side it shows immensely. I hear folks say it is too large. Not at all, to my eye. Some say, too, the columns front and rear of the Old Capitol part, there in the centre, are now so disproportionably slender by the enlargement, that they must be removed. I say no; let them stand. They have a pleasant beauty as they are; the eye will get accustomed to them, and approve them.

Of our Genius of America, a sort of compound of handsome Choctaw squaw with the well-known Liberty of Rome, (and the French revolution,) and a touch perhaps of Athenian Pallas, (but very faint,) it is to be further described as an extensive female, cast in bronze, with much drapery, especially ruffles,[10] and a face of goodnatured indolent expression, surmounted by a high cap with more ruffles. The Genius has for a year or two past been standing in the mud, west of the Capitol; I saw her there all Winter, looking very harmless and innocent, although holding a huge sword. For pictorial representation of the Genius, see any five-dollar United States greenback; for there she is at the left hand. But the artist has made her twenty times brighter in expression, &c., than the bronze Genius is.

I have curiosity to know the effect of this figure crowning the dome. The pieces, as I have said, are at present all separated, ready to be hoisted to their place. On the Capitol generally, much work remains to be done. I nearly forgot to say that I have grown so used to the sight, over the Capitol, of a certain huge derrick which has long surmounted the dome, swinging its huge one-arm now south, now north, &c., that I believe I shall have a sneaking sorrow when they remove it and substitute the Genius. (I would not dare to say that there is something about this powerful, simple and obedient piece of machinery, so modern, so significant in many respects of our constructive nation and age, and even so poetical, that I have even balanced in my mind, how it would do to leave the rude and mighty derrick atop o' the Capitol there, as fitter emblem, may be, than Choctaw girl and Pallas.)

ARMY WAGONS AND AMBULANCES.

Washington may be described as the city of army wagons also. These are on the go at all times, in all streets, and everywhere around here for many a mile. You see long trains of thirty, fifty, a hundred, and even two hundred. It seems as if they never would come to an end. The main thing is the transportation of food, forage, &c. Then the ambulances for wounded and sick, nearly as numerous.[11] Then other varieties; there will be a procession of wagons, bright-painted and white-topped, marked "Signal Train," each with a specific number, and over all a Captain or Director on horseback overseeing. When a train comes to a bad spot in the road this Captain reins in his horse and stands there till they all get safely by. If there is some laggard left behind, he will turn and gallop back to see what the matter is. He has a good riding horse, and you see him flying around busy enough.

Then there are the ambulances. These, indeed, are always going. Sometimes from the river, coming up through Seventh-street, you can see a long, long string of them, slowly wending, each vehicle filled with sick or wounded soldiers, just brought up from the front from the region once down toward Falmouth, now out toward Warrenton. Again, from a boat that has just arrived, a load of our paroled men from the Southern prisons, *via* Fortress Monroe. Many of these will be fearfully sick and ghastly from their treatment at Richmond, &c. Hundreds, though originally young and strong men, never recuperate again from their experience in these Southern prisons.

The ambulances are, of course, the most melancholy part of the army-wagon panorama that one sees everywhere here. You mark the forms huddled on the bottom of these wagons; you mark yellow and emaciated faces. Some are supporting others. I constantly see instances of tenderness in this way from the wounded to those worse wounded.

Then some smaller train of military wagons will be labeled "Officers' supplies." The magic initials U.S.A. are, of course, common. The regimental wagons have their regiment's number also lettered on them. There are generally four horses or mules, and the wagons are mostly covered with strong canvas. The drivers and teamsters sleep in them. They live a wild, hard life. Some of these teamsters are very handsome, vagabondish and picturesque. I go among them in their camps occasionally, and to their hospitals, for there are two or three here. In some respects I have found them the most interesting of the hospitals. Many of the teamsters are invalid soldiers.

The Transportation Department of the War-office is an immense branch. Few outsiders realize the countless wagons of all kinds, with more countless horses and mules, now owned and in the service of the Government for our campaigns. Few realize the great army of drivers and teamsters. These number tens of thousands. As a general thing they are left much to themselves, although ostensibly under military discipline. As to the ambulance and the driver thereof, they have become an institution. In Washington and all the war region you see them everywhere, and, indeed, gradually through other places. Every army has its hundreds; every post, every officer of rank here, every hospital, every headquarters and every State agency is continually employing them and wanting more. To-day here they far outnumber all the other vehicles in the city.

FIRST-CLASS DAYLIGHT.

As an item I feel to note something peculiarly intense and beautiful here in the quality of the daylight. The forenoon I indite this particular paragraph, (Aug. 31,) I have been wandering all around, quite smitten with the superb clearness, luxuriance, brilliancy, yet perfect softness, of the atmosphere and light. I have noticed it generally for months, but this forenoon set myself to give it particular attention. I know the effects of atmosphere and sky very well at New-York and Long Island, but there is something here that outvies them. It is very pure and very gorgeous. Somehow richer, more liberal, more copious of strength than in the North.

Then the trees and their dark and glistening verdure play their part. Washington,[12] being full of great white architecture, takes through the Summer a prevailing color-effect of white and green. I find this everywhere, and very pleasing to my sight. So, seen freed from dust, as of late, and with let up from that unprecedented August heat, I say I find atmospheric results of marked individuality and perfection here, beyond Northern, Western and farther Southern cities. (Our writers, writing, may pen as much as they please of Italian light, and of Rome and Athens. But this city, even in the crude state it is to-day, with its buildings of to-day, with its ample river and its streets, with the effects above noted, to say nothing of what it all represents, is of course greater, materially and morally, to-day than ever Rome or Athens.)

OUR COUNTRY'S PERMANENT CAPITAL.

Yet, a gloomy and ominous shape sits back there in the shade. It seems strange that one never meets here, in the people's talk of deeds, any consciousness of Washington's one day necessarily ceasing to be the Capital of the Union. None sees that the locale of America's Government must be permanently founded far West before many years. I say I never hear this alluded to here. Everything proceeds irrespective of it. Costly and large additions are this day being made to most of the public buildings—especially the Treasury—and the prices of real estate are kept up at high and advancing rates. So much architecture and outlay—and must all indeed be lost? A handsome and stately city, designed for a future it may never see; admirable in plan, only time and filling up needed. Yet, its fate would seem stern, certain, relentless. How can the prairie America, the boundless and teeming West, the region of the Mississippi, the California, Idaho and Colorado regions (two-thirds of our territory lies west of the Mississippi River) be content to have its Government lop-sided over on the Atlantic, far, far from itself—the trunk, the real genuine America? How long before the change, the abandonment, will be proposed, nay, demanded? When demanded in earnest who can gainsay it? Will that territorial, productive and populous two-thirds west of the Great River, with half the remaining one-third along its eastern line, not prove certainly potential over the Atlantic thin strip—commercial, financial, with European proclivities—whose nerves concentrate in Washington? There are questions affecting[13] this question deeper still; after the war what new combinations? Given the change of Capital[14] twenty, forty years hence, where the new one located? In the tongue formed by the Missouri and Mississippi? In Kansas? Nebraska? Illinois? Missouri?

But why may not Washington more and more tend toward a large city on its own hook, (perhaps, even, a first-class one in time,) apart from its political character? Its situation deserves it and its destiny points that way, far more than at first thought appears.[15]

A SUNSET VIEW OF THE CITY.

In my walks I never cease finding new effects and pictures, and I believe it would continue so if I went rambling around here for fifty years. The city being on a great V, and the shores backed[16] with small and large hills[17] up and down without end, and Georgetown with elevated grounds that overtop all from the upper end. You can go on looking forever, and never hit the same combination in two places.

I often watch the city and environs from the roof of an elevated building near the Treasury. Perhaps it is sunset. Sweep the eye around now on the scene. The dazzle of red and gold from over Virginia heights there, west, is thrown across full upon us. Turning, we see the dome of the Capitol lifting itself so calmly, southeast, there, with windows yellow-red. Not far below the [18]sombre-brown Smithsonian stands in the midst of shadows. Due east of us the severe and noble architecture of the Patent Office takes the last rich flood of the sun. The mist grows murky over in distance on the Maryland side. Northward the white barracks of the hospitals, and on a hill the Soldiers' Home; southward the queenly Potomac,[19] and the trailing smoke of a single steamer moving up this side the Long Bridge. Further down, the dim masts of Alexandria. Quite near again, the half-monument of the first President. Off far again, just visible, southeast, the low turrets of the United States Insane Asylum, on the Maryland side. But the day is fading fast.

In the street below me a long string of army wagons defiling along Fifteenth-street, and around into Pennsylvania-avenue. White canvas coverings arch them over, and each wagon has its six-mule team. The teamsters are some of them walking along the sides of the mules, with gads in their hands. Then I notice in the half-light squads of the Provost Guard. Then a galloping cavalry company, in their yellow-braided jackets.

WHITMAN.

NOTES

1. Transcribed from scanned original at search.proquest.com/hnpnewyorktimes. This editorial also appears in Walt Whitman, *The Uncollected Poetry and Prose of Walt Whitman*, ed. Emory Holloway (Gloucester, Mass.: Peter Smith, 1972), 2:29–36.

2. Holloway transcribes subtitle in italics. Original is in bold.

3. Holloway's transcription: "in the laying out of the City."

4. Holloway does not include this comma.

5. Holloway does not include the period.

6. While this semicolon appears in the original, it does not appear in Holloway's transcription.

7. In his transcription, Holloway places the period in this sentence outside of the parentheses.

8. Holloway places a space in between "may" and "be" in his transcription.

9. Holloway transcribes this as "if we accept what is called architecture [of] the orthodox styles . . . ,"

10. In Holloway, the sentence ends here.

11. Holloway's transcription: "Then the ambulances for wounded and sick, nearly as numerous."

12. Comma not in original.

13. In Holloway, the sentence reads "There are questions necessarily affecting . . . "

14. Holloway reads "Given the changes of Capital . . ."

15. This paragraph does not appear in Holloway.

16. ". . . back . . ." in Holloway.

17. ". . . large and small . . ." in Holloway.

18. ". . . below, the . . ." in Holloway.

19. Spelled "Patomac" in Holloway.

WASHINGTON.; The Last Hours of Congress—Washington Crowds, and the President. From an Occasional Correspondent. WASHINGTON, Monday, March 6, 1865.[1]

New York Times

MARCH 12, 1865

The just closed hours of the Nineteenth Presidentiad, and of the Thirty-Eighth Congress of the Nation, afford two or three items, merging into the inauguration of the Twentieth, which you will probably not receive by telegraph, but may be worth while for me to catch as they are flying, and jot them down. So I will skip what is latest up this morning—SHERIDAN's reported victory over EARLY,[2] the pending Departmental and other nominations, &c., (the forthcoming Ball in the Patent Office also,) and write my passing observations of last Saturday. Simply saying, first, however, that I have this moment been up to look at the gorgeously arrayed ball and supper-rooms, for the Inauguration Dance aforesaid, (which begins in a few hours;) and I could not help thinking of the scene those rooms, where the music will sound and the dancers' feet presently tread—what a different scene they presented to my view a while since, filled with a crowded mass of the worst wounded of the war, brought in from Second Bull Run,[3] Antietam[4] and Fredericksburgh.[5] To-night, beautiful women,[6] perfumes, the violins' sweetness, the polka and the waltz; but then, the amputation, the blue face, the groan, the glassy eye of the dying, the clotted rag, the odor of old wounds and blood, and many a mother's son amid strangers, passing away untended there, (for the crowd of the badly hurt was great, and much for nurse to do, and much for surgeon.) Think not of such grim things, gloved ladies, as you bow to your partners, and the figures of the dance this night are loudly called, or you may drop on the floor that has known what this one knew, but two short winters since.

To begin with the morning of Saturday last. The day just dawned, but in half-darkness, every thing dim, leaden, and soaking. In that dim light of dawn, under such circumstances, a strange occurrence happened in the Capitol, in the Hall of the House. The members were nervous, from long drawn duty, exhausted, some asleep, and many half asleep. The gas-light, mixed with the dingy day-break, produced an unearthly effect. The poor little sleepy, stumbling pages, the smell of the Hall, the members with heads leaning on their desks asleep, the sounds of the voices speaking, with unusual intonations, the general moral atmosphere also of the close of this important session, the grandeur of the Hall itself, with its effect of vast shadows up toward the panels and spaces over the galleries, all made a marked combination. In the midst of this, with the suddenness of a thunderbolt, burst one of the most angry and crashing storms of rain and wind ever heard. It beat like a deluge on the heavy glass roof of the hall, and the wind literally howled and roared. For a moment, (and no wonder) the nervous and sleeping Representatives were thrown into confusion. The slumberers waked with fear, some started for the doors, some looked up with blanched cheeks and lips to the roof, and the little pages began to cry; it was a scene. But it was over almost as soon as the drowsied men were actually awake. They recovered themselves; the storm raged on, beating, dashing, and with loud noises at times. But the House went ahead with its business then, I think, as calmly and with as much deliberation as at any time in its career. Perhaps the shock did it good. (One is not without an impression, after all, amid these members of Congress, of both the Houses, that if the flat and selfish routine of their duties should ever be broken in upon by some great emergency involving real danger, and calling for first class personal qualities, those qualities would be found generally forthcoming and from men not now credited with them.)

PENNSYLVANIA AVENUE

As the day advanced, of course Pennsylvania avenue absorbed all. The show here was to me worth all the rest. The effect was heterogeneous, novel, and quite inspiriting. It will perhaps be got at, by making a list in the following manner, to wit: Mud, (and such mud!) amid and upon which streaming crowds of citizens; lots of blue-dressed soldiers; any quantity of male and female Africans, (especially female;) horrid perpetual entanglements at the crossings, sometimes a dead lock; more mud, the wide street black, and several inches deep with it; clattering groups of cavalrymen out there on a gallop, (and occasionally a single horseman might have been seen, &c.;) processions of firemen, with their engines, evidently from the north; a regiment of blacks, in full uniform, with guns on their shoulders; the splendor overhead; the oceanic crowd, equal almost to Broadway; the wide Avenue, its vista very fine, down at one end closed by the capitol, with milky bulging dome, and the Maternal Figure over all, (with the sword by her side and the sun glittering on her helmeted head;) at the other, the western end, the pillared front of the Treasury Building, looking south; altogether quite a refreshing spot and hour, and plenty of architectural show with life and magnetism also. Among other items, our heavenly neighbor Hesperus,[7] the star of the West, was quite plain just after midday; it was right over head. I occasionally stopped with the crowds and looked up at it. Every corner had its little squad, thus engaged; often soldiers, often black, with raised faces, well worth looking at themselves, as new styles of physiognomical pictures.

THE PROCESSION AND THE PRESIDENT

In some respects the printed reports of Saturday's ceremonies here will give you a widely erroneous notion of the way they really transpired. For instance, the different parts of the procession were characterized by a charming looseness and independence. Each went up and down the Avenue in the way and at the time which seemed convenient, and was a law unto itself. The President very quietly rode down to the capitol in his own carriage, by himself, on a sharp trot, about noon, either because he wished to be on hand to sign bills, &c., or to get rid of marching in line with the muslin Temple of Liberty, and the pasteboard Monitor. I saw him on his return, at three o'clock, after the performance was over. He was in his plain two-horse[8] barouche, and looked very much worn and tired; the lines, indeed, of vast responsibilities, intricate questions, and demands of life and death, cut deeper than ever upon his dark brown face; yet all the old goodness, tenderness, sadness, and canny shrewdness, underneath the furrows. (I never see that man without feeling that he is one to become personally attached to, for his combination of purest, heartiest tenderness, and native Western even rudest forms of manliness.) By his side sat his little boy, of ten years. There were no soldiers, only a lot of civilians on horseback, with huge yellow scarfs over their shoulders, riding around the carriage. At the inauguration four years ago, he rode down and back again surrounded by a dense mass of armed cavalrymen eight deep, with drawn sabres, and carbines clanking at their sides, and there were sharp-shooters stationed at every corner on the route.

I ought to mention the President's closing Levee of Saturday night last. Never before was such a compact jam in front of the White House, all the grounds filled, and away out to the spacious sidewalks. But I forego that reception, and finish off with something I have on my mind about no more uncommon topic than simply the Weather. It refers to the hours and events immediately upon us, so is fit for a newspaper.

DO THE HEAVENS SYMPATHIZE WITH US?

Whether the rains, and the heat and cold, or what underlies them all, are affected with what affects man in masses, and follow his play of passionate action, strained stronger than usual, and on a larger scale than usual;—whether this, or no, it is certain that there is now, and has been for twenty months or more on this American Continent North, many a remarkable, many an unprecedented expression of the subtle world of air above us and around us. There, since this war, and the wide and deep national agitation, strange analogies. Different combinations, a different sunlight or absence of it, different products even out of the ground. After every great battle, a great storm. Even civic events, the same. On Saturday, a forenoon like whirling demons, dark, with slanting rain, full of rage; and then the afternoon, so calm, so bathed with flooding splendor from heaven's most excellent sun, with atmosphere of sweetness; so clear it showed the stars, long, long before they were due. As the President came out on the capitol portico, a curious little white cloud, the only one in that part of the sky, appeared like a hovering bird, right over him.

Indeed, the heavens, the elements, all the meteorological[9] influences, have run riot for weeks past. Such caprices, abruptest alternations of frowns and beauty, I never knew. It is a common remark that (as last Summer was different in its spells of intense heat from any preceding it) the Winter just completed has been without parallel. It has remained so down to the hour I am writing. Much of the daytime of the past month was sulky, with leaden heaviness, fog, interstices of bitter cold, and some insane storms. But there have been samples of another description. Nor earth, nor land ever knew spectacles of superber beauty than some of the nights have lately been here. The Western Star, in the earlier hours of evening, has never been so large, so clear; it seems as if it told something, as if it held rapport indulgent with humanity, with us Americans. Five or six nights since, it hung close by the moon, then a little past its first quarter. The star was wonderful, the moon like a young mother. The sky, dark blue, the transparent night, the planets, the moderate west wind, the elastic temperature, the unsurpassable miracle of that great star, and the young and swelling moon swimming in the west, suffused the soul. Then I heard, slow and clear, the deliberate notes of a bugle come up out of the silence,[10] sounding so good through the night's mystery, no hurry, but firm and faithful, floating along, rising, falling leisurely, with here and there a long-drawn note; the bugle, well played, sounding tattoo, in one of the army hospitals near here, where the wounded (some of them personally so dear to me) are lying in their cots, and many a sick boy, come down to the war from Ohio, Illinois, Wisconsin, and the rest.

WALT WHITMAN.

NOTES

1. Transcribed from scanned original at search.proquest.com/hnpnewyorktimes. This editorial also appears in W. T. Bandy, "An Unknown 'Washington Letter' by Walt Whitman," *Walt Whitman Quarterly Review* 2, no. 3 (1984): 23–27.

2. On March 2, 1865, General Philip Sheridan (1831–1888) defeated Jubal Early (1816–1894) at the Battle of Waynesboro in the Shenandoah Valley of Virginia, effectively ending Confederate activities there.

3. The Second Battle of Bull Run (or Manassas) took place in Virginia between August 28 and 30, 1862, and ended in a Union defeat.

4. The Battle of Antietam was fought in Maryland on September 17, 1862, and resulted ostensibly in a Union victory when Confederate forces retreated back into Virginia. It was the bloodiest single day of the war (and in U.S. history).

5. Fredericksburg is spelled this way in the original. The Battle of Fredericksburg was fought in Virginia between December 11 and 15, 1862, and ended in a Union defeat.

6. Bandy, in "An Unknown 'Washington Letter' by Walt Whitman," places a comma in between "beautiful" and "women"; however, the editors cannot find a comma between these two words in the scanned original.

7. Hesperus is the son of the goddess Dawn according to Greek mythology.

8. Hyphen in original.

9. Spelled "meteorolgical" in original.

10. Bandy's transcription reads "slience [*sic*]," but the word appears to be spelled correctly in the original.

Index

The Iowa Whitman Series

Conserving Walt Whitman's Fame: Selections from Horace Traubel's "Conservator," 1890–1919, edited by Gary Schmidgall

Democratic Vistas: The Original Edition in Facsimile, by Walt Whitman, edited by Ed Folsom

Intimate with Walt: Selections from Whitman's Conversations with Horace Traubel, 1888–1892, edited by Gary Schmidgall

Leaves of Grass, 1860: The 150th Anniversary Edition, by Walt Whitman, edited by Jason Stacy

A Place for Humility: Whitman, Dickinson, and the Natural World, by Christine Gerhardt

The Pragmatic Whitman: Reimagining American Democracy, by Stephen John Mack

Supplement to "Walt Whitman: A Descriptive Bibliography," by Joel Myerson

Transatlantic Connections: Whitman U.S., Whitman U.K., by M. Wynn Thomas

Visiting Walt: Poems Inspired by the Life and Work of Walt Whitman, edited by Sheila Coghill and Thom Tammaro

Walt Whitman: The Correspondence, Volume VII, edited by Ted Genoways

Walt Whitman and the Class Struggle, by Andrew Lawson

Walt Whitman and the Earth: A Study in Ecopoetics, by M. Jimmie Killingsworth

Walt Whitman, Where the Future Becomes Present, edited by David Haven Blake and Michael Robertson

Whitman among the Bohemians, edited by Joanna Levin and Edward Whitley

Whitman East and West: New Contexts for Reading Walt Whitman, edited by Ed Folsom

Whitman Noir: Black America and the Good Gray Poet, edited by Ivy G. Wilson

Walt Whitman's Reconstruction: Poetry and Publishing between Memory and History, Martin T. Buinicki

Walt Whitman's Songs of Male Intimacy and Love: "Live Oak, with Moss" and "Calamus," edited by Betsy Erkkila

Walt Whitman's Selected Journalism, edited by Douglas A. Noverr and Jason Stacy